The *Marchioness of Graham:* A Purser's Log

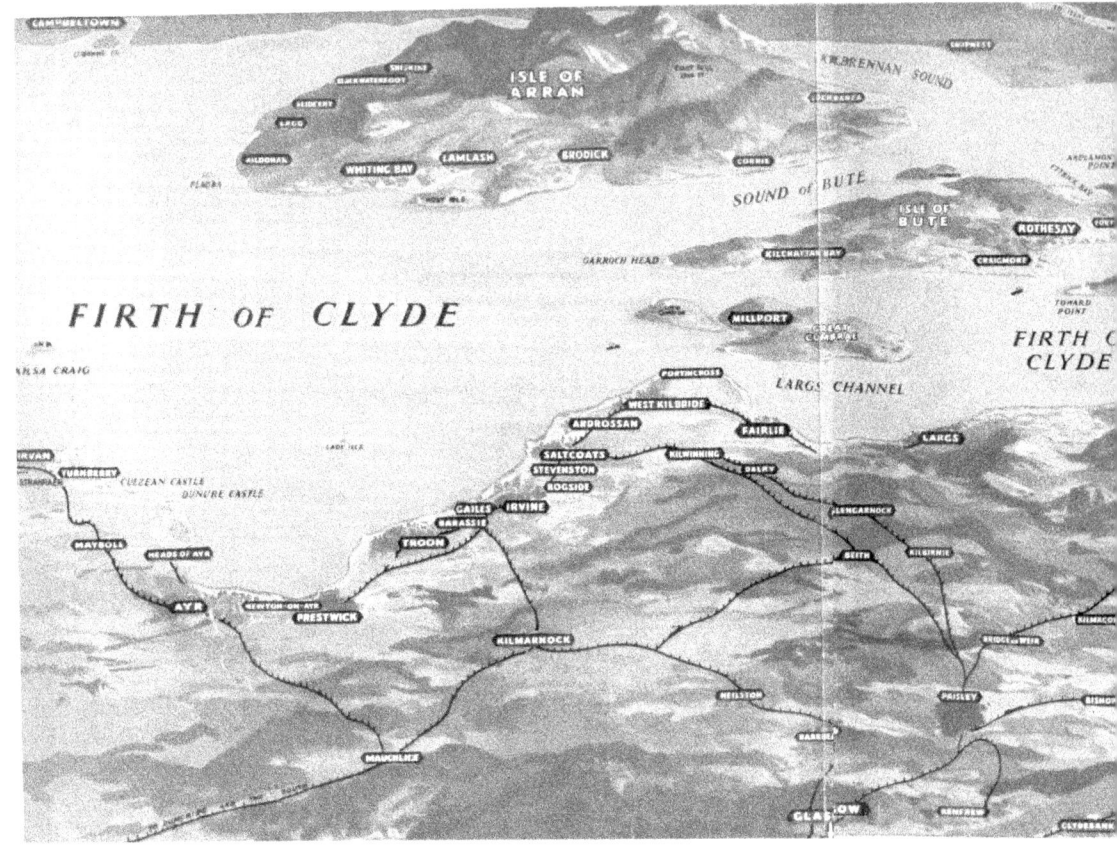

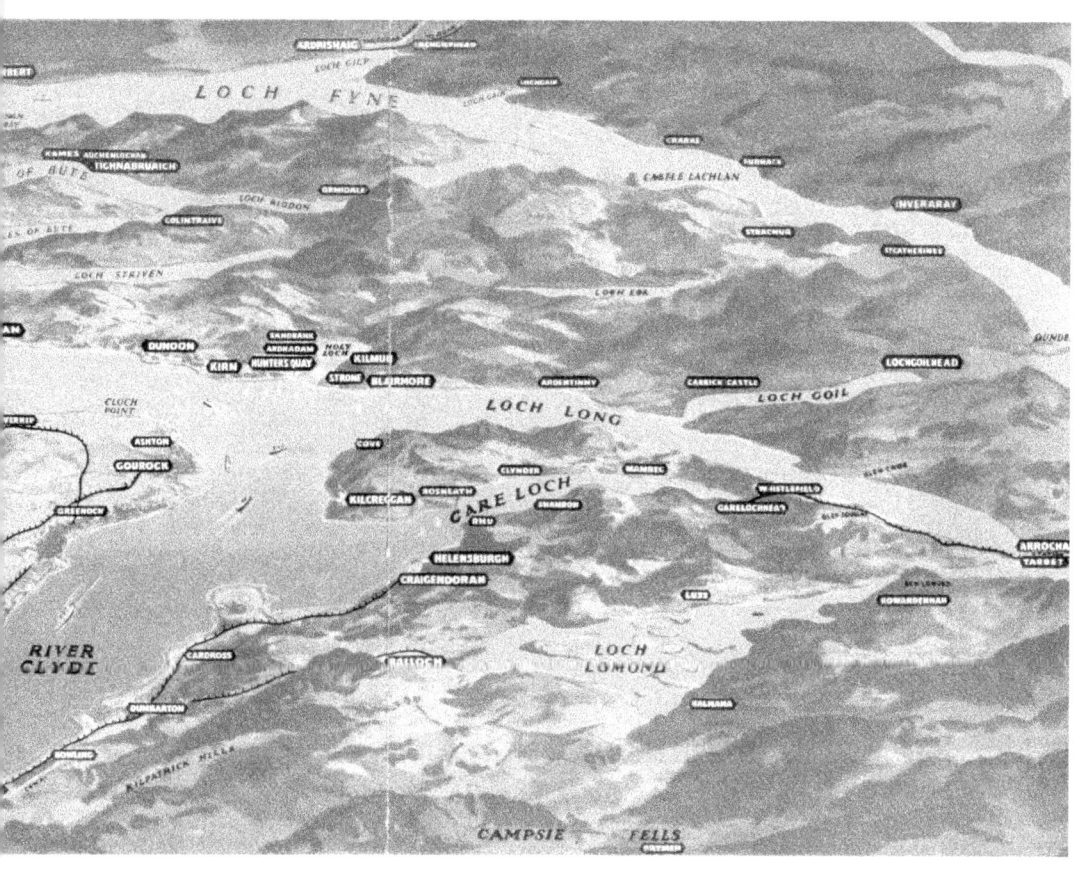

The ship in the frame

The *Marchioness of Graham:* A Purser's Log
A DIARY FROM A CLYDE STEAMER IN 1957

Richard M. Orr

The Grimsay Press

The Grimsay Press
an imprint of
Zeticula
57 St Vincent Crescent
Glasgow
G3 8NQ
Scotland.

http://www.thegrimsaypress.co.uk
admin@thegrimsaypress.co.uk

Text Copyright © Richard M. Orr 2010
First published 2010.
ISBN-13 978-1-84530-072-2

Every effort has been made to trace possible copyright holders and to obtain their permission for the use of any copyright material. The publishers will gladly receive information enabling them to rectify any error or omission for subsequent editions.

The right of Richard M. Orr to be identified as the author of the work has been asserted by him in accordance with the Copyright, Designs and Patents Act 1988.

All rights reserved. No part of this publication may be reproduced, stored in a retrieval system or transmited, in any form or by any means without the prior written permission of the publisher, nor be otherwise circulated in any form or binding or cover other than that in which it is published and without a similar condition being imposed on the subsequent publisher.

I am pleased to dedicate this book to the *Graham*, her crew and the many others, including friends and family, who figure in these pages. Without these, there would be no diary!

Pursers off duty - Dick in characteristic wellies gives me a searching look

Acknowledgements

Pride of place must go to the important contribution made by the Clyde River Steamer Club. Founded in 1932, the Club enrolled me among its members in the Fifties and has throughout the years whetted my interest with its frequent ship charters, instructive talks, social opportunities and valuable publications. It continues to play a key role.

Next come other books about the steamers which offer information, guidance and back-up. My diaries are not intended to provide full histories of the ships but concern themselves largely with life aboard as I found it, though admittedly a little is added about the later disposition of the ships involved. You must look elsewhere for greater detail.

My two books for first reference are:

Clyde River and Other Steamers – Duckworth and Langmuir – Brown, Son and Ferguson - invaluable for concise descriptions of the ships and easy of reference.

The Caledonian Steam Packet Company Ltd – MacArthur – Clyde River Steamer Club - this offers a good read and is crammed with information to interest anyone wishing to get a feel for the fleet and its development. It is not restricted to Caley Company ships!

Numerous other books can be found if one desires to delve further. For example,

The Clyde Passenger Steamer, 1812 to 1901 - Williamson – MacLehose and Sons

Clyde River Steamers of the last 50 Years – McQueen – Gowans and Gray.

Besides, there exist numerous books and booklets, well illustrated and each making its individual contribution, where *Marchioness of Graham* features. However, Peter Herriot's article in Clyde Steamers No 10, Autumn 1974, the Magazine of the Clyde River Steamer Club, is particularly detailed and gives extensive information about the ship and her sailings right from her launch through to her final years in Greece. Peter was a great admirer of the *Graham* and his article goes far beyond the parameters set for me in my diary for 1957.

This brings us to the illustrations. These are largely my own, supplemented by some few from other sources. The views in my personal collection have been amassed over many years and selected wherever possible to relate specifically to my text. One or two older views derive from the now defunct Robertson collection at Gourock or from commercial postcards. Likewise I include some obtained from Graham Langmuir, Jim MacAndrew, Bob Lindsay and members of the River Steamer Club, notably Iain Quinn and Andrew Clark. If I have included any uncredited picture from a source unknown to me, I apologise for this and acknowledge that contribution. No deliberate infringement of copyright is intended.

Last of all, I am indebted to my wife and family for their support without which this diary might never have reached the press.

Richard M. Orr
Glasgow
April 2010

Contents

Acknowledgements	*ix*
Illustrations	*xiii*
Foreword	*xvii*
The Very Firstlings of My Heart	1
Initiation	13
Day 1 *Saturday 29 June*	19
Day 2 *Sunday 30 June*	32
Digression	36
Day 3 *Monday 1 July*	64
Day 4 *Tuesday 2 July*	67
Day 5 *Wednesday 3 July*	70
Day 6 *Thursday 4 July*	73
Day 7 *Friday 5 July*	75
Day 8 *Saturday 6 July*	77
Day 9 *Sunday 7 July*	79
Day 10 *Monday 8 July*	80
Day 11 *Tuesday 9 July*	82
Day 12 *Wednesday 10 July*	86
Day 13 *Thursday 11 July*	89
Day 14 *Friday 12 July*	91
Day 15 *Saturday 13 July*	95
Day 16 *Sunday 14 July*	97
Day 17 *Monday 15 July*	99
Day 18 *Tuesday 16 July*	101
Day 19 *Wednesday 17 July*	103
Day 20 *Thursday 18 July*	105
Day 21 *Friday 19 July*	107
Day 22 *Saturday 20 July*	109
Day 23 *Sunday 21 July*	113
Day 24 *Monday 22 July*	116
Day 25 *Tuesday 23 July*	118
Day 26 *Wednesday 24 July*	120
Day 27 *Thursday 25 July*	124
Day 28 *Friday 26 July*	127
Day 29 *Saturday 27 July*	130
Day 30 *Sunday 28 July*	132
Day 31 *Monday 29 July*	134
Day 32 *Tuesday 30 July*	136

Day 33 *Wednesday 31 July*	138
Day 34 *Thursday 1 August*	140
Day 35 *Friday 2 August*	141
Day 36 *Saturday 3 August*	143
Day 37 *Sunday 4 August*	146
Day 38 *Monday 5 August*	148
Day 39 *Tuesday 6 August*	151
Day 40 *Wednesday 7 August*	*153*
Day 41 *Thursday 8 August*	156
Day 42 *Friday 9 August*	158
Day 43 *Saturday 10 August*	160
Day 44 *Sunday 11 August*	162
Day 45 *Monday 12 August*	164
Day 46 *Tuesday 13 August*	166
Day 47 *Wednesday 14 August*	169
Day 48 *Thursday 15 August*	171
Day 49 *Friday 16 August*	174
Day 50 *Saturday 17 August*	175
Day 51 *Sunday 18 August*	178
Day 52 *Monday 19 August*	181
Day 53 *Tuesday 20 August*	183
Day 54 *Wednesday 21 August*	186
Day 55 *Thursday 22 August*	189
Day 56 *Friday 23 August*	191
Day 57 *Saturday 24 August*	192
Day 58 *Sunday 25 August*	194
Day 59 *Monday 26 August*	196
Day 60 *Tuesday 27 August*	198
Day 61 *Wednesday 28 August*	199
Day 62 *Thursday 29 August*	201
Day 63 *Friday 30 August*	203
Day 64 *Saturday 31 August*	205
Day 65 *Sunday 1 September*	207
Day 66 *Monday 2 September*	208
Change of Life - Aboard *Glen Sannox*	210
Metamorphosis - A Life Hereafter	213
Index	*221*

Illustrations

The ship in the frame	iv
Pursers off duty - Dick in characteristic wellies gives me a searching look	viii
Waverley leaves Lochgoilhead in 1947 season, dressed overall for her first day in service.	3
Cock of the Walk - *Saint Columba* glides into Rothesay in 1957 with depot ship *Adamant* beyond.	3
Duchess of Fife off Craigmore in summer 1949. You can see how you could get up to the very tip of the bow in an effort to escape the crowd!	4
Duchess of Fife in winter garb approaches Gourock in 1953. Gone now are the summer crowds.	4
Halliday puffer *Norman* at Carradale lands her load on to the horse and cart waiting in the shallows.	7
MacBrayne's cargo ship *Loch Carron* leaves Kingston Dock with a Clyde Navigation Trust hopper ahead. Plenty of river traffic is evident around.	8
The wee *Marchioness of Lorne* on her Holy Loch run which suited her well. Events proved she was safer there!	8
Car ferry *Arran* crosses from Gourock in 1958. Here she appears as built with business like Samson posts.	11
Maid of Argyll en route for Innellan seen from the *Graham*. One of the four very similar *Maids* which appeared in 1953.	11
Caledonia flying the Glasgow High School flag comes alongside the new look *Queen Mary II* in May 1957 at Glasgow. Sloan's Line ship and river dredging work ahead.	12
Caledonia passes John Brown's at Clydebank on that same day with the High School flag at her main mast. One of the three Cunard sisters lies in the background.	12
Letter of possibility - BTC are still in charge and they got my middle initial wrong with L for M! My first approach is acknowledged.	14
Letter of probability - power still rests with BTC. Employment looks certain!	15
Letter of confirmation - the excitement rises! *Marchioness of Graham* comes out the hat!	17
Letter of transfer - change of arrangements and an earlier start date. The *Glen Sannox* certainly played havoc with the precise timings given in the letter!	18
Glen Sannox makes her first arrival in the rain at Gourock after trials on 27 June 1957 - not her prettiest angle in my view! Car ferry *Cowal* lies beyond.	21
Glen Sannox at Brodick dressed overall for her first day of service, 29 June 1957. She was running late!	21
Some of the tickets collected.	22
Glen Sannox heads upriver at the end of her first day and I await transfer to *Graham* at Brodick.	24
Proposed Timetable for *Caledonia* had fate not intervened.	25-30
Kildonan laid up at Ardrossan with Burns Laird *Lairdscrest* ahead of her.	31

Lairds Isle ex Southern Region's *Riviera* of 1911 - Denny built and a flier!
In summer 1955 it was she that took our school cadet force over to
Ireland for summer camp. 31

Fleet list as it appears in 1957 timetable. First the steamers and then the
motor vessels - *Talisman* is a misfit! 34

Duchess of Montrose dressed overall at Dunoon. Note the unfortunate,
black painted steam whistle. 37

Duchess of Hamilton draws out of Rothesay. 38

A well-crowded *Queen Mary II* arrives at Rothesay in September, 1956.
Her last day in service with 2 funnels. Depot ship *Adamant* lies beyond. 38

Queen Mary II at Barclay Curle's yard, May 4, 1957. She is still awaiting
her name - and note the alien crouching in that transformational funnel! 39

Marchioness of Graham ready for trials. Even the belting is being hosed
down for the occasion! 41

Jeanie Deans cannily approaches Rothesay. She is viewed here across the
putting green from our top flat. 41

Caledonia beats a retreat from Ardrossan on 30 June while the *Graham* lies
at Jerry's Quay. Her mishap came the following Sunday. 43

Talisman brings a good crowd to Rothesay from Millport and Largs in
September, 1956. *Jupiter* leaves in the background. 43

Jupiter takes her usual wide berth approaching Rothesay. 44

Waverley lingers off Ardbeg shore while awaiting a vacant berth at Rothesay. 44

Maid of Argyll approaches Rothesay in 1956. 46

ABC car ferry *Arran* loads up while MacBrayne's *King George V* lies off. 46

Countess of Breadalbane in Lamont's dry dock, Greenock in 1959. 49

Ashton nears Gourock while Ritchie's *Grannie Kempock* comes over from
Kilcreggan. An *Empress* creeps into the picture. 49

1906 *Atalanta*, G and SW fleet's only turbine steamer, shown here after
amalgamation with LMS. The *Graham* displayed some similarities. 50

1926 turbine *Glen Sannox* makes haste off Arran. 50

Captain Colin MacKay stands beside *Duchess of Fife*. 53

Chief engineer, Leslie Rosser contemplates his dials over a pipe (or several!).
True to form, he keeps at a distance! 54

Dick Raines holds our attention at Bridge Wharf under the dock
policeman's watchful eye. 54

Bennie Martin, or Hooch, prepares the ropes hopefully, all ready for a
pirouette. 56

Empress of Scotland, ex *Empress of Japan*. She was a regular visitor at the time. 66

Waverley puts up a half hearted race out of Rothesay. 66

Marchioness of Graham at Campbeltown, offering a poor substitute for the
Duchess. 69

Talisman comes alongside the *Graham* at Fairlie. Our crew watch on. Relief
skipper Forster to left and Mate Campbell with his back to us at gangway. 69

Skipper in shirt sleeves on top of the wheelhouse with TV engineer to discuss arrangements for Pleasure boat while lying at Fairlie. The barman and galley boy are busy with chores.	72
Coaling time at Jerry's Quay, Ardrossan.	72
Talisman alongside at Fairlie about to transfer her passengers across us - our mate and relief skipper (in civvies) look on.	74
Caledonia, dressed overall, berths at Brodick.	81
Duchess of Montrose speeds away from Bute with a fine bow spray.	83
Marchioness of Graham at Bridge Wharf, seen from the King George V Bridge.	84
All action! A BBC trailer inches over the planks at a mercifully favourable tide. Coal is wheeled aboard over another plank!	84
Events were to prove that Steamer Services took precedence over Pleasure boat and we headed off for Fair Saturday at Arran.	88
Watching in the rain - Pleasure boat in the rain at Gourock with *Cowal* beyond.	94
My sole souvenir from the ship! The Notice for the Cancellation Office which of course served as my cabin at night.	100
A view up on the after deck on a day when both upper decks are open to the public – with supervision by yours truly!	102
The *Graham* graces Troon and shows her attractive view from the rear.	102
Red Handbill, with AMENDED PLEASURE SAILINGS FROM AYR AND TROON TILL 9TH AUGUST when *Caledonia* was expected to be back.	110/111
Marchioness lies low at the end of lengthy Whiting Bay pier.	115
Coming into Rothesay with a good crowd from the Ayr sailings.	115
Three popular booklets:	123
Preparation for TV Pleasure boat Round 2 - out of Rothesay this time, still in the rain and oilskins!	126
Fraternising- from left to right, TV engineer, our waitress Jean, Dick and myself- I am now sporting a less lumpy plastic white top!	126
Coming up from Ayr. A typical busy scene at Largs. The skipper would have cleared the pier if at all possible!	129
Loading cars on planks on to *Talisman* - a familiar if scary scene on the *Graham*.	129
Mona's Queen leaving Ardrossan viewed from *Graham* at Jerry's Quay	142
Meeting the *Queen Mary* off Greenock as our ship returns from Upriver sailing.	145
In familiar waters approaching Brodick.	145
The *Graham* having a quiet smoke at Brodick pier.	149
AMENDED SAILINGS – GIRVAN AND MAYBOLE.	150
The *Marchioness* meets up with the *Duchess of Hamilton* at Campbeltown.	155
Our ship heads off blank from Rothesay to Gourock.	155
We meet *Flying Merlin* towing *Bardic Ferry* while *Hopper no 9* lies ahead.	168
To the rear, *Chieftain* tows *Joseph Lykes* past *Bardic Ferry*. Busy times indeed upriver!	168

Landing passengers at Gourock, with *Maid of Argyll* beyond.	173
Duchess of Hamilton takes the last Sunday run out of Rothesay with what appears to be an impressive overload.	173
Time to relax on a blank run down to Ayr off Skelmorlie. The pilot sits under the bridge - his favoured spot - having a smoke before going up to take the wheel.	177
A sheep run on *Waverley* - our skipper preferred to see the sheep at the bow!	180
Here we act as tender to the Cunarder *Sylvania* at the end of August.	180
The *Graham* cants in Ayr Harbour at the end of a quiet day.	182
MacBrayne's *Loch Frisa* and *Loch Ard* at Kingston Dock, Glasgow.	188
Lying at Berth 1 in Rothesay the morning after Smart's Circus sailing, with the *Countess* adjacent in Berth 1A.	188
Preparing to leave Ardrossan for the last time on 2 September. The mate stands by the funnel and big Donald stands proud over to his left. The skipper commands the show from his eyrie.	209
Marchioness of Graham bows out of Ardrossan- stern first!	209
Wee John Cameron looks down from the bridge on the *Sannox* to the *Talisman* alongside her at Fairlie.	212
Festooned with toilet rolls, *Glen Sannox* at Brodick in September, 1957.	212
Marchioness of Graham and *Jupiter* awaiting disposal in Greenock's Albert Harbour.	214
Marchioness of Graham prepares to leave for Greece under new ownership, as signified by the Greek letter delta (D) for Diapoulis on the funnel.	214
Transformed to *Ellas*, now converted to diesel and serving Rhodes from Peiraeus in September, 1962 - yes, once our Clyde *Marchioness*.	216
That frightful funnel close up.	216
Renamed *Nea Ellas* in 1963, with new insignia on that awful funnel.	218
The plunge pool replaces a cargo hold belonging to pre-cruise days.	218
A backward look — a last look at the *Graham* that I knew.	220

Foreword

1957 was for me a momentous year. That June, I finished secondary school in Glasgow and I had till October and the start of University before resuming studies. That meant I was free as a bird! Or, more realistically, I could take a job, earn some spending money and get a taste of this new life of liberty. I already knew what I hankered after. My target was to work as an assistant purser aboard a Clyde steamer and for this post I realised that there would be fierce competition. Many were the attractions but few the openings.

Perhaps you are wondering that it should have taken me so long to set down this record in print. Other priorities, I suppose, pressure of work, lack of time and suchlike excuses would be my explanation. But now has come retirement and time is more generous though, sadly, I have delayed so long that the post of purser no longer exists on the Clyde car ferries! Only *Waverley* remains true to Clyde steamer tradition and retains the post. Indeed, *Waverley* alone survives as an example of the famed Clyde cruising steamers which I knew and loved. Still, I have always intended to share these unique experiences and in this I am helped greatly by the fact that I kept a daily log of my activities recorded faithfully in an old Accounts book from my grandmother's hat shop in Rothesay. Indeed, I suppose the existence of the daily log more than anything else has prompted the publication of the record. Diary keeping began for me in 1953 with secondary school, and brief, daily accounts burgeoned out into much lengthier affairs during life shipboard when employed as a summer purser, or on foreign trips leading school groups round the Mediterranean in quest of Greek and Roman sites. So now I can rely on my diary for the daily detail of the 66 days that I spent signed on shipboard that memorable summer and elucidate or expand on the detail in the explanatory sections which I have grandly called Commentaries, though these are inevitably rather subjective in style. As with any diary account, some parts will be summary, others more extensive, some close knit and others disjointed. All views expressed will necessarily be mine and mine alone. But I shall for the most part stick to my original, using the Commentaries as backup.

Whatever the reason for my tardiness in going into print, 1957 was certainly an unforgettable summer, allowing me to masquerade as ship's officer around the decks of a steamer whose yacht-like lines well disguised her primary role as year-round transport for passengers and cargo around the Clyde piers of the lower Firth. And this is what I mean to record and in so doing to recall something of the magic and mystique which I enjoyed. My steamer log will be a key player.

But do not look here for a word-for-word account of actual happenings. Nor seek in these pages for an accurate history of Clyde steamers, which can readily be found elsewhere. While actual people and happenings are central to my story, these will have no doubt been twisted to suit my interpretation. They are presented as they appeared to me in that glorious summer of 1957 when I was fresh from sixth year at the High School of Glasgow and preparing to read Classics at Glasgow University. Life on the Clyde was to prove an eye-opener. I was still starry eyed so far as steamers were concerned and had much to learn. So come along and share this learning experience with me.

The Very Firstlings of My Heart

My romance with Clyde steamers began early. The advent of the new paddler *Waverley* in 1947 did not escape me, albeit I was but a mere eight year old (or should that not more properly read eight year young?). That steamer's antics in Rothesay bay as she tackled teething problems with her engines were duly noted and yet, surprisingly, I have no clear memory of her actual appearance then, in her LNER (London North Eastern Railway) colours with red, white and black funnels and teak wood effect deckhouses. For that was to be the only year she wore these pleasing colours before assuming the dull mantle of uniformity under British Rail in 1948. Thereafter, uniform yellow and black funnels became standard for the Clyde fleet. I trust I'll remember to say more later about *Waverley*'s colours, should the occasion arise. Suffice to say for the moment that she was an early favourite and her looks and lines drew praise.

But around this time, other vessels were making their mark on my affections. First and foremost was the magnificent three funnelled turbine *Saint Columba*. This splendid old ship had originally been built at Denny's of Dumbarton in 1912 as *Queen Alexandra*, a two funnelled turbine on traditional lines and second to bear that name. Now renamed and transformed, she carried the mail from Gourock to Ardrishaig every summer for David MacBrayne and was regarded as a cut above the rest in speed and appearance. With her three red stacks, she was a real eye-catcher and bore her years with aplomb. Favoured too, but for quite different reasons, was the gaunt but graceful *Duchess of Fife* of 1903. Every summer she transported me, my sister and my parents, along with the dog, bikes and luggage-hamper, to Kilchattan Bay on the magical island of Bute. The hamper preceded the party, being sent in advance - PLA or Passenger Luggage in Advance - to our miniscule seafront cottage, courtesy of Malcolm Kelso, the ageing, stooped pier master, with his horse and cart and stalwart assistant, Danny. But to revert to the *Duchess*! After this delightful old paddler had reversed out of Wemyss Bay pier amid much paddle froth and headed along the Skelmorlie coast for Largs, a visit to the engine room was *de rigueur*. Adults may have used this as their cover to mask a furtive session in the bar in the very bowels of the ship. But for me it was to witness the real thing. Down amid the heady atmosphere of oil and steam, the two great connecting rods thrust forward and back purposefully, driving the paddle wheels, while joy of joys, the heavy gates into the paddles on either side were wide open and provided an uninterrupted view of the paddles as they splashed about their important business. What bliss! In these early days,

I took little cognisance of the fact that the later paddlers that I knew had three connecting rods, an improvement introduced to the Clyde fleet by *Jeanie Deans* in the thirties. On the old *Duchess* there was a slight swaying occasioned by the thrust of the two connecting rods while triple expansion all but removed this sensation on the later paddlers.

Nor was this the *Fife*'s only service for my pleasure. Come winter, her open bow section, so typical of the old Caledonian Company steamers, was plated up, exposed forward windows were shielded by protective guards and the inner, allegedly water tight paddle gates, that beloved summer viewing point, were tightly sealed. Thus equipped she was ready to do battle with the elements on the Wemyss Bay-Rothesay run. Here again I would join her on my regular winter visits to stay with (and to be spoiled by) my grandmother and my great aunt (always known as Anta). A feature of these winter expeditions to Rothesay was travelling alone, after being put in the care of some other traveller, preferably a mature female selected as suitable by my mother, in the third class compartment of the steam train at Central Station. Excitement rose as we neared Lamont's shipyard outside Port Glasgow where steamers could regularly be spotted, albeit briefly, as we sped past them high on the stocks for winter overhaul. Then we huffed and puffed our way up the steep hill to Upper Greenock station before passing Inverkip and the first chance to identify the Rothesay steamer lying at Wemyss Bay pier. Darkness merely added to the thrill of identification! On boarding ship at Wemyss Bay, I would slip the reins and roam freely until I was met by my adoring relatives at the pier head and whisked off up steep Chapel Hill to their eyrie at Ardarach, perched loftily above the bay. My mother was a Rothesay Halliday and her father prominent in the sphere of sawmills and pier building. The three strikingly positioned houses up on Chapel Hill were also within his demesne. Though before my time, his brother George had owned three puffers in connection with the sawmill. These were *Elizabeth*, *Norman* and *Craigielea*. So here perhaps we can identify another factor in my fondness for the Clyde and Rothesay in particular. The means of conveyance to Ardarach was a taxi, usually a Daimler of ample proportions to accommodate my grandmother's equally ample frame.

Returning to the *Fife*, perhaps she was sparsely fitted, with single mast, pencil funnel and scant deck cover, but she was thoroughly reliable and much loved. It was a great delight to stand under the starry sky on a winter's night as we beat our way past Toward lighthouse, with the wind whistling in the rigging and the tall funnel exuding a glow of welcome warmth. The intermittent beam from the lighthouse momentarily illuminated the deck before we plunged again into Stygian blackness. Stormy crossings

Waverley leaves Lochgoilhead in 1947 season, dressed overall for her first day in service.

Cock of the Walk - *Saint Columba* glides into Rothesay in 1957 with depot ship *Adamant* beyond.

Duchess of Fife off Craigmore in summer 1949. You can see how you could get up to the very tip of the bow in an effort to escape the crowd!

Duchess of Fife in winter garb approaches Gourock in 1953. Gone now are the summer crowds.

brought their own special excitement. With so little in the way of deck cover, a soaking was commonplace when spray swept across the deck. Indeed, I once had to be dried off at the ship's boiler following a foolhardy escapade when mimicking a figure-head stationed at the ship's heaving bow. But, of course, I viewed this as a personal triumph and a chance to reach those parts where others were not permitted! With the coming of spring and increased passenger traffic, the *Fife* would resume her Cumbrae connection and the capacious paddler *Caledonia* took over the busy Rothesay run. This gave greater scope for hide and seek or running around deck - not at all popular with crew or fellow passengers - although the numerous metal wheeled trolleys stacked with cases, luggage and milk-churns, not to mention the occasional car, were well designed to put a brake on deck sports. Still, with spacious saloons, upper decks and wide alleyways below, *Caledonia* did all a ship could to satisfy the aspirations of youth and frustrate the efforts of elders to control such energetic, even dangerous, frolics. Unsuspecting and unexpected, other deck users were at risk as we raced headlong around the ship, and wet decks often gave rise to nasty falls, sometimes accompanied by even nastier splinters!

At this stage in my life, if I was not watching or sailing on steamers, I was frequently mimicking them. Thus in upper primary school at Netherlee, while saner classmates were taken up with football, playing peever or clustering in mixed sex groups to talk or scheme among themselves, I would join forces with one or two of like mind and lunacy, mark out suitable "piers" around the playground and assume the role of steamers. To be told, as I ran between these makeshift piers, resplendent in red blazer and with arms rotating, that I "looked like the *Waverley*" was the very acme of praise! Paddlers were the preferred role models: turbine steamers with their propulsion at the rear were not so appealing and imitators might have been exposed to ribald comment from the uninitiated. Even at home, ways were devised for feeding the obsession. Here, the trusty Singer sewing machine with foot treadle could take on a new role and its busy needle would rattle round a prepared map drawn on paper as it followed *Caledonia* or other vessel round the hand drawn piers. This was a particularly effective way of passing time during my occasional bouts of bronchitis and made a welcome change from noting the numbers of the 5 and 13 tramcars as they passed before the house. My regular visits to Rothesay produced other steamer related activities. The favourite was facing up to the wash of steamers as they approached the pier. Mighty sand ramparts were the usual bulwark against the waves but occasionally my pals and I would find an old tyre and perch on this out in the deeper water and see if we could remain tolerably dry. The late evening runs, *Caledonia* from Wemyss Bay and *Jupiter* circling the bay on her arrival from Gourock, were favourite tyre times! Only when there was a lull in the pier arrivals would I drift over to the Children's Corner where, resplendent in faded fez and felt backed moustache, Uncle Phil presented Punch and Judy or encouraged youngsters to display their talent in singing such contemporary pop songs as Chickory Chick or Doin' the Tennessee Wig Walk. But the mere toot of a whistle or sight of a steamer was enough to recall me to my customary station on the miniscule beach.

Then came secondary school and the interest was notched up a few points. Collecting postcards of steamers or piers with steamers became the new obsession. This led me naturally to track down shops like Adamson in Rothesay, Robertson in Gourock or Spencer in Tighnabruaich, places which at that time catered for the needs of the professional collector as well as the impecunious enthusiast. Adamson was my main port of call, where an asthmatic salesman brought out his selection of steamers old and new on sale at a shilling apiece. Along at Gourock, I made similar searches and, when the business there was being dispersed, I managed to make a few purchases before the collection was sold off. Friends too at school and elsewhere added photographs to my collection. On another front, newspaper cuttings on steamers, captains and shipping incidents were avidly amassed. My diaries, started in the early 50's, were larded with steamer names, especially in summer, rather like a train spotter's notebook. Then there was a brief dalliance with sailing models in the oily swamp down the road at Muirend. Here I had a hulk which I likened to the 1842 *Balmoral*. The resemblance was weak but my enthusiasm dispelled any deficiencies! There followed contact with Clyde steamer *cognoscenti* like retired teacher Cameron Somerville in his aging villa Athelstane at Craigmore and Graham Langmuir operating from a law office in Glasgow. Both these worthy gentlemen, deservedly acclaimed in steamer circles, fed the flames of my passion so that Clyde steamers of years gone by were now encompassed by my collecting fever, with occasional diversions too into the world of trams and trolleybuses. To be sure, Cameron Somerville vainly endeavoured to persuade me to show restraint and set bounds on my collecting. But I was past redemption and already copying slides from paintings of old steamers in Glasgow Art Galleries! All this proved costly but absorbing and opened new lines of enquiry. Discovery of the Clyde River Steamer Club kept me on the straight and narrow, with meetings at the once splendid but crumbling and creaky floored Christian Institute in Bothwell Street where monthly seances were held with illustrations supplied by glass slides on a magic lantern. Club members were fewer in those days but the enthusiasm was unbounded.

Halliday puffer *Norman* at Carradale lands her load on to the horse and cart waiting in the shallows.

MacBrayne's cargo ship *Loch Carron* leaves Kingston Dock with a Clyde Navigation Trust hopper ahead. Plenty of river traffic is evident around.

The wee *Marchioness of Lorne* on her Holy Loch run which suited her well. Events proved she was safer there!

Time marched on relentlessly but my support never faltered and was constantly being stimulated. My diaries record frequent steamer trips in 1953 and 1954 when we were still based at Kilchattan Bay for the month of July. For by now, every August saw me resident in Rothesay where opportunities for sailing were enhanced. 1954 brought a novelty in the shape of a ten day Highland voyage out of Kingston Dock in Glasgow on MacBrayne's sturdy cargo ship *Loch Carron* to Harris and islands between. We managed some forty calls in the course of our trip. My father had in his youth gone a similar cargo sail with his father and so this was a kind of pilgrimage or re-enactment for him. At all events it was a shared delight. *Loch Carron* carried only four passengers and our two mess fellows were English. Our relatively lively crossing of the Minch excited Dad and me but gave our companions alarm and nausea. I regarded their discomfiture with some satisfaction: it offered recompense for our daily exposure at breakfast to lurid and stomach turning descriptions by one of the pair of his erratic and colourful bowel movements. Ugh! I can almost hear him even now! At Harris, time allowed for a nerve racking, 14 shilling trip on an antique boneshaker bus to see Stornoway and then a chance to witness the silent Sabbath in Tarbert, meticulously recorded in my daily diary.

1955, often referred to as the great summer owing to an unusually fine spell of weather, saw the family abandon Kilchattan Bay and purchase a top flat on the sea front in Rothesay, next to the Victoria Hotel. It was a time of change. My grandmother had died in April so that Ardarach was cleared in readiness for selling. I can well remember the continual conflagration as masses of papers, clothes and other real treasures were torched at the bottom of the garden. It is so often the same at the time of a death: there is an urgent, almost frenzied desire to close the record and move on. So it was with us that summer. Our abandonment of Kilchattan did not go unnoticed. At the end of 1955, the summer service to the Bay was terminated. The old *Fife* had been withdrawn and scrapped in 1953, the attractive little *Marchioness of Lorne* had been found wanting after a single season in 1953 - her speed was abysmal - and it fell to the noisy, diesel electric paddler *Talisman* to terminate the service. Our family made use of her for our final fling at the Bay in 1954. As I have remarked, it was indeed a time of change. Earlier in the year, on 4th January, I had witnessed the arrival at Dunoon of Denny's *Arran*, inaugurating car ferry services on the Clyde. Other car ferries would follow and, far in the future, would oust the traditional Clyde steamer. As if a presage of things to come, the old turbine *Glen Sannox* was towed off to be scrapped at Ghent on 28th July that summer by the tug *Flying Enterprise* and her departure from the Clyde was noted by another young enthusiast, George Train, and me from our stance at the Red Rocks *en route* Garroch Head. We had united in our desire to have a last glimpse of her, he abandoning the tennis court with female challengers and I the rock pools with their evasive shrimps along the shore.

So far as I was concerned, our move to the esplanade in Rothesay had obvious advantages. Like Ardarach, it was ideally situated for steamer watching but also made possible a rush down to the adjacent pier whenever something of note was observed. It also encouraged increased participation. That summer of 1955, I took out two consecutive eight day season tickets of the Runabout, Any pier variety. Steamer traffic was flourishing in the fine weather, with two steamers regularly needed to clear the hordes waiting at Glasgow Bridge Wharf. Basking sharks were also much in evidence. Indeed, on 1st August, *Saint Columba* speared one as she rounded Ardlamont Point and it was with her till Tighnabruaich pier! Brodick bay was another hotspot for encounters with these giants of the sea. As I was still under 18, I travelled half price on my Runabout ticket - a mere seventeen shillings and sixpence! This was real value for money and so, not surprisingly, I repeated the exercise in 1956 with a fourteen day ticket. The diary carefully estimates the potential savings made as I endeavoured to take full advantage of the ticket. Even ferry runs at dawn and dusk were considered fair game! In the course of these sailings, I consorted with a coterie of enthusiasts, both young and old, and came to know some new Clyde experts or fanatics who presented challenging views on the future shape of Clyde cruising. Many of these thoughts, then seeming fantastic, have sadly been proved right. Most of us were equipped with sandwiches to be consumed on deck at a suitable point in the cruise. We longed for a force 8 gale in the Kilbrannan Sound to toss the turbine *Duchess of Hamilton* as she made for Campbeltown and to force us to duck down behind the parapet forward of the bridge as spray enveloped the deck. Yes, we were quite mad! If it was raining, we rarely noticed the extra moisture. Storms too made the new diesel *Maids* popular. These smaller vessels, new to the Clyde in 1953, were normally eschewed as being cramped and noisy. But they were extremely lively in heavy seas. Rough weather gave the *Maid of Skelmorlie* a chance to show her paces on an evening trip round both Cumbraes and we would be there. The afternoon cruise to Dunagoil Bay was another exhilarating opportunity but the *Duchess* in Kilbrannan Sound would usually be preferred as a full day excursion. Apart from these frantic forays into stormy seas, the over-riding object was to board as many steamers as possible each day and so to maximise the gain from use of the ticket. Good timetabling skills were essential!

Car ferry *Arran* crosses from Gourock in 1958. Here she appears as built with business like Samson posts.

Maid of Argyll en route for Innellan seen from the *Graham*. One of the four very similar *Maids* which appeared in 1953.

Caledonia flying the Glasgow High School flag comes alongside the new look *Queen Mary II* in May 1957 at Glasgow. Sloan's Line ship and river dredging work ahead.

Caledonia passes John Brown's at Clydebank on that same day with the High School flag at her main mast. One of the three Cunard sisters lies in the background.

Initiation

However, by this time everything was propelling me towards my goal of securing a post as assistant purser on the steamers. Life shipboard on *Loch Carron* had proved pleasurable; on a Clyde steamer it had to be idyllic. Assistant purser jobs could be had but they were highly sought after and I needed some leverage to jump the queue!

The fates were with me. I had made early contact in October 1956 with Gourock office, nerve centre of the Clyde fleet and popularly known as the Kremlin. As head boy, or captain as I was designated, I had been responsible for the charter of *Caledonia* by the High School to take place in May 1957. Preparing the ground and route for this whole school charter to Brodick from Glasgow offered significant opportunities to become known in the Kremlin - for the rector was most supportive and allowed me great scope in planning and running the charter, even to organising the Art department into preparing a flag for the occasion!

Ralston, the photographers, further marked the great day by choosing to produce a post card of *Caledonia* as she passed John Brown's yard at Clydebank with a Cunarder in the fitting out basin and the school flag at our mainmast. This charter, generously supported by both pupils and weather, brought me acclaim in school and, I believe, useful external recognition.

At all events, I was never called to Gourock for interview but, in late April 1957, a letter from Gourock headed BTC (British Transport Commission) Clyde Shipping Services arrived, intimating that my services would be required and on 10th June, another letter, this time under the heading Caledonian Steam Packet Company, requested me "to arrange to report to *Marchioness of Graham* at Ardrossan, 10am, Friday 5 July". A travel ticket from Glasgow to Ardrossan was provided. I had a placement!

True, this was not a paddler but neither was it a diesel. I had pinned my hopes on a paddler, preferably the capacious *Caledonia* sailing out of Ayr on the lower Firth. Beggars cannot be choosers. The *Marchioness of Graham* was in fact something of a mystery to me as being closely identified with Arran sailings summer and winter, as well as having acted as Ayr steamer until summer 1954. She was therefore rather a stranger at Rothesay and up river piers. Indeed, my best memory of her was as she headed out past Craigmore bound for Ayr and amazed me by producing a mighty wave, not the usual assortment of lesser waves more commonly produced by the steamers. She had won my attention then and here now was my chance to get better acquainted.

BRITISH TRANSPORT COMMISSION

A. STEWART
Manager

Telephone
GOUROCK 3126   ext. 11.

Telegraphic Address
MARINE RAILWAY GOUROCK

CLYDE SHIPPING SERVICES
SCOTTISH REGION
GOUROCK

Our Reference

Your Reference 1709

5th October, 1956.

Mr. Richard L. Orr,
   630 Clarkston Road,
      Netherlee,
         GLASGOW, S.4.

Dear Sir,

   ASSISTANT PURSERS : SEASON, 1957.

   Referring to your letter of 4th October, I have to advise you that your name has been placed on the list of applicants for a situation as Assistant Purser, and will receive consideration when arrangements are being made for Season, 1957.

   It will be appreciated that the position with regard to the re-engagement of Assistant Pursers employed during Season 1956 must be dealt with before new application can be considered.

                              Yours faithfully,

                              A. STEWART
                              PER

Letter of possibility - BTC are still in charge and they got my middle initial wrong with L for M! My first approach is acknowledged.

BRITISH TRANSPORT COMMISSION　　B.R. 13500/9

A. STEWART
Manager

Telephone
GOUROCK 31261　　ext. 11.

Telegraphic Address
MARINE RAILWAY GOUROCK

CLYDE SHIPPING SERVICES

SCOTTISH REGION

GOUROCK

Our Reference

Your Reference 1709

23rd April, 1957.

Mr. R. Orr,
630 Clarkston Road,
GLASGOW, S.4.

Dear Sir,

ASSISTANT PURSERS : SEASON,
1957.

With reference to your letter of 15th April, I am pleased to advise you that your services will be required as Assistant Purser for the coming summer season.

I shall write you again in course giving you detailed instructions.

Yours faithfully,

A. STEWART

Letter of probability - power still rests with BTC. Employment looks certain!

But before I could board the *Marchioness* at Ardrossan, again the fates intervened. Another letter from the Gourock Kremlin, dated 25 June, arrived with a change of instructions:

" Further to my letter of 16 June, [*or more accurately 10 June - the Kremlin was evidently not infallible*] please join *Glen Sannox* at Ardrossan at 10.0 am on Saturday 29 June instead of 5 July as already advised to you.

You will leave *Glen Sannox* at Brodick at 6.15 pm the same evening and thereafter join *Mars*. [*sic*] *of Graham* at that pier at 7.35 pm for the season."

So my start date had been brought forward! I was to serve on the brand new diesel car ferry *Glen Sannox* on her inaugural sailing to Arran. We would both be novices that day.

Well, that meant I had to reorganise my schedule and prepare myself for a summer afloat. The main items of luggage were a large brown canvas bag of decidedly worn appearance and a small case. These carried white shirts, of which several had detachable paper or plastic collars, a splendid doeskin uniform, kindly supplied by a teacher at school who had previously served as a naval officer - this was a class item! - stout black shoes with which to brave the elements, wellington boots too, for particularly inclement days - these were guaranteed in a Scottish summer - and a couple of civvy outfits for my deportment ashore. Besides this, I had necessary toiletries for shaving and personal grooming, pen and paper, diary, addresses of various friends to contact and a selection of reading material - Latin and Greek texts prescribed by the University for summer reading were not yet included. I did not imagine for a moment that such prescriptions were to be taken seriously! To render me the complete officer, I lacked only cap and badge. These were to be supplied on boarding ship but I had to find for myself the all-important white top.

Saturday 29 June could not come quickly enough and for the first account let us look to my log for that day.

TELEGRAPH:
"MARINE RAIL GOUROCK"

BR 13500/30

TELEPHONE No.:
GOUROCK 31261

THE CALEDONIAN STEAM PACKET CO. LIMITED

GENERAL MANAGER'S OFFICE

GOUROCK 10th June 19 57

Our ref. 1709.

A. STEWART,
General Manager

Mr. R. Orr,
   630 Clarkston Road,
      GLASGOW, S.4.

Dear Sir,

ASSISTANT PURSERS : 1957

Please arrange to report to "Mars. of Graham" at Ardrossan at 10. 0 a.m. on Friday 5th July, bringing with you your National Insurance Card.

I enclose free ticket for your journey from Glasgow to Ardrossan.

Yours faithfully,

A. Stewart
per

Letter of confirmation- the excitement rises! *Marchioness of Graham* comes out the hat!

BR 13500/30

Telegraph:
"Marine Rail Gourock"

Telephone No.:
Gourock 31261

THE CALEDONIAN STEAM PACKET CO. LIMITED

GENERAL MANAGER'S OFFICE

GOUROCK 22nd June, 1957

Our ref. 1709.

A. STEWART,
General Manager

Mr. E. Orr,
630 Clarkston Road,
GLASGOW, S.4.

Dear Sir,

Further to my letter of 15th June, please join "Glen Sannox" at Ardrossan at 10. 0 a.m. on Saturday 29th June instead of 5th July as already advised to you.

You will leave "Glen Sannox" at Brodick at 6.15 p.m. the same evening and thereafter join "Mars. of Graham" at that pier at 7.35 p.m. for the season.

Yours faithfully,

A. Stewart
per

Letter of transfer - change of arrangements and an earlier start date. The *Glen Sannox* certainly played havoc with the precise timings given in the letter!

Day 1 *Saturday 29 June*

Bright with showers later. Light West wind.

Left home with large bag and case at 8.05 - free pass. Took 8.50 special from St. Enoch station and reached Ardrossan at 10.10. Boarded *Glen Sannox*, dressed overall for her maiden voyage but, due to trouble with new car lift, did not sail till after 11.00, almost an hour late. Saw round her in my spare time - she's a lovely job inside but not a beauty outside! Her speed is around 21 knots but 17 on service. Very manoeuvrable and the Marine Superintendent seems proud of her. Officials buzzing everywhere, eg General Manager of the Company and his side-kick. Clyde River Steamer Club also well represented. She achieved only two double crossings and her third ended at Brodick when she left for Gourock. The first arrival at Arran was met by a tape cutting deputation. We carried few passengers, about 900 in all and about 100 cars. The ferry *Arran* took most of our runs since we were late. She and the *Graham* (on Whiting Bay run) carried the brunt. Gradually learned a little of the job. Left *Sannox* at 6.30 at Brodick, joining the *Graham* there at 7.40. We returned to Ardrossan at 9.00 for the weekend and, after much debate, I ended up in the chief purser's bed temporarily. Food excellent all day. A nice beginning. Vibration on *Sannox* very bad.

Commentary Day 1

You will note from the log that I was told to report to the ship at 10.00 although she was meant to sail at 10.20. This allowed me to travel on the connecting passenger train in possession of a free pass, altogether a most civilised way to begin! And we made our start from the imposing edifice that was Glasgow St Enoch station, starting point for piers on the lower firth. Now a mighty glass menagerie occupies the site, providing covered shopping where once the station had bustled, smoked and whistled.

At Ardrossan, we were greeted by the mighty *Sannox*, towering over Winton pier and resplendent with flags for her maiden voyage. This was not in fact my first sighting of the monster. I had already waited to witness her arriving two hours late at 7.00pm at Gourock after trials on Thursday 27 June. I had not much liked what I saw and I should have noted that lateness was to be her trademark for the season. Then as now she was certainly impressive, nay overwhelming, when viewed from the bow, with the CSP (Caledonian Steam Packet) red lion emblazoned there and her mighty superstructure resembling a floating tenement alongside Winton Pier. No Clyde steamer had ever looked like *this*! But her squat and dumpy funnel had no charm for me and her stern view was even less becoming. Indeed, from this angle she appeared to me at her worst, with her massive beam and no redeeming features. Vibration, too, was considerable and as for the supposed 21 knots - pure fantasy! A service speed of 17 knots was however quite attainable.

My late appearance meant that I was quickly put to work. I had barely time to clamber aboard, dump my gear and report to the tall, pockmarked and welcoming purser whose laugh filled the ship, before snatching cap and badge, which marked me out as a real crewman, and taking my station at the head of the gangway. There I found the second assistant purser, a local lad called Robbie. He would serve the season on her and had an agreeably relaxed approach to his duties. This was a decided advantage for me. I was raw, nervous and feeling very exposed. He introduced me to the counter, a key item in our armoury. Its purpose was to count the passengers as they boarded by clicking a button on the counter with the thumb. These counters came in various guises - here, on the *Sannox*, we used dull, grey oval objects with the push button on the top to record each person boarding, but on *Caledonia* they were circular and metallic silver in colour. Classier the latter may have been, but they did not sit so easily in the palm of the hand. Keeping count with the clicker and recording passenger numbers constituted a key role for an assistant purser. Robbie also schooled me in the basic and approved rope lashings for securing the gangways while we were at piers. No training, only sheer brute effort could heave the gangway up into position, especially when the tide was high and we towered above the pier. Gangway mechanical hoists were as yet unknown. Then there were the safety measures to observe, such as ensuring that no space was left between gangway and ship through which a determined or wayward child might plunge into the sea below. Besides all this, there was of course the all-important task of ticket collection. Efficient performance of this host of unfamiliar duties was the more needful that day with so much officialdom in evidence. The general manager, Alex Stewart, was conspicuous in dark Homburg hat (worn with or without gabardine coat) and with heavy rimmed spectacles. Never far from his side went his traffic clerk, alias side-kick, John Gunn, favouring a trilby hat and grey raincoat. On their faces they wore their changing moods: smiles when things were going according to plan, frowns when the car lift was proving troublesome and an altogether inscrutable look if the situation was unpredictable - not much different from politicians, I suppose.

But Robbie and I had other concerns. Once we set off on the 50 minute crossing to Brodick, I had to be shown how to deal with tickets.

Glen Sannox makes her first arrival in the rain at Gourock after trials on 27 June 1957 - not her prettiest angle in my view! Car ferry *Cowal* lies beyond.

Glen Sannox at Brodick dressed overall for her first day of service, 29 June 1957. She was running late!

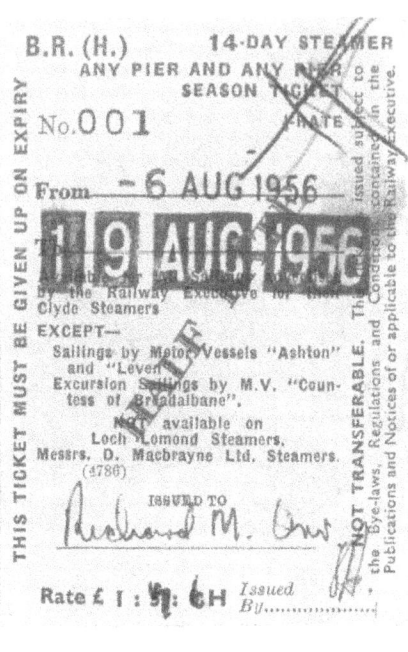

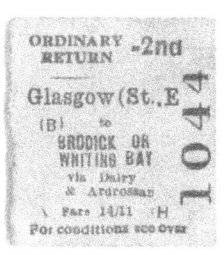
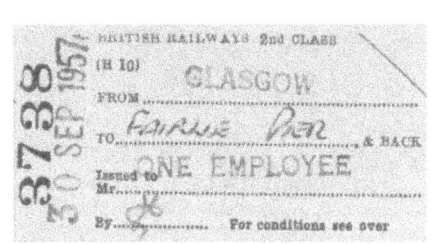

Some of the tickets collected, clockwise from top left:
My two week ticket in 1956. You will note I did *not* give up my runabout on expiry! So much for rules.
Blue Embarkation ticket for new *Glen Sannox* sailing.
Yellow half day excursion outward and return portion between Ardrossan and Arran.
White single for crossing from Arran to Ardrossan.
My green free pass to join *Glen Sannox* at Fairlie in September.
Green return portion from Glasgow St Enoch to Brodick.

And what a collection of these there were! Blue embarkation tickets to torment you on peak crossings - and of course this had to be such a one - white ordinary return tickets, yellow day return tickets, red ones for dogs and bikes, white privilege tickets identifiable by a large red P and reserved for railway and Company employees, single tickets (double size, of course) and finally these infernal little third portions of the green rail connection tickets. Our task was to collect these from disembarking passengers, cancel them with clippers, sort them in trays according to type, and often, as an added nuisance, in numerical order, always so at month ends. When all this was duly completed, we tied them in separate bundles, parcelled them in newspapers or confectionery boxes, (an interesting shape of parcel was often a particular delight!) and sent them off to the Kremlin where they might be checked before being forwarded to the main sorting office.

This done, there was time to look around. The new ship was extremely spacious and bright in her lounges and assembly areas. The purser's office was tucked away in a gloomy corner next the men's toilet but, outside the window, the purser's view was enhanced by a huge CSP flag emblazoned on the flooring of the assembly area. If the ticket office was a room with little view, it was far otherwise with the cancellation ticket office where the assistant pursers were to live, move and have their being. This was a delightful room abaft the bridge and the captain's accommodation. From it, one had a commanding outlook over the stumpy funnel and upper deck. It was thoughtfully equipped with two lounge seats and matching curtains and carpet. But, of course, there was a catch! The room was to be available for any visiting VIP and at such times we had to vacate and leave the tickets till later. An inconvenience, certainly, but the compensating comforts were considerable. We were really not meant to sprawl about on the easy chairs but the temptation was all too great! For our lesser needs there were supplied a wooden table and two small chairs. Now, the captain was most anxious to exclude us totally from his bridge area but there was no alternative, sadly for him! When installing a bed for one assistant was proposed, the captain went ballistic but that all came later.

Let us get back now to the main public accommodation. Passenger movement at the gangways was to be a problem. The alleyways at the head of the gangways were narrow and caused crowding. The ship's great height, requiring long, steep gangways at high tides, added to our problems. It would be a long time before specially designed gangways addressed this difficulty. But these were trifles when compared with the operation of the exciting new hydraulic lift. This system was devised to obviate the electrically operated wires and pulleys used on the smaller ferries serving Dunoon and Rothesay. Tidier the new lift certainly was but it was slow, unreliable and regularly jammed when it went off alignment. The result was long delays and long faces for the manager and his clerk. I suppose we were lucky to get away at 11.00, considering the number of cars attracted by our first sailing! Anyway, Lady Jean Fforde of Arran waited and was there at Brodick to cut the tape and welcome the first car driver from the ferry. Thereafter, the lift ensured that we were confined to two double crossings in total and a late final crossing to Brodick. We certainly had an easy time, while the ferry *Arran*, released from duties upriver, and the *Graham*, which was to be my ship for the summer, maintained the service times as far as the *Sannox*'s bulky presence permitted. Yes, it was an easy initiation both for me and for the new ferry. I jumped ship at this point with all my gear, as per instructions, leaving the *Sannox* to head off up river to Gourock for adjustments. It was not till Friday 5 July that she resumed her service run.

On boarding the *Graham* at the end of the day and commencing my season aboard this attractive little turbine, my first concern was to find a bed for the night. She had accommodation for only one assistant purser and that was already taken. Fortunately for me, the chief purser was both genial and accommodating and heading up river for home. No doubt he thought I should do the same but instead I readily chose to take his bed for the night. It was the beginning of my dream. Why on earth would I want to go back home? Nor was there any suggestion of going ashore for drink. Yes, I was very much a novice!

Glen Sannox heads upriver at the end of her first day and I await transfer to *Graham* at Brodick.

PROGRAMME
OF
PLEASURE SAILINGS
FROM
AYR, TROON and ARDROSSAN
SEASON 1957

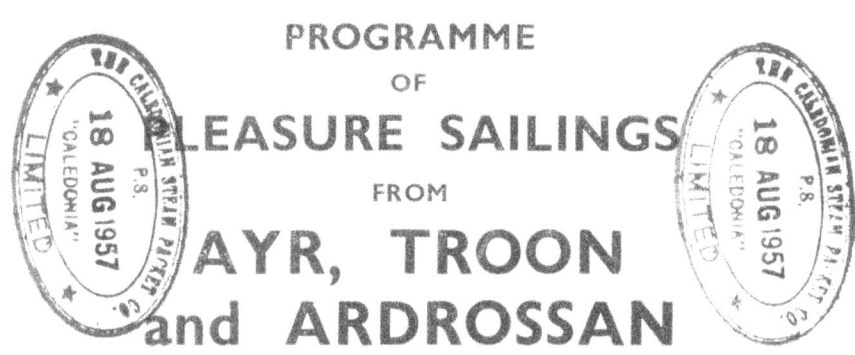

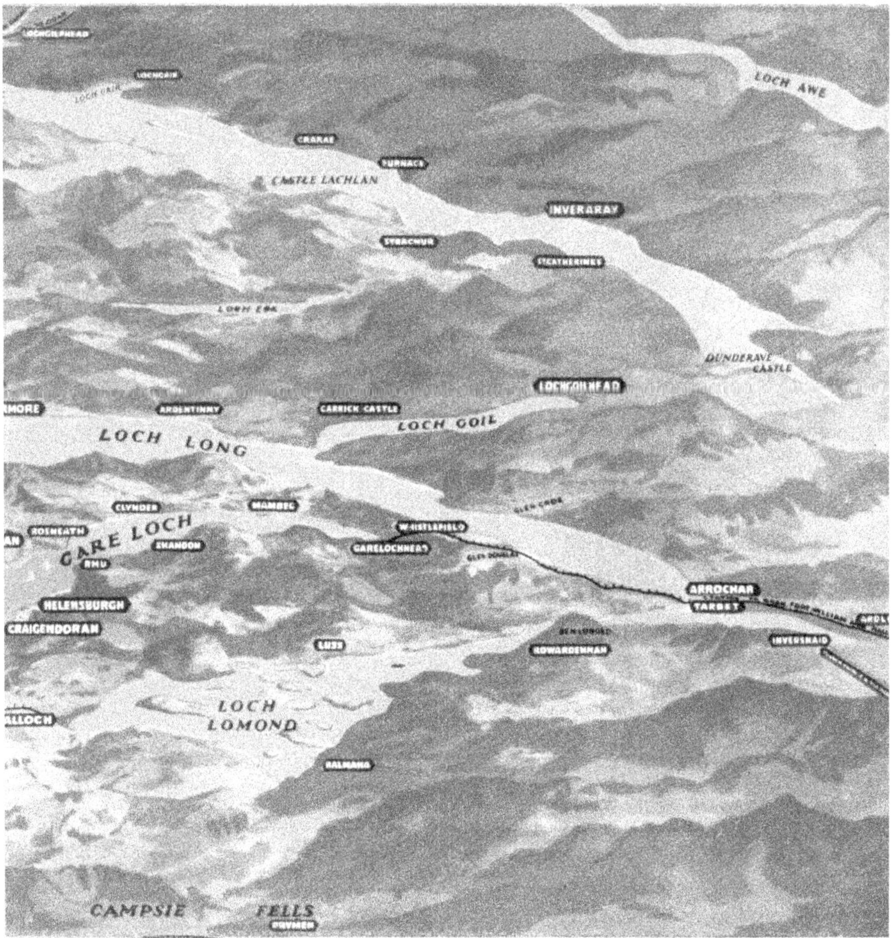

THE CALEDONIAN STEAM PACKET COMPANY LIMITED
in association with
BRITISH RAILWAYS

PROGRAMME OF EXCURSION SAILINGS

FROM

AYR, TROON and ARDROSSAN (Winton Pier)

Date	To	Page
JUNE		
Sunday 30th	Dunoon and Cruise to Gare Loch	2
JULY		
Monday 1st	Rothesay via Brodick and Kyles of Bute	2
Tuesday 2nd	Tighnabruaich (Kyles of Bute) via Rothesay	3
Wednesday 3rd	Afternoon Cruise to Millport (Isle of Cumbrae)	4
	Evening Cruise to Brodick Bay	4
Thursday 4th	Campbeltown (Kintyre) via Whiting Bay	3
Saturday 6th	Afternoon Cruise Round Ailsa Craig	4
	Evening Cruise to Brodick (Time Ashore)	4
Sunday 7th	Rothesay and Cruise to Loch Riddon (Kyles of Bute)	2
Monday 8th	Dunoon via Brodick	2
Tuesday 9th	Dunoon and Cruise to Loch Goil via Millport	3
Wednesday 10th	Afternoon Cruise to Brodick (Arran)	4
	Evening Cruise to Pladda	4
Thursday 11th	Campbeltown (Kintyre) via Whiting Bay	3
Saturday 13th	Afternoon Cruise Round the Islands of Cumbrae	4
	Evening Cruise to Whiting Bay (Time Ashore)	4
Sunday 14th	Dunoon and Cruise to Gare Loch	2
Monday 15th	Rothesay via Brodick and Kyles of Bute	2
Tuesday 16th	Tighnabruaich (Kyles of Bute) via Rothesay	3
Wednesday 17th	Afternoon Cruise to Millport (Isle of Cumbrae)	4
	Evening Cruise to Holy Isle	4
Thursday 18th	Campbeltown (Kintyre) via Whiting Bay	3
Saturday 20th	Arran Bays Afternoon Cruise	4
	Evening Cruise to Brodick (Time Ashore)	4
Sunday 21st	Rothesay and Cruise to Loch Riddon (Kyles of Bute)	2
Monday 22nd	Dunoon via Brodick	2
Tuesday 23rd	Dunoon and Cruise to Loch Goil via Millport	3
Wednesday 24th	Afternoon Cruise to Brodick (Arran)	4
	Evening Cruise to Pladda	4
Thursday 25th	Campbeltown (Kintyre) via Whiting Bay	3
Saturday 27th	Afternoon Cruise Round Ailsa Craig	4
	Evening Cruise to Whiting Bay (Time Ashore)	4
Sunday 28th	Dunoon and Cruise to Gare Loch	2
Monday 29th	Rothesay via Brodick and Kyles of Bute	2
Tuesday 30th	Tighnabruaich (Kyles of Bute) via Rothesay	3
Wednesday 31st	Afternoon Cruise to Millport (Isle of Cumbrae)	4
	Evening Cruise to Brodick Bay	4
AUGUST		
Thursday 1st	Campbeltown (Kintyre) via Whiting Bay	3
Saturday 3rd	Arran Bays Afternoon Cruise	4
	Evening Cruise to Brodick (Time Ashore)	4
Sunday 4th	Rothesay and Cruise to Loch Riddon (Kyles of Bute)	2
Monday 5th	Dunoon via Brodick	2
Tuesday 6th	Dunoon and Cruise to Loch Goil via Millport	3
Wednesday 7th	Rothesay via Whiting Bay and Kyles of Bute	3
	Evening Cruise to Holy Isle	4
Thursday 8th	Campbeltown (Kintyre) via Whiting Bay	3
Saturday 10th	Afternoon Cruise Round the Islands of Cumbrae	4
	Evening Cruise to Whiting Bay (Time Ashore)	4
Sunday 11th	Dunoon and Cruise to Gare Loch	2
Monday 12th	Rothesay via Brodick and Kyles of Bute	2
Tuesday 13th	Tighnabruaich (Kyles of Bute) via Rothesay	3
Wednesday 14th	Afternoon Cruise to Millport (Isle of Cumbrae)	4
	Evening Cruise to Brodick Bay	4
Thursday 15th	Campbeltown (Kintyre) via Whiting Bay	3
Saturday 17th	Afternoon Cruise Round Ailsa Craig	4
	Evening Cruise to Brodick (Time Ashore)	4
Sunday 18th	Rothesay and Cruise to Loch Riddon (Kyles of Bute)	2
Monday 19th	Dunoon via Brodick	2
Tuesday 20th	Dunoon and Cruise to Loch Goil via Millport	3
Wednesday 21st	Afternoon Cruise to Brodick (Arran)	4
	Evening Cruise to Pladda	4
Thursday 22nd	Campbeltown (Kintyre) via Whiting Bay	3
Saturday 24th	Afternoon Cruise Round the Islands of Cumbrae	4
	Evening Cruise to Whiting Bay (Time Ashore)	4
Sunday 25th	Dunoon and Cruise to Gare Loch	2
Monday 26th	Rothesay via Brodick and Kyles of Bute	2
Tuesday 27th	Tighnabruaich (Kyles of Bute) via Rothesay	3
Wednesday 28th	Afternoon Cruise to Millport (Isle of Cumbrae)	4
	Evening Cruise to Holy Isle	4
Thursday 29th	Campbeltown (Kintyre) via Whiting Bay	3
Saturday 31st	Dunoon for Cowal Highland Gathering	3
SEPTEMBER		
Sunday 1st	Rothesay and Loch Riddon (Kyles of Bute)	2

SPECIAL AFTERNOON CRUISE FROM AYR

by Turbine Steamer "DUCHESS OF HAMILTON"
EVERY FRIDAY—7th JUNE until 20th SEPTEMBER
TO
ARRAN COAST AND ROUND HOLY ISLE

Leaving **AYR** at 1.45 p.m.   Arriving back at 4.0 p.m.
CRUISE 4/6 FARE

DAY CRUISES from AYR, TROON, ARDROSSAN
by Paddle Steamer "CALEDONIA" (WINTON PIER)

Note:—In connection with these sailings the Western S.M.T. Company's 'Buses will run between Prestwick and Ayr Stations and Ayr Harbour also between Troon Cross and Harbour.

SUNDAYS

To DUNOON and CRUISE TO GARE LOCH
on 30th June, 14th and 28th July also 11th and 25th August.

OUTWARD		a.m.	RETURN		p.m.
Ayr Harbour	leave	11 15	Dunoon	leave	4 0
Troon Harbour	,,	11 55	Largs	,,	4 45
Ardrossan (Winton Pier)	,,	12 45p	Ardrossan	arrive	5 45
Largs	arrive	1 45	Troon	,,	6 35
Dunoon	,,	2 30	Ayr	,,	7 15
thence cruise					

CRUISE FARES

FROM AYR OR TROON TO		FROM ARDROSSAN TO	
GARE LOCH 12/-	DUNOON 11/-	GARE LOCH 9/6	DUNOON 7/6

To ROTHESAY and CRUISE TO LOCH RIDDON (Kyles of Bute)
on 7th and 21st July also 4th and 18th August also 1st September

OUTWARD		a.m.	RETURN		p.m.
Ayr Harbour	leave	11 15	Rothesay	leave	4 5
Troon Harbour	,,	11 55	Largs	,,	4 45
Ardrossan (Winton Pier)	,,	12 45p	Ardrossan	arrive	5 45
Largs	arrive	1 45	Troon	,,	6 35
Rothesay	,,	2 25	Ayr	,,	7 15
thence cruise					

CRUISE FARES

FROM AYR OR TROON TO		FROM ARDROSSAN TO	
LOCH RIDDON 12/-	ROTHESAY 11/-	LOCH RIDDON 9/6	ROTHESAY 7/6

MONDAYS

To DUNOON via BRODICK (Allowing time ashore)
8th and 22nd July also 5th and 19th August

OUTWARD		a.m.	RETURN		p.m.
Ayr Harbour	leave	10 0	Dunoon	leave	3 0
Troon Harbour	,,	10 40	Largs	,,	3 45
Brodick	arrive	11 55	Brodick	,,	5 0
Largs	,,	1 15p	Troon	arrive	6 15
Dunoon	,,	2 0	Ayr	,,	7 0

RETURN FARES FROM AYR OR TROON TO
DUNOON 12/-   BRODICK 7/-

To ROTHESAY via BRODICK and KYLES OF BUTE returning via Garroch Head
on 1st, 15th and 29th July also 12th and 26th August

OUTWARD		a.m.	RETURN		p.m.
Ayr Harbour	leave	10 0	Rothesay	leave	3 30
Troon Harbour	,,	10 40	Brodick	,,	5 0
Brodick	arrive	11 55	Troon	arrive	6 15
Rothesay	,,	2 15p	Ayr	,,	7 0

RETURN FARES FROM AYR OR TROON TO
ROTHESAY 12/-   BRODICK 7/-

ISLE OF ARRAN COACH TOUR
FROM WHITING BAY (OR BRODICK)

Messrs. Lennox Motor Coaches await the arrival of the Ayr and Troon excursion steamer at Whiting Bay on Thursdays and at Brodick on Mondays to convey passengers on the tour round the Island of Arran (three hours drive).

MOTOR 7/6 FARE (Juvenile 4/-)

Tickets for the motor tour should be obtained on board the steamer.

CONNECTING TRAIN SERVICES
AND THROUGH RAIL AND STEAMER FARES FROM
GIRVAN AND MAYBOLE via AYR

On Mondays, Tuesdays and Thursdays (also Wednesday, 7th August)

OUTWARD		a.m.	RETURN		p.m.
Girvan	leave	8 48	Ayr	leave	7 37
Maybole	,,	9 8	Maybole	arrive	7 55
Ayr	arrive	9 21	Girvan	,,	8 17

THROUGH SECOND CLASS RAIL AND STEAMER RETURN FARES

From	LARGS and MILLPORT	BRODICK and WHITING BAY	DUNOON (direct)	ROTHESAY (direct)	DUNOON (via Brodick) and ROTHESAY (via Brodick and Kyles of Bute)	CAMPBELTOWN LOCH GOIL and TIGHNABRUAICH
GIRVAN	12/6	11/-	15/-	16/-	16/-	16/-
MAYBOLE	10/3	8/9	12/9	13/9	13/9	13/9

Through First Class Rail Fares can also be obtained

2

DAY CRUISES from AYR, TROON and ARDROSSAN
By Paddle Steamer "CALEDONIA"

Note:—In connection with these sailings the Western S.M.T. Company's 'Buses will run between Prestwick and Ayr Stations and Ayr Harbour also between Troon Cross and Harbour.

TUESDAYS

To LOCH GOIL via MILLPORT and DUNOON
on 9th and 23rd July also 6th and 20th August

OUTWARD		a.m.	RETURN		p.m.
Ayr Harbour	leave	10 0	Dunoon	leave	3 30
Troon Harbour	,,	10 40	Largs	,,	4 15
Ardrossan (Winton Pier)	,,	11 30	Millport	,,	4 40
Millport (Old Pier)	arrive	12 20p	Ardrossan	arrive	5 30
Largs	,,	12 45	Troon	,,	6 15
Dunoon	,,	1 30	Ayr	,,	7 0
thence Cruise					

CRUISE FARES

FROM AYR OR TROON TO — LOCH GOIL 12/-   DUNOON 11/-   MILLPORT 8/6
FROM ARDROSSAN TO — LOCH GOIL 9/6   DUNOON 7/6   MILLPORT 5/6

To TIGHNABRUAICH (Kyles of Bute) via ROTHESAY
2nd, 16th and 30th July also 13th and 27th August

OUTWARD		a.m.	RETURN		p.m.
Ayr Harbour	leave	10 0	Tighnabruaich	leave	3 5
Troon Harbour	,,	10 40	Rothesay	,,	3 55
Ardrossan (Winton Pier)	,,	11 30	Largs	,,	4 30
Largs	arrive	12 30p	Ardrossan	arrive	5 30
Rothesay	,,	1 5	Troon	,,	6 15
Tighnabruaich	,,	2 0	Ayr	,,	7 0

RETURN FARES

FROM AYR OR TROON TO — TIGHNABRUAICH 12/-   ROTHESAY 11/-
FROM ARDROSSAN TO — TIGHNABRUAICH 9/6   ROTHESAY 7/6

WEDNESDAYS

To ROTHESAY via WHITING BAY and KYLES OF BUTE
on 7th August only

OUTWARD		a.m.	RETURN		p.m.
Ayr Harbour	leave	10 0	Rothesay	leave	3 30
Troon Harbour	,,	10 40	Whiting Bay	,,	5 0
Whiting Bay	arrive	11 55	Troon	arrive	6 15
Rothesay	,,	2 30p	Ayr	,,	7 0

RETURN FARES FROM AYR OR TROON TO — ROTHESAY 12/-   WHITING BAY 7/-

THURSDAYS

To CAMPBELTOWN (Kintyre) via WHITING BAY
From 4th July until 29th August

OUTWARD		a.m.	RETURN		p.m.
Ayr Harbour	leave	10 0	Campbeltown	leave	3 15
Troon Harbour	,,	10 40	Whiting Bay	,,	5 0
Whiting Bay	arrive	11 55	Troon	arrive	6 15
Campbeltown	,,	1 45p	Ayr	,,	7 0

RETURN FARES FROM AYR OR TROON TO — CAMPBELTOWN 12/-   WHITING BAY 7/-

SATURDAY, 31st August, only

To DUNOON for COWAL HIGHLAND GATHERING

OUTWARD		a.m.	RETURN		p.m.
Ayr Harbour	leave	10 0	Dunoon	leave	6 45
Troon Harbour	,,	10 40	Largs	,,	7 30
Ardrossan (Winton Pier)	,,	11 30	Ardrossan	arrive	8 20
Largs	arrive	12 20p	Troon	,,	9 10
Dunoon	,,	1 5	Ayr	,,	9 50

RETURN FARES

FROM AYR OR TROON TO — DUNOON 11/-
FROM ARDROSSAN TO — DUNOON 7/6

TICKETS OBTAINABLE IN ADVANCE

Note.—Steamer tickets can be obtained, in advance if required, at the following Stations and accredited Rail Ticket Agencies

Steamer from Ayr ... At Ayr, Newton-on-Ayr, Prestwick and Heads of Ayr Stations, and at Messrs. Scott's Tourist Agency, 36 Newmarket Street, Ayr.
Steamer from Troon ... At Troon Station and at the Town Clerk's Office, Troon.
Steamer from Ardrossan ... At Ardrossan (Winton Pier) Station.

3

Proposed Timetable for *Caledonia* had fate not intervened.

AFTERNOON CRUISES from AYR and TROON
By Paddle Steamer "CALEDONIA"

Note:—In connection with these sailings the Western S.M.T. Company's 'Buses will run between Prestwick and Ayr Stations and Ayr Harbour also between Troon Cross and Harbour.

WEDNESDAYS

To MILLPORT (Isle of Cumbrae) (Allowing time ashore)
on 3rd, 17th and 31st July and 14th and 28th August

OUTWARD	p.m.	RETURN	p.m.
Ayr Harbour .... leave	2 0	Millport .... leave	4 50
Troon Harbour .... ,,	2 40	Troon .... arrive	6 0
Millport (Old Pier) .... arrive	3 50	Ayr .... ,,	6 40

CRUISE 5/6 FARE

To BRODICK (Arran) (Allowing time ashore)
on 10th and 24th July also 21st August

OUTWARD	p.m.	RETURN	p.m.
Ayr Harbour .... leave	2 0	Brodick .... leave	4 50
Troon Harbour .... ,,	2 40	Troon .... arrive	6 0
Brodick .... arrive	3 50	Ayr .... ,,	6 40

CRUISE 5/6 FARE

AFTERNOON CRUISES from AYR

FRIDAYS
By Turbine Steamer "DUCHESS OF HAMILTON"

7th JUNE until 20th SEPTEMBER

TO ARRAN COAST
AND
ROUND HOLY ISLE

Leaving AYR at 1.45 p.m.   Arriving back at 4.0 p.m.

CRUISE 4/6 FARE

SATURDAYS
By Paddle Steamer "CALEDONIA"

6th and 27th July also 17th August	13th July also 10th and 24th August	20th July also 3rd August
ROUND AILSA CRAIG	**ROUND ISLANDS OF CUMBRAE**	**ARRAN BAYS CRUISE** (Whiting, Lamlash and Brodick Bays)

Leaving AYR at 2.15 p.m.   Arriving back at 5.30 p.m.

CRUISE 5/- FARE

EVENING CRUISES FROM AYR

WEDNESDAYS
By Paddle Steamer "CALEDONIA"

3rd and 31st July and 14th August	10th and 24th July and 21st August	17th July and 7th and 28th August
TO BRODICK BAY	**TO PLADDA**	**TO HOLY ISLE**

Leaving AYR at 7.15 p.m.   Arriving back at 9.45 p.m.

CRUISE 4/6 FARE

SATURDAYS
By Paddle Steamer "CALEDONIA"

6th and 20th July also 3rd and 17th August	13th and 27th July also 10th and 24th August
BRODICK (Time Ashore)	**WHITING BAY** (Time Ashore)

Leaving AYR at 6.30 p.m.   Arriving back at 10.0 p.m.

CRUISE 4/6 FARE

SERVICES BETWEEN ARDROSSAN or FAIRLIE PIER and BRODICK and WHITING BAY

MONDAYS TO SATURDAYS
1st JUNE until 30th SEPTEMBER

FROM FAIRLIE PIER TO BRODICK	FROM ARDROSSAN (Winton Pier)		TO FAIRLIE PIER FROM BRODICK	TO ARDROSSAN (Winton Pier)	
	TO BRODICK	TO WHITING BAY		FROM BRODICK	FROM WHITING BAY
a.m.	a.m.	a.m.	a.m.	a.m.	a.m.
6 40	—	—	—	7M5	6M25
—	10†10	10A10	—	8 35	1*25p
—	10*20	10*20	—	11*45	3C50
—	1*30	—	11†50	—	5*10
2†15p	—	—	—	3* 0p	—
—	4*30	3*10p	—	4†40	—
—	6† 5	7 F 5	—	6*20	—
—	6B45	—	7†20p	—	—
—	7 F 5				

* Saturdays only. † Except Saturdays. M Mondays only.
A 1st and 15th July, 1st, 5th and 7th August only. B Saturdays, 22nd June until 31st August, inclusive.
C 28th June, 15th and 31st July, 5th, 7th and 30th August.
F Fridays only, 28th June until 30th August, also Friday, 20th September.

RETURN FARES
ARDROSSAN (Winton Pier) or FAIRLIE PIER to BRODICK or WHITING BAY

ORDINARY RETURN	DAY EXCURSION	AFTERNOON EXCURSION
(Valid three months)	(Valid on date of issue)	(Valid on date of issue)
7/3	6/6	5/6

EVENING CRUISES TO BRODICK
MONDAYS TO FRIDAYS by T.S.M.V. "GLEN SANNOX"

Leaving ARDROSSAN (Winton Pier) 6 5 p.m. Returning via FAIRLIE PIER thence train to ARDROSSAN (South Beach). Arriving back 9.15 p.m.

CRUISE FARE **5/6** (2nd CLASS RAIL)

SATURDAY AFTERNOON CRUISES
From ARDROSSAN (Winton Pier)
by T.S.M.V. "GLEN SANNOX" or Turbine Steamer "MARCHIONESS OF GRAHAM"
TO ARRAN (BRODICK AND WHITING BAY)

OUTWARD	p.m.	p.m.	p.m.	RETURN	p.m.	p.m.	p.m.
Ardrossan (Winton Pier)...leave	1 30	3 10	4 30	Whiting Bay ....leave	—	5 10	—
Brodick............arrive	2 20	—	5 20	Brodick .... ,,	3 0	—	6 20
Whiting Bay .... ,,	—	4 15	—	Ardrossan (Winton Pier)......arrive	3 50	6 15	7 10

CRUISE **5/6** FARE

ROUND ARRAN MOTOR COACH TOUR
FROM BRODICK

Messrs. Ribbecks' Motor Coaches run in connection with 10.10 a.m. sailing from Ardrossan to Brodick daily, Mondays to Saturdays, to convey passengers on the **ROUND ARRAN TOUR** (No. 10A) (three hours drive).

MOTOR **7/6** FARE
(Juveniles 4/-)
Motor tickets should be obtained on board the steamer.

ARRAN CAR FERRY SERVICE
FAIRLIE PIER or ARDROSSAN (Winton Pier) and BRODICK (Arran)

FAIRLIE TO BRODICK	ARDROSSAN TO BRODICK	BRODICK TO FAIRLIE	BRODICK TO ARDROSSAN
6 40 a.m.	10†10 a.m.	11†50 a.m.	8 35 a.m.
2†15 p.m.	10*20 a.m.	7†20 p.m.	11*45 a.m.
—	1*30 p.m.	—	3* 0 p.m.
—	4*30 p.m.	—	4†40 p.m.
—	6† 5 p.m.	—	6*20 p.m.

* Saturdays only. † Except Saturdays.

CHARGES FOR ACCOMPANIED MOTOR CARS AT OWNER'S RISK (including Driver)

	Single Journey	Return Journey
Not exceeding 13' 0"........	£2 7 0	£3 10 0
Over 13' 0" and not exceeding 14' 6"........	3 4 0	4 15 0
Over 14' 6"........	4 0 0	6 0 0

It is advisable for motorists to reserve shipping space prior to date of travel—especially on Saturdays.
For Car Reservations, apply to:—GENERAL MANAGER, THE CALEDONIAN STEAM PACKET COMPANY LIMITED, GOUROCK STATION. Telephone Gourock 31261.

Kildonan laid up at Ardrossan with Burns Laird *Lairdscrest* ahead of her.

Lairds Isle ex Southern Region's *Riviera* of 1911 - Denny built and a flier! In summer 1955 it was she that took our school cadet force over to Ireland for summer camp.

Day 2 *Sunday 30 June*

Warm and sunny. Little wind.

Lay inactive all day at Ardrossan - coaling in morning. I got up at 8.00 and had breakfast at 9.00. Took snaps of *Graham* and of *Kildonan* (now rusting in the inner harbour and displaced by *Sannox*) and also *Caledonia* when she called at 12.45 on a cruise from Ayr to Gareloch, returning at 5.25. Apart from *Caley*, no other CSP boats were to be seen. I bought two film spools in a chemist to feed my habit, walked around a bit and sunbathed in the afternoon. Apart from fatty chops at dinner and hard lumpy mince for tea, the meals were quite good. The captain seemed quite sociable at the times when he appeared for meals. My fellow purser, another Richard, vanished to Troon or Largs for the day once we had finished sorting yesterday's tickets. The Isle of Man steamer, *Mona's Queen*, arrived about 4.15 and docked skilfully in the inner harbour. Bought Sunday Post but had little use for it. The relief purser is very friendly and among the most pleasant on board. Looked over next week's sailing roster and wrote to Mum and Dad and also to Tubby MacCormick. *Lairds Isle* arrived from her day trip to Dublin and also docked in the inner harbour. Chatted with the galley boy and had supper with him at 9.00. Not the most eventful day.

Commentary Day 2

It is very clear from the report just how starry-eyed I was at the outset. The *Graham* had no Sunday roster and so I stayed put with the ship, whereas most of the crew, relief purser included, headed home if they were not paid to work. I was clearly different! Without the possible incentive of a rail pass, I chose to stay with my new ship. There was plenty to interest me in the harbour and photos to be taken of the now redundant Arran cargo vessel *Kildonan* - *Glen Sannox* obviated the need for this aging vessel - and arrival of *Mona's Queen*. *Kildonan* dated back to 1933 and bore the name *Arran* till 1953 when she was renamed to allow the name *Arran* to pass to the new car ferry. The other assistant went off up river but I remained where I was. I even helped with the tickets from the previous day - a clear indication of my fanaticism. I was there for my beloved *Caledonia* each time she called and took my meals aboard ship. I even seemed anxious to enjoy them although they don't sound any too attractive as described. And, of course, I had my first meeting with the captain. I held him in awe but as yet I did not find him scary. He seemed human enough. But for company, my preference was the galley boy, another rookie. The relief purser too seemed amiable when he appeared late in the day to prepare for the early morning start. So far, so good.

This was the down side of my having been rushed into service early. Sunday sailings were standard up river but Arran was a different story. Religious considerations held sway down in these waters and it was not till 1959 that the turbine *Duchess* was allowed to call at Whiting Bay on a Sunday evening as she proceeded back from Campbeltown on her way up river. A regular ferry service to Arran on Sundays did not come to pass till 1965. Now, for an assistant purser, Sunday sailings were important. They added a full pound to the weekly wage of a little over £2. Three whole pounds and more! For me, a summer season without Sundays was the expectation and I don't think I was greatly upset by the prospect.

Oh, and one other thing to note. You will see that I was immediately into letter writing. This I have always enjoyed. It gives you time to reflect and plan out what you wish to say. Phone conversations are less satisfactory. You so often forget to mention things. With a letter you can always revisit it until it is finally posted. And anyway, phones were not always conveniently placed at piers for steamers and usually proved costly. The convenience of e-mail was far in the future. And I suspect internet cafes would never have been my scene anyway! So here I was, already writing to my parents, schoolmates and friends. A pattern was being established. Iain MacCormick (*alias* Tubby, later the Toad – these were among his more respectable nicknames, and at an age when nicknames were fashionable. With advancing years, we tend to revert to more normal nomenclature. Of course, there are exceptions but for me today to address Iain as Toad or Tubby is hard to imagine) was a loyal friend both in the school corps and as my vice captain in school. He wrote a fine copper-plate hand and was a good correspondent in these early years on the Clyde. Highet Rodger too, a local pal, was a regular writer and even embellished his epistles with the occasional artwork. I greatly valued these contacts with my other world.

THE CALEDONIAN STEAM PACKET COMPANY LIMITED

CLYDE COAST STEAMER FLEET

"CALEDONIA" (Paddle—Triple Expansion). Built 1934 by Wm. Denny & Bros. Ltd., Dumbarton. Length 230 feet. Gross tonnage 624.

"DUCHESS OF HAMILTON" (Turbine—3 screws). Built 1932 by Harland & Wolff Ltd., Glasgow. Length 272 feet. Gross tonnage 801.

"DUCHESS OF MONTROSE" (Turbine—3 screws). Built 1930 by Wm. Denny & Bros. Ltd., Dumbarton. Length 273 feet Gross tonnage 795.

"JEANIE DEANS" (Paddle—Triple Expansion). Built 1931 by Fairfield Shipbuilding and Engineering Co., Glasgow. Length 258 feet. Gross tonnage 840.

"JUPITER" (Paddle—Triple Expansion). Built 1937 by Fairfield Shipbuilding and Engineering Co., Glasgow. Length 231 feet. Gross tonnage 642.

"MARCHIONESS OF GRAHAM" (Turbine—Twin screw). Built 1936 by Fairfield Shipbuilding and Engineering Co., Glasgow. Length 231 feet. Gross tonnage 586.

"QUEEN MARY II" (Turbine—3 screws). Built 1933 by Wm. Denny & Bros. Ltd., Dumbarton. Length 263 feet. Gross tonnage 918.

"TALISMAN" (Paddle—Diesel Electric). Built 1935 by A. & J. Inglis Ltd., Glasgow. Length 223 feet. Gross tonnage 544.

"WAVERLEY" (Paddle—Triple Expansion). Built 1947 by A. & J. Inglis Ltd., Glasgow. Length 240 feet. Gross tonnage 694.

Fleet list as it appears in 1957 timetable. First the steamers and then the motor vessels - *Talisman* is a misfit!

THE CALEDONIAN STEAM PACKET COMPANY LIMITED

CLYDE COAST MOTOR VESSEL FLEET

"ARRAN" (Motor—Twin Screw). Built 1954 by Wm. Denny & Bros. Ltd., Dumbarton. Length 179 feet. Gross tonnage 568.

"BUTE" (Motor—Twin Screw). Built 1954 by Ailsa Shipbuilding Co., Troon. Length 179 feet. Gross tonnage 568.

"COWAL" (Motor—Twin Screw). Built 1954 by Ailsa Shipbuilding Co., Troon. Length 179 feet. Gross tonnage 569.

"GLEN SANNOX" (Motor—Twin Screw). Built 1957 by Ailsa Shipbuilding Co., Troon. Length 257 feet. Gross tonnage 1,000.

"MAID OF ASHTON" (Motor—Twin Screw). Built 1953 by Yarrow's, Glasgow. Length 165 feet. Gross tonnage 509.

"MAID OF ARGYLL" (Motor—Twin Screw). Built 1953 by A. & J. Inglis, Ltd., Glasgow. Length 165 feet. Gross tonnage 509.

"MAID OF CUMBRAE" (Motor—Twin Screw). Built 1953 Ardrossan Dockyard Co. Length 165 feet. Gross tonnage 509.

"MAID OF SKELMORLIE" (Motor—Twin Screw). Built 1953 by A. & J. Inglis, Ltd., Glasgow. Length 165 feet. Gross tonnage 509.

"COUNTESS OF BREADALBANE" (Motor—Twin Screw). Built 1936 by Wm. Denny & Bros. Ltd., Dumbarton. Length 95 feet. Gross tonnage 106.

"ASHTON" (Motor—Twin Screw). Built 1938 by Wm. Denny & Bros. Ltd., Dumbarton. Length 63 feet. Gross tonnage 39.

"LEVEN" (Motor—Twin Screw). Built 1938 by Wm. Denny & Bros. Ltd., Dumbarton. Length 63 feet. Gross tonnage 39.

Digression

Before we launch ourselves on to Day 3 and our summer programme of sailings on the river, there are some matters which require clarification to make our activities more comprehensible. You need to know something of the other Clyde steamers we are likely to meet, you must be better informed about our own ship, and you certainly have to be introduced to the officers and crew with whom I worked that summer. We shall consider these in turn.

The Clyde Fleet in 1957

This year marked the high water mark in the fortunes of the post war fleet. Clyde cruising was still popular, sometimes even profitable, and the traditional fleet members maintained reasonably high standards of comfort. The number of sizeable vessels in the Clyde fleet was also impressive: five turbines, five paddle steamers, four smaller *Maids* and now, with the arrival of *Glen Sannox* in June, four car ferries.

The turbines were designed like mini liners and undertook the main long distance summer cruises. All of these, except for the *Marchioness of Graham*, passed the winter in dock. First, there was MacBrayne's sleek *Saint Columba*. She had been launched from the famous yard of Denny at Dumbarton in 1912 as *Queen Alexandra*, but passed in 1935 into the fleet of David MacBrayne where she was renamed and transformed. The most obvious change was the addition of a third dummy funnel and main mast. Yet she retained much of her impressive speed and two years later was converted to burn oil instead of coal - a sensible improvement which was only effected on the coal burning Caley fleet some twenty years later! Innovation was never the Company's strong point! The *Saint's* summer station was the Ardrishaig mail run from Gourock. I always found her a delight to travel aboard. She alone had red and black funnels while the main Clyde fleet displayed buff and black.

Next came the 1930 *Duchess of Montrose*, another beauty from Denny's yard. Her internal fittings were superb, markedly superior to those on her sister and on *Queen Mary* and her profile delightful. Both she and her sister were converted to oil burning in 1956. Prior to this, the *Montrose* had often been dogged by a combination of poor coal and poor ship handling so that her timings on cruises to Inveraray, Campbeltown and Ailsa Craig were adversely affected. After conversion to oil and with John Macleod in command, she reverted to her original form as a true racer. Her sister,

Duchess of Montrose dressed overall at Dunoon. Note the unfortunate, black painted steam whistle.

Duchess of Hamilton draws out of Rothesay.

A well-crowded *Queen Mary II* arrives at Rothesay in September, 1956. Her last day in service with 2 funnels. Depot ship *Adamant* lies beyond.

Queen Mary II at Barclay Curle's yard, May 4, 1957. She is still awaiting her name - and note the alien crouching in that transformational funnel!

Duchess of Hamilton, came from the yard of Harland and Wolff, Govan in 1932. She may not have been as sumptuous in her fittings as the *Montrose* but she more than compensated for this in her sailing performance under the command of Fergie Murdoch, her captain from 1946 till her withdrawal in 1970. His handling of the ship was masterful, making him something of a legend and his ship, less deservedly, with him. He also used his undoubted influence to secure favourable treatment for his vessel. Her cruising programme included Campbeltown, Ayr, and Arran via the Kyles of Bute. Finally, up at Glasgow in the heart of the city, was the summer home of *Queen Mary II*. Yet another Denny masterpiece, she was built in 1933 specifically for the Doon the Watter sailing to Dunoon, Rothesay and Tighnabruaich. Space and cover were her hallmarks and, with sofa seating in the observation lounge and her dining saloon placed forward, she was a class apart. When converted to oil for the 1957 season, she was given a new boiler and emerged rejuvenated, with one fine funnel instead of two and with her speed enhanced. Weighing in now at 1,014 tons, she was the first Clyde steamer to exceed the 1,000 ton mark, though *Glen Sannox* was soon to win the accolade for tonnage. The last turbine in the fleet was our little *Marchioness of Graham*, built by Fairfield's in 1936. She was the sole coal burner in the fleet in 1957 and this was clearly ominous. Throughout her career, she had been closely identified with the Arran sailings, both summer and winter, and from 1947 to 1954 she was Ayr excursion steamer. 1957 saw her as effectively spare vessel.

Turning now to the paddle steamers, these too could satisfy the needs of cruising when so required but their strength lay in pier to pier services, where passenger numbers were high and distances between piers were short. Oldest was the Craigendoran based *Jeanie Deans*, built by Fairfield's in 1931 for the London and North Eastern Railway (LNER). Her 3 crank triple expansion engine drove her at a speed in excess of 18 knots and she was intended as the LNER response to the new cruising turbines across the water at Gourock. She was fine and spacious, with two funnels bearing the LNER colours of red, white and black, until British Railways assumed control in 1948 and brought buff and black uniformity throughout the railway fleet. Converted to oil burning in 1957, she was much associated with the popular afternoon cruise Round Bute. *Caledonia* appeared in 1934 from Denny's yard. She was extremely roomy and comfortable, with one bulky funnel and two masts. A significant and indeed controversial feature was her disguised paddle boxes whereby the traditional paddle sponsons were concealed and she masqueraded as a turbine when viewed from the side. She was converted to oil in 1955,

Marchioness of Graham ready for trials. Even the belting is being hosed down for the occasion! The first group of 4 windows from the bow was covered over in the early '50s, becoming portholes. This explains the gloominess in the forward lounge.

Jeanie Deans cannily approaches Rothesay. She is viewed here across the putting green from our top flat.

the year in which she took over as Ayr excursion steamer, and was an invaluable passenger carrier at peak times. *Talisman* came from the yard of A and J Inglis at the mouth of the river Kelvin in 1935 and was the world's first direct acting diesel electric paddle vessel. She was another LNER product, transferred from her Craigendoran base to the Millport station from summer 1954, and regularly employed as spare vessel in winter. Although certainly economical, she was no beauty, spoiled by her gaunt, unattractive funnel. The whine of her engines is best forgotten, while a visit to view the engine area was a huge disappointment. Her propulsion came of an object reminiscent of a front loading industrial washing machine! Fairfield's yard produced the *Jupiter* in 1937, another disguised paddler like *Caledonia*. However she was much more pleasing to the eye, with two well proportioned funnels and two masts. Again like *Caledonia*, she was spacious and an excellent passenger carrier, but her speed let her down - and her engineers liked it this way - so that she was rarely to be found on cruises. This significant drawback did not prevent her costly conversion to oil in 1957. Finally we come to *Waverley*, launched in 1946 from A and J Inglis. She was similar in looks to *Jeanie Deans* and a most attractive steamer with fine lines. She had a good turn of speed but was rather cramped aboard and her fittings were inferior. She suffered a bit from the aftermath of the War. An oil burner from 1957, she was singled out for some longer cruises such as Arran via the Kyles of Bute in addition to her regular excursion to Lochgoilhead and Arrochar. She alone survives today, restored to her attractive LNER colours, to remind us of what we have lost, thanks to the determined efforts of her backers, the Paddle Steamer Preservation Society, aided by public support and lottery funding.

Moving away from the ten traditional Clyde steamers, we come to the four *Maid* class diesels which appeared on the Clyde in 1953. These were very similar to one another in appearance but not quite identical. *Maid of Ashton* hailed from Yarrow's and was normally found on the Holy Loch service. *Maid of Argyll* from Inglis was largely associated with Craigendoran and Rothesay, while *Maid of Skelmorlie*, also from Inglis, commonly served Wemyss Bay, Innellan, Rothesay and Largs. *Maid of Cumbrae*, built by the Ardrossan Dockyard, often found herself employed on short cruises or service runs from Craigendoran and Gourock. The *Maids* introduced to the Clyde scene a new programme of morning Café cruises, offering coffee and a biscuit to partakers of the sail. They also made possible an expansion in afternoon and evening cruises and took over a large part of the uneconomic winter sailings. Being small, they were

Caledonia beats a retreat from Ardrossan on 30 June while the *Graham* lies at Jerry's Quay. Her mishap came the following Sunday.

Talisman brings a good crowd to Rothesay from Millport and Largs in September, 1956. *Jupiter* leaves in the background.

Jupiter takes her usual wide berth approaching Rothesay.

Waverley lingers off Ardbeg shore while awaiting a vacant berth at Rothesay.

not great people carriers and were lively in choppy seas but they proved efficient and were quite attractive, with short funnel and two masts. In addition to these four *Maids*, there were the dual purpose vessels, the new breed of Clyde car ferry. *Arran* was the first to appear in January 1954 on the Gourock - Dunoon crossing, having been launched at Denny's in 1953. *Cowal* and then *Bute* followed from the Ailsa Shipbuilding Co. at Troon. These three ferries almost immediately revolutionised the Clyde scene and gave a phenomenal boost to car traffic. Over the years, they were destined to supersede the cruise steamer - the dual purpose carrier of passengers and cars satisfied all needs! *Arran*, *Bute* and *Cowal* (the ABC ferries) were soon completely taken up on the upper river services - Gourock to Dunoon, Wemyss Bay to Rothesay and occasional support runs to Millport and Arran. Although not intended to be beautiful so much as functional, they conveyed a satisfying air of purpose. Like the *Maids*, they were rather cramped in their passenger accommodation and, when busy, this led to severe congestion at disembarkation. Yet for all their noise and vibration, they provided warm travel conditions in winter and were reliable and economical. The ABC ferries were joined in 1957 by the mighty *Glen Sannox*. Built by the Ailsa yard at Troon, she was designed for the Arran crossing and was the largest Clyde vessel so far built, weighing in at over 1,000 tons. She was diesel propelled and fast, at over 17 knots. After initial teething troubles, she settled down on the Arran run where her extraordinary capacity for passengers and cars made her much appreciated.

The fleet list in 1957 also included a handful of little motor ships: Denny-built *Countess of Breadalbane* of 1936 and the sisters *Ashton* and *Leven* of 1938, again from Denny. These were all twin screw motor ships, too small to warrant a funnel and of no interest to me so far as pursering was concerned. And yet they all played their part in the big picture.

Mention of pursering reminds me that now may be a good time, with the full complement of Clyde vessels considered, to pick up on this point. As I observed earlier, purser jobs on the Clyde steamers were in great demand by students. They were also hard to get! Each of the traditional steamers carried two assistants in July and August and this number often dropped to one at the start or finish of the season. All the diesel *Maids* and ABC ferries carried one assistant while the *Sannox* allowed two. The little *Countess* took one student purser, elevated to the rank of junior purser and in sole command of the ticket office. Her small capacity was not thought worthy of a regular full purser! But as in most matters, *Queen Mary* was a law to herself. Her tremendous booking potential at

Maid of Argyll approaches Rothesay in 1956.

ABC car ferry *Arran* loads up at Gourock while MacBrayne's *King George V* lies off.

Glasgow was met by providing three student pursers to assist their chief: two junior pursers to assist with bookings in addition to gangway work and one ordinary assistant purser performing regular gangway tasks and ticket cancellation.

Now that we have got these matters cleared and looked at the whole Clyde fleet in 1957, it is time to home in on our *Marchioness* and take a closer look at both the ship and her crew.

The *Marchioness* – Close up and personal

First then come the boring statistics. Gross tonnage 585; length 220 feet; breadth 30 feet; draught 10 feet. Propulsion: 4 steam turbines driving twin screws with single reduction gearing (if geared turbines mean little to you, join the club. We're in the same boat! But perhaps it is worth observing that she differed in her propulsion from her Clyde turbine sisters where 3 direct drive turbines drove triple screws). Speed: 17.87 knots on trial. Her dimensions marked her out as the smallest of the turbines.

Steel hulled like her turbine consorts, she was launched from Fairfield's yard in Govan on 6 March 1936. She carried a single tall funnel and two masts and had an attractive cruiser stern. A gate in her funnel allowed access to a spark arrester to catch any ash emitted from her funnel. This must have worked quite effectively - I cannot recall any passenger complaining of smuts from the funnel and that though we were coal burning! On her long promenade deck she had a small forward deckhouse which carried, one level up, the captain's cabin and a useful forward observation rail. This observation deck was normally closed to passengers in spite of its being fully railed. There was also a disembarkation point here to suit awkward tides, though I can hardly recall seeing it so used. At yet another level up towered the high overhanging wheelhouse and bridge. Inside this deckhouse at promenade deck level on either side were alcoves with seating, much favoured by the ship's pilot as he waited on his moment to take the wheel on approaching a pier. It should be stressed that this was not an observation lounge of the kind fitted to her contemporaries of the thirties - even the little *Marchioness of Lorne* boasted such a lounge! Those responsible for the small ship models once sold on the fleet could not believe the omission and added a small lounge to their representation of our ship. I suppose it was the need for extra cargo space which explained the lack of a forward lounge. At any rate, the after deckhouse was altogether larger, and contained a sizeable lounge with spartan but typical wooden seats and large windows affording a fine view of the adjacent deck and beyond. Above this deckhouse were more wooden seats containing buoyant apparatus and two lifeboats on either side of the ship. The rail here was interrupted around the lifeboats to allow ready access and the inevitable result was that passengers were barred for safety reasons, despite the excellent stairway up from the promenade deck. An immediate consequence was the provision of a splendid, private sunning spot for assistant pursers on longer sailings, of which there were plenty in 1957! The main deck below was reached by two stairways located in the two deckhouses on the promenade deck. At the forward end of the main deck was a rather gloomy and damp lounge with padded seating around its sides. This was glorified by the title of "observation" lounge, there being a lack of this feature on the deck above, but in truth there was little in the way of windows and so little in the way of observation! From this a further stairway down into the bowels of the ship led to an even darker saloon, which had originally served the needs of diners in third class but class divisions had long been abolished. Artificial lighting was always necessary here and the room was rarely used. Proceeding along the main deck towards the stern took you past the engine room and to the main dining saloon. On the deck below this were a tea room where supper was laid out for the officers at the end of the day, a smoke room and bar, and most of the officers' quarters. All three of these areas were approached by separate stairways from the main deck, though I must admit that my memory of this layout is now hazier than I could wish. Perhaps this can be explained by the fact that I rarely used these quarters and had to find alternative accommodation aboard. Back up on the promenade deck, you could not fail to note the extensive space for cars and cargo around the funnel and would recognise the significance of this provision in a ship designed to serve Arran for much of the year. All in all, the *Graham* was functional but also an attractive, trim vessel with a striking profile. Her high, overhanging bridge and slim lines gave her a decidedly top heavy look when seen from the bow but she was one of the few steamers which looked well even from the stern - in marked contrast to *Caledonia*, the *Duchesses* and of course *Glen Sannox*, all of which I regarded as major offenders in this regard.

From the outset, the *Marchioness* was earmarked for the Arran service where she proved reliable if lively! The Arran folk held her in high regard and were already well accustomed to a one funnel turbine with a tendency to roll in pretty well any sea. After all, her predecessor on the route was Glasgow and South Western's *Atalanta*, a turbine on lines not dissimilar to those of the *Graham* and with a like predilection to roll. So, for most of

Countess of Breadalbane in Lamont's dry dock, Greenock in 1959, with *Ashton* or *Leven* beyond.

Ashton nears Gourock while Ritchie's *Grannie Kempock* comes over from Kilcreggan. An *Empress* creeps into the picture.

1906 *Atalanta*, G and SW fleet's only turbine steamer, shown here after amalgamation with LMS. The *Graham* displayed some similarities.

1926 turbine *Glen Sannox* makes haste off Arran.

her active life, the *Marchioness* assisted the turbine *Glen Sannox* in summer but took over the winter service alone and unaided while the older turbine was laid up. During the war years, she was mostly to be found on the Millport run while the *Sannox* served Arran. The *Graham* became Ayr excursion steamer from 1947 to 1953 and supported the ageing turbine *Glen Sannox* with Arran summer traffic at weekends. When the old *Sannox* was withdrawn, *Marchioness of Graham* became main Arran steamer from 1954, with weekend help provided by the paddler *Caledonia* which that year had become the new Ayr based steamer. The car ferry *Arran* was also called down from up river to move car traffic at peak times. At the end of summer the *Graham* resumed the Arran winter service out of the more sheltered pier at Fairlie instead of the more costly and exposed Ardrossan. 1957 saw the arrival of the car ferry *Glen Sannox* and the *Graham* was displaced. But during all of June and the first week of July in that year she struggled manfully, with assistance from the car ferry *Arran*, to maintain the enhanced service that the new ferry was designed to introduce. Thereafter she became effectively spare vessel on the river with an intriguing if light roster. However, as we have noted, the *Graham* had not been converted to oil burning along with the rest of the fleet. Nor had she been favoured with a cafeteria when most others had been so fitted in the mid fifties. Again, she was denied her annual major overhaul for the 1957 season so that she was a little sluggish owing to the build up of weed on her hull. Worse still, the coal supplied was not the small lump type which suited her stokehold, with the result that she suffered embarrassing blockages, causing loss of steam and power. Her daily consumption of coal was some 16 tons and she was normally fuelled every second day wherever a suitable coaling place was found. Coaling was a messy business, often performed at unusual times and places, with the coalmen wheeling the coal in barrows over planks and dumping it down manholes in the deck. The captain made every effort to keep his charge spick and span but, given these circumstances, it was an uphill struggle!

1957 saw the *Graham* featuring as relief steamer with a big question mark over her future. She was a versatile unit and yet, sadly, she no longer quite suited either of her two main roles. Her car carrying capacity, realistically six vehicles, was totally inadequate for the burgeoning car trade created by the new ferries and her down river passenger complement of 891 often fell short of summer requirements though in the upper river the tally rose to 1300. Her single level on the promenade deck for landing passengers - for we have observed that the small landing point below the bridge was little favoured - caused awkward problems at extremes of the tide. Again, as a cruise steamer she fell short of the mark. Her accommodation was spartan and she was woefully short of deck seating. We even resorted to tarpaulin-covered planks poised between two drums to offer some respite on busy cruises. The standard seats with buoyant apparatus and the deck chairs issued free to discourage revolt among the passengers were but a drop in the ocean! Her slim lines and Arran base made for many a lively ride on the *Graham*. So prone was she to lift her screws out the water in stormy seas that she carried a permanent load of small cement blocks deep down in the stern. This I even viewed, to satisfy my curiosity, through a manhole cover aft near the windlass. In choppy seas, she readily shipped water over the bow and you had to keep on the alert as you teetered along the plunging decks if you were anxious to avoid a soaking! If she were not leaping about and tossing, she was a fine roller and was known on occasions to take a second roll before righting herself. This was particularly scary, as were the changing moods of the captain, as we shall see.

And so to the crew

First and foremost there was the captain, Colin MacKay. His Clyde career had started as seaman on the famed Arran paddler *Glen Sannox* in 1919. Thence he worked his way up to mate in 1933 and became captain of the *Duchess of Fife* in 1946. He served here for some years and attracted notice for his eccentricities. Master of the *Waverley* in 1956, he had been advanced to captain the *Graham* for the 1957 season. He had a wondrous way with ships and his knowledge of channels and depths around the Clyde was uncanny. He could perform marvels with the *Graham* in Ayr harbour without the aid of bow thrusts or other new fangled devices. Yes, he certainly could handle ships - but it was very different when it came to handling people. No doubt he was at heart a shy Highlander from the isle of Lewis but he was hard on his men and put the fear of death in every one of us. He was certainly one scary individual! His face was squarish and weathered, with red and purple mottling. When released from its customary white topped cap, his head was satisfyingly bald across the pinnacle with a thin rim of grizzled hair edging the cranium. I thought his eyelids hooded and slightly hawk-like but early prejudice may have influenced my view. He spoke slowly and deliberately as if translating directly from the Gaelic, but his moods changed swiftly and were totally unpredictable. He was said to have sacked the entire crew for its attitude on one occasion when captain on the *Duchess of Fife*. This I could believe,

Captain Colin MacKay stands beside *Duchess of Fife*. He has a Caley company cap badge and visible watchstrap in his breast pocket. Absolutely typical!

Chief engineer, Leslie Rosser contemplates his dials over a pipe (or several!). True to form, he keeps at a distance!

Dick Raines holds our attention at Bridge Wharf under the dock policeman's watchful eye. Murdo MacLean, Ian Thorburn and Tommy MacLoon, luggage man, stand from left to right. There am I too, in the lumpy cap!

as I was to discover that he had a penchant for sackings! He tended to keep very much to himself; when he broke the pattern we were all likely to suffer, himself included. Meal times in our curtained seclusion off the dining saloon were tense, often silent occasions and frequently ended with his wiping his mouth with the edge of the table cloth. But this diversion was far preferable to his occasional altercations with the chief engineer or public shaming at the table of chef or steward for the quality or quantity of food proffered. His closest confidante was Flora, the elderly stewardess who held sway in the lower tea room and who regularly brought supper up to his cabin at night, while we lesser and malicious mortals spied cautiously upon her, wondering if there could possibly be some sexual significance, even a coupling, in this unlikely liaison. We never knew. On one or two occasions he seemed to sense our proximity and burst from his cabin, glowering around and sniffing the breeze. We for our part fled, fading into corners or, if concealment proved impossible, trying to appear preoccupied and with our thoughts engaged elsewhere. Perhaps after all it was really innocent and all they sought was company and the chance to enjoy the radio together! If the stewardess found favour with him, it was a different matter with the male stewards and all of these were subjected to his frequent outbursts. His favoured pronouncement to conclude and justify a row was "I am the master". There was no more to be said! He had risen from the deck on Clyde steamers of the past and knew high standards. Hence his obsession with his ship's appearance, timekeeping and performance. He also inherited a healthy disregard for passenger numbers and set at nought the limitations enjoined by the ship's certificate. His fascination with timings seems to have been infectious as you may observe when reading through my daily log.

When his time came for a day or weekend off, he was relieved by either of two very different skippers. The one was a delightful, spruce old gentleman who gave the appearance of a retired bank manager. He was certainly not noteworthy for his ship handling but his relaxed attitude made a welcome change. The other was a gravel voiced salt from Arran with a pawky sense of humour. So for these reliefs and the comparative relaxation they brought with them, much thanks.

The mate, Murdo Campbell, too was Highland like the skipper but there the likeness stopped. His was an easy, affable manner and he was a keen gambler, specialising in horses. If he was not intent on studying form, he would read paperback Westerns and follow this pursuit to the cinema in Ayr or any other resort. For in these days bingo was not gobbling up cinema crowds and cinemas too. There were still several cinemas from

Bennie Martin, or Hooch, prepares the ropes hopefully, all ready for a pirouette.

which to choose in most Clyde coast resorts. He was a good listener and walked with a splendid splay-footed gait which served him very well when the *Graham* was prancing about in stormy seas as was her wont. He handled the captain with consummate skill so that we all marvelled. It was a different matter with the regular relief mate. He was in constant fear of the skipper and his partiality for drink, no doubt to relieve this fear, made a bad situation a great deal worse. His weekend reliefs on the *Graham* must have been for him the stuff of nightmares.

The chief engineer, Leslie Rosser, was another fine specimen! He was Welsh and a tall, stooped lugubrious being who favoured wearing his naval cap without its white top. The darker look better suited his wintry nature. His hair was grey and lank to match his complexion. He rarely smiled - did he ever? - but complained much and grunted or grumbled under his breath, while keeping a firm grip of a small bowled pipe between clenched teeth. Indeed, he could well have substituted for the dour ferryman Charon who bore the dead across the waters of the Styx in the Underworld. He was a man of few words and these usually well chosen, acrid, withering. His exchanges with the captain were indescribable - there was no love lost between these two! Poor quality fuel was a godsend, as he would never force the engines and was content to sail at a leisurely pace. His favoured stance was just outside the engine room at the little railed air space nearby. There he could watch the world - and other steamers! - passing by. But he did not welcome any intrusion into his reverie and quickly cut off any attempt to make conversation. He must have hated being wide open to the public gaze while working in his engine room, responding to the ring of the bridge telegraph! Now, the chief had identified an oil flow pipe which was prone to block if the ship listed too much to starboard. Ever inventive, he tried to counter this by keeping the bath in the officers' quarters on the port side filled with cold water. If this sounds improbable, the engineer on the *Jupiter* employed the same strategy. Perhaps they were in league with each other or had attended the same training school! At all events, I can scarcely believe that a filled bath could make a great impression on the ship's buoyancy and surely, if it did, it must have accentuated the list to port? Still, doubtless that was his intention. It certainly was a mighty inconvenience for anyone wanting a hot bath when we were sailing! I can recall no access to showers on the *Graham*. Perhaps the chief saw these as a steam loss and so we passed steam through the bath water to secure the desired effect. There had been a time when cold baths would have suited me well. The Sunday Post doctor had pronounced these an effective means of reducing winter colds and for several years, first as pupil and then as student, I started the day with a bracing cold plunge in summer and winter. But my enthusiasm for this form of masochism was now fading so that hot baths were back on my agenda and clashes with the chief were inevitable. Strangely enough, my father managed to strike up a rapport with the chief on the odd occasion that he came aboard. So perhaps there was a better side to the chief after all.

The second engineer, Hugh Campbell, was thoroughly self-effacing and, like his senior, a man of few words. He was probably from Glasgow or Greenock and he kept a back seat so far as the occasional rows were concerned. He was a mild man with white hair and pock marked face but he had a good sense of humour and must have needed this to coexist with the gloomy chief. His main concern was ensuring efficient operation by the fireman and greaser to keep the engines running smoothly despite the indifferent fuel. This was a major task. He shared with the mate his surname as well as a love for Westerns.

And so we come to the purser, Donald MacNaughton, with whom we, the assistants, were fated to share our lives. Big Donald was tallish with a tendency to stoop. Round shouldered and rather gangly, his weight gathered around waist and hips, giving him a vaguely diamond shape. His features were rather gannet-like and he kept a commendable cover of grey hair, which I attributed to his reluctance to wear his cap except when officialdom required it. But when it came to complaining, he was without equal! He was adept at finding grounds for a grouse and also at identifying or devising "wee jobs" for his unfortunate assistants to perform. More of that anon! The nightly balance or check of revenue against ticket sales was for Donald a mighty labour, reaching truly gargantuan proportions when it came to the month end. I have no clear memory of the books ever balancing, though the actual figures of gain or loss were usually small. But certainly these were times to make yourself scarce before you were entrapped in some tedious, unprofitable task. Our astonishingly varied programme of sailings required numerous ticket stocks and this in turn necessitated the manhandling of stout and sturdy mahogany ticket cases around the cramped office or even from ship to ship when we were deputising for another vessel. At such times the ticket stocks - hopefully undisturbed and not dislodged out of their proper tubes by the movement - had to be checked and the tubes replenished in correct running order. Meal tickets on cruises were a further complication - again a good time to be busy elsewhere. The ceremony of the mats was another big event. This entailed the dragging of our two rope mats from side to side to protect the decks from being gouged by the gangways and mat movement was expected of us at every pier to suit variations in tide, gangway length etc. No such treatment was given to the two planks when these were stretched out from ship to pier for cars to make their precarious passage aboard. The planks seemed to constitute no threat to the welfare of our decks. Gangways alone were the offenders! Lessons in mat handling by Donald were supplemented by displays of efficient methods of lashing or tying gangway ropes. Another gem was the demonstration of how best to collect tickets to prevent fraud. Here, Donald would fling himself into the gangway opening and into the way of the approaching passengers and flail about like a windmill, assailing passengers as if meaning them some mischief and not simply wishing to relieve them of their ticket! There was a very real risk to the unwary of a knee in the groin, although I was never witness to such a moment of painful truth! I must confess that neither of us, the assistants, adopted the approach and preferred a more people-friendly style which seemed no less effective.

Relief pursers were drawn from two possible quarters. The one was a craggy, easygoing drinker who smoked like a chimney. His brown stained fingers attested to his nicotine abuse and his craggy features would have made him an ideal model for a Toby jug or ceramic wall plaque. His range of expletives when the balance belied its name was quite marvellous. He it was who had so readily offered me his cabin on my first night aboard. The other was a suave, urbane operator with receding reddish hair and a tendency to plumpness. He was cool and unflappable and a fond follower of the fair sex. This combination made him particularly hard to find in emergencies when he was pleasantly diverted. These relief pursers, like the relief skippers, were seen by us, the assistants, as god sent.

As I have remarked earlier, there were two assistant pursers assigned to the *Graham*, although sleeping accommodation was provided for only one. The chosen one was a seasoned salt who had served the previous season on the Millport based paddler *Talisman*. Dick Raines was therefore my senior and mentor, ready, even anxious indeed, to take over at the window, issuing tickets at the rare opportunities allowed him by big Donald. You could say there was a lack of trust evident in their relationship! Dick studied at Dublin University so that I often wondered how he had secured a placement on the Clyde. He certainly warranted the description of kenspeckle, being short of stature, round shouldered and with a mop of brown, curly hair reaching over his collar. If you add to this the dark glasses which he invariably wore, the well crushed naval cap (also much favoured), the dark blue, striped suit and wellingtons turned over at the tops, you can see that he was every inch a true salt! He spoke in a throaty but relaxed fashion which well disguised any Irish brogue, and he was impressively eccentric, if also a trifle lazy. Thus he displayed enviable skill in evading the purser's wee jobs and preferred days off and drinking sessions. Needless to say, both captain and purser disliked his manner and made their feelings abundantly clear. Not that it made the slightest impression upon our Dick. Perhaps, in fact, it strengthened his resolve! Viewed alongside this star performer, I was a real rookie. My cap never seemed to acquire the desired look of venerable age but remained doggedly large and lumpy. But on the plus side, my doeskin uniform (acquired from that friendly teacher who had served in the Merchant Navy) certainly scored me a few points. I eschewed the wearing of wellington boots in all but the worst of weather and endeavoured to present the appearance of a dashing ship's officer, while acknowledging that my lumpy cap let me down a bit. Pay was not commensurate with image. My weekly pay packet on a Friday was not much more than two pounds, soaring to just above three pounds when Sunday work was included. It was hardly even adequate as pocket money but in these heady days it seemed a princely ransom!

The chief steward, Kenny MacDonald, concerned me less in my daily round but he was normally well turned out for work and his appearance was impeccable. He had a round face and bullet head crowned with sparse reddish brown hair. But, for all his fine appearance, he was far from flawless in his delivery and I found him hard to comprehend. He directed the flow of his speech from one corner of his mouth and I supposed this caused the problem, which was aggravated by frequent licking of the lips. However, it dawned on me with experience that drink was a contributory factor to this difficulty in communication and certainly I never was entirely sure whether his accent was Scottish or Irish - it was well disguised by the limited movement of his lips. His attempts to conceal inebriation made him appear furtive and his eyes too were a give away. The captain had obviously found him wanting and made this abundantly plain in any dealings with him. This made for uncomfortable confrontations at meal times. Not that the steward ever ate with us in the little side alcove reserved for us - he was much too shrewd for that! Rather, he was summoned to the mess table to answer for some perceived shortcoming and sparred with the captain from the table edge before darting back to the cover of his office when the ordeal was over. Big Donald, our welcoming purser, tholed the steward but there was no love lost there. And on cruise days, when the steward was constantly popping in and out the ticket office to catch up on numbers dining, the atmosphere was electric. A blast of whisky-tainted breath amid ticket tensions was ill received.

The second steward, George Anderson, was quite different from his boss. He conveyed the impression of a spiv, with sleek, wavy black hair and a shiny single-breasted suit. As being a male steward, he was a natural butt for the captain's ire but he was not one to be overawed. Indeed, as the season progressed, he showed himself capable of meeting the master head-on! The third male steward was unassuming and scarcely noticed - a good way to be on the *Graham*.

Then, of course, there was the cook. He was elderly, with a sparse sprinkling of white hair on a small head and wore the greasiest overalls imaginable. It was as if he thought it important to have his day's work on show for all to see! He was regularly called to account by the captain, sometimes alone, sometimes in company with the cringing chief steward. Whatever the occasion, be it complaint over quantity, quality or preparation of food, he bore it all with amazing calm and stood there like an ancient oak in a gale, apparently unmoved by the captain's tantrums. I was full of admiration and marvelled often at his composure, even nonchalance. Rarely did he offer any response to the master's onslaught, a wise tactic as was often shown. Still, he liked his sleep and perhaps this fortified him for these shows of strength.

Flora Scott, the elderly stewardess, was the last member of the catering department to warrant a special mention. She it was whom we noted earlier as sharing the captain's confidence and his cabin. She was a tough old character and not given to lavishing comestibles on hungry student pursers. She tended to make her home in the lower tea room. In addition, there were two, rather tarty, young waitresses who passed between tea room and dining room according to need, and also a barman who rarely issued up into the light of day from his abode in the bowels of the ship. A regularly changing selection of galley boys completed the catering roll.

Back on open deck again, and away from all the scheming and backbiting, were the nine seamen who comprised the deck crew. On these depended the daily functioning of the ship, always under that watchful eye in the eyrie, the pinnacle of power from which the captain kept constant vigil. My direct dealings with the deck hands were confined largely to the pilot and luggage man, though others might take on gangway duty when the situation required this. Busy days or blustery weather conditions would call up all our manpower reserves to help at the rail.

The pilot, Jimmy, was delightful and hailed from Rothesay on the island of Bute. He was totally self contained and unflappable, and wore a wry smile as he watched the world go by. A kindly man, he puffed on his pipe whenever leisure permitted. He particularly favoured the wooden sparred seat on the deck, right under the shelter of the bridge. Handy for access to the bridge for piloting the ship into piers, he was also completely hidden from that eye of Mordor in the eyrie above! Once the ship was positioned at the pier, he made himself available for gangway duty. He was, like the cook, marvellously able to shut himself off from the captain's moods and I admired his self sufficiency. Tommy, the luggage man, was a great support. He recognised my rawness and did all he could to answer my needs and hide my blunders. He spoke with a wonderful drawl which would have done credit to a Yankee Southerner. Perhaps his lack of teeth was a contributory factor. At all events, appearance was of no concern to him and he traded smartness for reliability. Of the others, two may be singled out for mention. First there was Eddie, who carried an impressive paunch before him and was appropriately stationed at the waist rope. His task was to hold the ship steady when the gangways or car planks were in position and he achieved this by an additional rope wound round a pair of bollards amidships. When the luggage man had a day off, Eddie deputised. Then there was Bennie, or Hoochmagandy as he preferred to be known. This character fancied himself as a sex symbol as well as an athlete and pirouetted and pranced around the ship when engaged in flinging the forward rope. His task was to get a casting line ashore from the bow as the ship drew level with the pier. Once this was done, the heavier bow rope could be hauled to land and slung round a bollard on the pier when the windlass would take over. Thereafter, the screws would bring the stern alongside and the same rope procedure would follow at the stern. Failure to get the casting line ashore meant that the vessel swung out and an embarrassing second approach to the pier was often necessary. All too often our Hooch missed, for all his palavers, to his discomfiture, to the delight of the gallery and to the wrath of that all-seeing eye aloft. Those seamen charged with the windlasses and the main ropes fore and aft were normally far removed from my daily dealings.

One more person should get a mention. The old night watchman, true to his title, used to slip aboard most evenings. Our varied roster must have given him some headaches as he endeavoured to track us down from his starting point in Arran. The suppliers of our coal certainly found us reminiscent of the Scarlet Pimpernel as they scoured the Firth to locate us and for that the roster was wholly responsible.

The Runabout Roster

I remarked earlier that service on the *Graham* had never entered into my reckoning as I considered my preferred options for that summer. The *Caledonia*, subject of my charter with the school earlier that year, was my first ambition, although the Craigendoran paddlers, *Jeanie Deans* or *Waverley*, would have been very acceptable. The cruising *Duchesses*, I imagined, were beyond my aspirations and likely to be the preserve of the experienced or specially favoured. Of course, it could so easily have been a diesel, one of the paltry *Maids* or, worst of all, a car ferry, pinned perpetually on the daily drudgery between Gourock and Dunoon or Wemyss Bay and Rothesay. Certainly, the car ferry *Glen Sannox* would have been more palatable with a fifty minute crossing from Ardrossan or over an hour out of Fairlie, and this in open waters with a less demanding schedule. But the *Marchioness of Graham*! This came totally out of the blue.

Yet the gods must have favoured me in the selection of the *Graham* that season. All unknown to me, she was to act as spare vessel that summer, as her future was in doubt. Heavy operating losses had required that the fledgling Caledonian Company under railway governance must achieve economies and the *Graham's* fate was sealed unless a miracle occurred in the shape of an outstanding summer. Thus she had missed out on her full winter overhaul before the 1957 summer season and she alone of the fleet still burned coal. Every effort was made to give her a chance to survive. The Upriver run from the Clyde resorts to Glasgow city was revived on Wednesdays and proved popular. Attractive, new afternoon cruises Round Bute and to the Arran Coast from Rothesay and Largs were created for her and she was identified as passenger relief vessel on busy crossings to Dunoon and Rothesay during the Glasgow Fair holiday. She also deputised for the new *Sannox* on the Arran run for all of June and the first week of July. Besides all this, she took special charters, relieved steamers required for other duties and maintained her traditional weekend services to Arran. The grounding of *Caledonia* in the Kyles of Bute early in July changed everything yet again and back she went to her former base at Ayr.

But we are running ahead of ourselves. It is time to return to the diary.

Day 3 *Monday 1 July*

Very warm. Fresh westerly winds.

Up at 5 am and left Ardrossan at 5.10. Reached Whiting Bay at back of 6.00 and left again at 6.25 for Brodick after breakfast. We carried about 230 passengers to Ardrossan. Left again 15 minutes late at 10.25 for Brodick with 957 people, 5 cars and miles of trunks (our downriver complement is 891). Next we crossed blank to Fairlie which we left with one motor bike and passenger to relieve ferry *Arran* at Brodick. We did the 4.30 relief, taking 232 passengers to Brodick. Before this, we played around Brodick bay while the skippers of the two boats quarrelled about who should go in first. Our skipper gave way and the *Arran*'s captain actually hid in the wheelhouse rather than signal to allow us alongside him! We then went up blank to Gourock and lay with *Glen Sannox*, the *Duchesses*, *Arran* and *Cowal*. Checked and cancelled our tickets during spare time. Took an odd photo or two. *Lairds Isle* left Ardrossan a little before us in the morning, about 9.50. A pretty quiet day - changed our ticket boxes for those on the *Hamilton* for tomorrow's cruise. Most of the crew went home when we tied up at Gourock at 7.20. *Hamilton* and *Sannox* both did tender work to the *Empress of Scotland* which followed us all the way to Gourock in the evening. Her turn around was a mere 2 hour stop. *Sannox* undergoing trials and adjustments till Friday so we're doing her sailings this week.

Commentary Day 3

This was the first day of my summer stint on the *Graham*. Most of this week was spent deputising for the absent *Glen Sannox* - we took the passengers while the *Arran* carried much of the cars and cargo. *Arran*'s passenger certificate down river was very restricted and our captain showed a total disregard for certificate restrictions so that together, in the manner of Jack Sprat and his wife, we cleared the waiting traffic. We also took cars and cargo on the *Marchioness* if the tide suited. Loading five cars for our 10.25 crossing was quite impressive and I marvelled at the drivers inching their cars across the planks. She could have squeezed another car on board but a suggestion that she could take ten cars must be suspect - they would have needed to be in the nature of minute Minis or Smart cars!

This was my first taste of the Death run, which we performed most Mondays that summer. The purpose of this early morning crossing was to get businessmen and other like-minded early birds up to the city for

9.00. A 6.25 departure from Whiting Bay necessitated a 5am start for us at Ardrossan. It would be hard to say whether passengers or crew looked more dishevelled and deathlike at this unearthly starting time. Burns Laird's fine old steamship *Lairds Isle* (or Smoky Joe, as she was known, owing to her unfailing plume of black smoke) readily caught my attention when she was on the move. This was her last season in operation and she was fast. Her departure from service signalled the end of the daylight crossing to Belfast at that time, as her diesel successor was far slower. Then again, I could not fail to note the splendour of the three funnelled *Empress of Scotland*, still a regular visitor to Clyde waters in these days. Built at Govan in 1930 as *Empress of Japan*, she was inevitably renamed in wartime as *Empress of Scotland*. With her three great yellow smoke stacks towering over her gleaming white hull she presented quite a spectacle. Glimpses of visiting liners were always exhilarating and seeing them sailing at speed off Arran was the crowning glory, granted to the select few! I was hardly aboard adjusting to the requirements of the job and here we were we were preparing to go off on the Campbeltown run with all the movement of ticket stocks which that entailed. We could not match the *Hamilton*'s speed on that run but the only alternative was the even tardier *Jupiter*. Clearly, it was thought preferable to place the slower ship on the Arran crossing, freeing us for Campbeltown. Just consider already the amount of blank sailing in which we were involved. For me, without a care or passenger, it was the life of Reilly!

Then there were the antics of the two captains in Brodick bay to consider. I had never imagined grown men, let alone Clyde captains, behaving so childishly. Before the season was over, I would have plenty more examples of peculiar or unexpected behaviour to chalk up on my list.

Empress of Scotland, ex *Empress of Japan*. She was a regular visitor at the time.

Waverley puts up a half hearted race out of Rothesay.

Day 4 *Tuesday 2 July*

Bright and a light wind.

Up at 6.00. Walked along Gourock pier after breakfast. Left 15 minutes late owing to train delay and set off with about 350 passengers. Got steadily later and were 30 minutes late at Fairlie. 1,300 aboard between Fairlie and Keppel pier, so I got the captain's permission to open the upper decks and watch them. This, as well as extra deck chairs, failed to seat the throng. Reached Campbeltown at 2.40 and had to leave again at 3.15 to the anger of many. I took a few photos. Raced *Waverley* out of Rothesay at 7.00 and gradually drew ahead but she didn't seem to be trying and our chief engineer was certainly not for pushing us. 30 minutes late at Gourock and then blank to Fairlie for the night. My partner Dick left at Fairlie for his day off. Was busy with tickets most of the evening. *Hamilton* on charter and *Jupiter* on Arran sailing. *Sannox* shown on TV using her new BOT dinghies.

Commentary Day 4

Considering the demands of the day, I am surprised that the diary should be so brief. Perhaps I was exhausted and unable to give full expression to my feelings. Much needs to be added to the account.

An early rise at 6.00 presented no problem after two days of relative relaxation on the Arran crossing and a Sunday off. Anyway, I was still happily ensconced in the chief purser's bunk, as the regular incumbent was yet to reappear. After breakfast, I stretched my legs on the pier and admired the fine lines of the *Duchesses* lying off "on the wires". This was a measure taken at Gourock to protect them from chafing against the pier at night should there be wind or waves and entailed their being hauled off on hawsers to lie clear of the pier.

The Campbeltown run highlighted our shortcomings as stand-in for the *Duchess*. The connecting train was late and we left Gourock at 8.55 for Dunoon, Wemyss Bay, Rothesay, Largs, Fairlie, and Keppel pier for Millport before venturing out into the open waters of the outer Firth, crossing to Lochranza and then proceeding down the splendid Kilbrannan Sound to Campbeltown, feasting our eyes the while on the west coast of Arran, Kintyre and Davaar island. This was a splendid prospect from the decks of the *Duchess* as she sped gracefully between the pier heads towards her goal. But for us on the little *Marchioness*, it was awesome. We had neither the speed to make up lost time between piers nor adequate gangway positions to speed up embarkation. Unlike pretty well every other ship in the fleet, our gangway points were effectively all at one level and we were severely affected by awkward tides resulting in steep gangways. No amount of good ship handling by our captain could remedy this deficiency and the old chief down below was certainly not prepared to push his precious engines. So it was that we were a full hour late on reaching Campbeltown. Adding insult to injury we left, as per schedule, 30 minutes later. The passengers were furious and made their feelings heard!

Fine weather aggravated the difficulties, as more were tempted to travel. Thus we were well over complement to Millport and Lochranza for, as I remarked earlier, the skipper was never one to turn away trade. In an attempt to alleviate the situation, we issued additional free deckchairs and stretched our car planks over oil drums and boxes. Add a bail of canvas and you have a makeshift seat further to clutter the crowded decks! Space was at a premium. So I boldly approached the skipper asking if we could perhaps open the upper decks. You know what they say about fools rushing in….! Still, permission was granted. The forward observation deck presented no problem but the gaps in the rail around the lifeboats on the after deckhouse were quite another matter. So I agreed to supervise this and ensure the safety of the public! Sometimes I wonder what would have happened if some unmanageable child had fallen overboard. After all, I was left alone to command the rear deck. Later research has produced a picture or two showing passengers crowding the after deck house without any attempts at restraint or supervision. We were not the first! Then again, our dining facilities were greatly overstretched by the crowds. The chief steward hovered about continuously at the ticket office to keep a tally of the numbers - his panic gradually dispersed and he became more loquacious if less comprehensible as the day progressed and the drink took effect. The air in the office was blue - and not just with cigarette smoke. I cannot recall nor did I record if the books balanced but I can be fairly confident that they did not!

At the end of that testing day we were glad to unload the ticket cases and extra deckchairs and then to scuttle off down to Fairlie, sailing blank, of course. As the sun sank in the west, there would be time to stand forward, right up at the very bow and watch our slim prow cutting through the calm waters. No doubt we would see the *Jupiter* paddling up on the reverse leg from Fairlie as she returned up river, blank again, having done her slow stint on our normal Arran crossing.

While all the work downriver was left to us, the new *Sannox* meanwhile posed for the TV cameras at Gourock, showing the shape of things to come with her new buoyant apparatus.

Marchioness of Graham at Campbeltown, offering a poor substitute for the *Duchess*.

Talisman comes alongside the *Graham* at Fairlie. Our crew watch on. Relief skipper Forster to left and Mate Campbell with his back to us at gangway.

Day 5 *Wednesday 3 July*

Misty and showers early.

Up at 6.30. Left Fairlie at 6.40 with 9 passengers. Had breakfast and shaved before Brodick. Over 100 out of Brodick but arrived late at Ardrossan and had to wait for *Lairds Isle* leaving for Ireland. 10.10 to Arran was busy but quieter back to Fairlie. *Maid of Cumbrae*, acting for *Talisman* on Rothesay roster, came alongside at Fairlie. All other crossings were quiet until the 7.20 back to Fairlie which was well filled. *Jupiter* was on our Upriver run to Glasgow so *Talisman* standing in for her. Naturally, *Jupiter* was about 30 minutes late on return to Largs. Dick, nicknamed Sunshine, was off today, so I was in complete control. Big Donald, the regular purser, returned from his weekend off. Several Transport Commission VIP's sailed with us to Brodick and back. An enjoyable day. Not so for steward of *Waverley* who fell overboard and was charged!

Commentary Day 5

It was a relief after our Campbeltown venture to be back at Arran with less traffic and less pressure. Even the rain came as offering some relief! Yet it was surprising to find the *Jupiter* designated for our Upriver sailing. Economics would have kept her for a second day at Arran, especially when we were already available up river on Tuesday night. The Kremlin thought otherwise. Perhaps they liked to see their ships running blank around the river or maybe the BTC (British Transport Commission) celebrities were assessing our performance that day on the *Sannox* relief. So it was all change!

The impact of the *Graham*'s early movements on my activities is noteworthy. Shaving in time for the first sailing was to be unusual and an early unkempt look was favoured. But shaving was now an essential start to my day. Long past were the early attempts to disguise my heavy growth by the use of Hydrogen Peroxide which had featured in 4th year at school. I doubt whether the Peroxide treatment did much for my skin! So, breakfast followed by shaving was the regular pattern and this meant an encounter in the washroom with the cantankerous chief, who would grunt at the doorway and withdraw on seeing the basin occupied. Any feelings of grandeur that Dick's day off encouraged were quickly dispelled by the return of the regular purser. I had heard plenty about him but this was our first meeting. Big Donald was quick to make known his disenchantment with Dick and his wish that I would pursue a more acceptable line. I have no idea who had christened Dick Sunshine.

Certainly not Donald, as his nature would not have permitted such a frivolity as a nickname! The mate was the most likely origin, with a tilt at Dick's fondness for affecting sunglasses in most weather conditions. At all events, I was immediately and unceremoniously evicted from my bed in his bunk and seized a temporary place in Dick's vacated space. The stewards were quick to produce fresh bed linen for every contingency and to ensure that I did not feel unwanted.

But in most other regards, this was an enjoyable day. Watching the *Maid* come alongside us while we lay at Fairlie was for me quite fascinating and enabled me to display my importance at the gangway as I directed passengers over our deck and on to the pier. The long crossing times and relative quietness in passenger terms were appreciated and I could enjoy the sail, with the observation deck providing a particularly attractive point of vantage. Once the used tickets were sorted, cancelled and parcelled, the time was my own and I was able to mingle; for an attractive feature of the Arran run was the considerable number of school friends and other acquaintances who made this crossing. Arran was always a popular holiday venue, so that I could usually meet up with someone for a gossip.

And yet I can only marvel how successfully we were able to cope with the traffic demands in these days before the *Sannox* took over. For the whole of June and the first week of July, here we were, alone and unaided, except on Saturdays when one of the ABC car ferries came down to offer much needed support with cars. Fortunately for us, car traffic was slow to develop at Arran and the figures bear this out.

It is astonishing from that last diary entry how quickly news passed around the steamer fleet and how blasé I could be about that steward's misfortune aboard *Waverley*!

Skipper in shirt sleeves on top of the wheelhouse with TV engineer to discuss arrangements for Pleasure boat while lying at Fairlie. The barman and galley boy are busy with chores.

Coaling time at Jerry's Quay, Ardrossan.

Day 6 *Thursday 4 July*

Dull, becoming sunny.

We left Fairlie at 6.40 and followed yesterday's roster. The relief skipper took over when we got to Ardrossan. Dick rejoined us at Ardrossan at 10.00, so that I was free to join *Talisman* at Fairlie when she came alongside us at 1.30 on her way to Rothesay. Returned to mainland on ferry *Bute*'s last crossing out of Rothesay at 7.45. I get free passage on the steamers around the river. *Jupiter* on tender to *Carinthia*, and *Cowal* took over her Cumbrae circle and cut 20 minutes from *Jupiter*'s timings. Excursion steamers well filled despite poor weather early. I am now sleeping in the forward saloon rather than consider travelling home. There is no other place available. Got my pay - seven shillings after tax and insurance deductions! Called in at meeting in Fairlie to celebrate.

Commentary Day 6

This was my first official day off but I was obviously in no hurry to leave. Much preferable was to watch the *Talisman* come alongside and join her at Fairlie for the no cost run to Rothesay, arriving there at my parents' new flat next the Victoria Hotel on the seafront at 3.30. Fresh shirts and underwear were then exchanged for soiled clothes, as this was one of the main purposes of the visit! On returning to Wemyss Bay at night, - a mere five hours ashore at Rothesay sufficed for this first official day off! - I took the bus to Largs and walked along the coast to join the *Graham* at Fairlie. I have always enjoyed a walk and this put me in the right condition for a late pub call at Fairlie with Dick as my aider and abetter - after all, I was still not 18 and was being circumspect! Indeed, the diary entry has changed "pub" to "meeting". Perhaps I was afraid of someone reading my diary and was anxious to disguise the truth.

I well remember my dislike of the watery taste of beer, whether in pints or bottled. Whisky or other spirits were more palatable but unrealistic in view of my meagre earnings. The crew all worked on me to change my attitude - the learning curve had begun. My pitiful pittance also explains my delight at finding that free transport aboard other members of the fleet was the norm for assistants. This was a valuable privilege indeed and one to be savoured.

Had we not been acting for *Glen Sannox* at Arran, we would probably have done tender to the Cunarder at the Tail of the Bank. *Jupiter* was chosen instead and this afforded the *Cowal* an opportunity to show her paces and show up *Jupiter* for her tardiness on the Cumbrae circle or indeed anywhere she happened to be sailing!

That night, instead of availing myself of the comfort of a bed in the Rothesay flat, I spent in the stuffy, damp-smelling airlessness that was typical of the *Graham*'s forward saloon. I shared it with other lads from the galley whose more substantial earnings enabled them to insulate themselves better against the unattractive surroundings. It proved a noisy and disturbed night. But then I saw no alternative: Donald had returned to claim his bunk as chief purser and Dick, as my senior, claimed the one berth available aboard for an assistant purser. A comfortable bed at home was considered unacceptable!

Talisman alongside at Fairlie about to transfer her passengers across us - our mate and relief skipper (in civvies) look on.

Day 7 *Friday 5 July*

Very warm and sunny.

Normal 6.40 start. I did not sleep well, as one of the galley lads sleeping in the saloon was very sick and he succeeded in covering my shirt and cap cover with the stuff. So I was up at 5.45 and busy! Only 4 passengers. Relief captain left at Fairlie at 2.00. *Sannox* down to take the 6.05 pm crossing and 15 minutes late owing to hydraulic lift. She then returned upriver to Gourock. We did the 7.05 evening run to Brodick and Whiting Bay. Two brothers, Stuart and Colin Ferguson, whom I knew from school days, were aboard and they invited me to stay for the weekend at their cottage in Corrie. After the previous night, this was a very acceptable proposition and I consented with alacrity. The old *Kildonan* made her last cargo run today, assuming all goes well with the *Sannox*. I was kept busy pricing the new ticket rates by the purser. We got back to Ardrossan by 9.30 and completed most of our ticket checking before stopping for the night. On our last run out of Fairlie, the pier staff ceremoniously cut away the wooden stanchions and brought them to pier level as they seemed likely to interfere with the *Sannox*'s touchy car lift.

Commentary Day 7

This was our last day acting for the *Sannox* and she appeared for the evening 6.05 crossing. Again, she was running late and seemed to feel more at home in her Gourock berth where the manager could admire her while she was safely out of service. For the rest of the day we coped well with the traffic, though 4 passengers on the first run was no trial at all!

For me the start of the day was spent cleaning the vomit from my clothes. The shirt was a fresh one from my Rothesay visit and I was anxious to continue wearing it. This called for a determined cleaning effort and my double-breasted uniform jacket provided useful cover for any inadequacy in my cleaning. The cap was less of a concern. So here I was having my first lesson on the dangers of the demon drink. But the message that I took from this experience was that I must seek alternative sleeping accommodation. The invitation to Corrie came at an ideal time – a veritable *deus ex machina*! Here was a chance for a night away in a peaceful cottage in the company of old friends. But next, I would need to seek out a longer term solution. Travelling home was an extreme option. The folks were now on holiday at the coast so that there was little to attract me from my steamer to an empty house, particularly when there was washing of clothes to be considered!

By now we knew that we had been selected to play Pleasure Boat on national television the following Friday. No sooner had the relief skipper left at Fairlie when along came some of the TV technical back up to button hole our skipper and look over the ship. Before they were finished, they had the skipper up on the roof of the wheelhouse in shirt sleeves and I dared a furtive photo for the record. It seemed too good to miss!

With the arrival of the *Sannox*, it was expected that we would now assume our varied programme of sailings up river with Arran sailings at weekends only. The weather had been fine all day but any fond thoughts of enjoying the glory of an Arran sunset from the stern that evening as we sailed back to Ardrossan were dashed by the purser's call to a new chore - revision of ticket prices to take account of a fares' increase. After that, there was the cancelling and parcelling of tickets to be done. No peace for those learning to be wicked!

Day 8 *Saturday 6 July*

Warm and humid till evening when thunder, lightning, hail and rain took over.

Glen Sannox appeared at Ardrossan this morning so that we had to use the inner berth next to *Lairds Isle* for our Whiting Bay crossing at 10.20. This was a little late owing to the train. The Sannox did all the Brodick services today without problems although the car lift remains painfully slow. Our crossings were very quiet and only 650 passengers were carried all day. There was a lively scene at Whiting Bay at 5.10 when songs and coin throwing accompanied our departure from the pier. *Empress of Scotland* visited today. Meals aboard were very good. Tired, as I did not sleep well in the lower bow saloon owing to the heat. Helped big Donald to amend fares for all stations. On the 6.45 crossing, the sea was quite rough with a rising easterly wind. I got off at Brodick before the *Graham* went out to let the *Caledonia* call from Ayr and in time for the connecting bus to Corrie. This was taking up the invitation of the previous day. The fare was 2/6d return and it was a bumpy journey amid sheets of rain. There at Corrie I was met by my friends who escorted me to their cottage on the hill. Then we bathed in the harbour while the rain lashed us. It was great! I stayed in and dozed while my friends went to the local dance. I had not the necessary range of clothes to suit the situation.

Commentary Day 8

This concluded our stint as main Arran ferry though we continued Arran sailings at weekends, especially serving Whiting Bay while the *Sannox* confined her attention to Brodick. The *Sannox*'s bulk required that we give her more space and we moved into the inner harbour berth at Ardrossan. Actually, this was a blessing for the passengers: for our usual berth at Jerry's quay in the outer harbour beside the lighthouse presented something of an obstacle race for the intending traveller. Lumps of coal, mostly our own, broken cobble stones, muddy puddles, rusting railway lines - these were some of the obstacles put in the path of elderly couples or parents weighed down by such *impedimenta* as cases, dogs, prams and children. It was quite a spectacle watching them fight their way along from the station and determined to reach their goal.

The scene described at the evening departure from Whiting Bay was very typical of the time. The end of a holiday period, even of a weekend, was invariably marked in some such fashion. Tears at parting were followed by waving, then by shouting and singing of appropriate material.

Material of a different sort usually marked the final stages when toilet rolls (mostly purloined from the toilets aboard before the ship sailed) were hurled from and to the ship as a last demonstration of affection and regard. The prize cast was to get the unravelling roll down the funnel and this evoked roars of satisfaction. Scoring a hit on the captain fulminating on the bridge came a poor second best.

Our final 6.45 sailing from Ardrossan was provided on Saturdays only in the height of summer. We would normally berth at Brodick for the weekend, but the Saturday evening cruises from Ayr had begun and *Caledonia* was approaching, so that there was need for speed if I was to disembark and catch the connecting bus for Corrie. I had no wish to sleep aboard any more than absolutely necessary! You must appreciate that sleeping in the lower lounge forward was no bed of roses. The lounge seats lining the ship's sides were firm and a little damp despite the stuffy heat emanating from the steam engines. Ventilation was non-existent so that a spell of hot weather, coupled with the fetid breath and smell of sweat coming from the many denizens of the ship's galley who shared this space, resulted in an unimaginable cocktail of savours. Hence my enthusiasm for that bed in Corrie! The fact that the invitation came from school friends of long standing made it all the more attractive. We had been close friends at primary school. Indeed, the younger brother, Colin, had been one of those who took on the role of steamer with me in the playground! We had all then joined the cadet force in secondary school and so our friendship had continued although we were in different school classes. It was good now to be back in their company in a new location. Soaked as we all were by the short walk from the bus stop, a bathe in the sea was an obvious move, as it is always said that sea bathing is warmer in the rain and there was plenty of that! Wet clothes were also a convenient excuse for dodging the dance and catching up on my sleep.

Day 9 *Sunday 7 July*

Was up at 10.30 and went to church after breakfast. Poor service, boring minister. After dinner, I lay down for a while before a walk in the rain with my friends to Sannox where we had a coffee. After our evening tea, we went up the hill behind the house where one of my pals played bagpipes and we all got positively drenched. Rather a wild Sunday night. Intended to bathe again but gave up the idea and packed for the morning. Set alarm for 5.30 and, after washing and pubbing, got to bed about 11.00.

Late news
Caledonia ran ashore in Narrows in Kyles of Bute during her cruise from Ayr. She grounded near Loch Riddon and began to list so that the heat was not evenly distributed in the boiler, which began to collapse. She managed to get refloated and proceeded to Ayr, arriving 30 minutes late. But, owing to the fallen boiler heads, she is likely to be off for some time. Ayr cruises cancelled from Monday.

Commentary Day 9
This would probably have been a typical weekend for the rest of the season had the *Caledonia* not gone aground. The *Graham* would have lain idle all Sunday at Brodick, I would have got no Sunday pay and my Corrie pals would have got no peace. A bed ashore was far preferable to the miseries of the forward lounge aboard ship! Church attendance was a small price to pay for a decent sleep.

Bad weather seems to have made little impact upon us, when in holiday mood, and we even contemplated a second swim! But first a brief snooze after a hefty dinner ensured full recovery from the previous night's excesses. Then came the inevitable walking in the rain before filling the hills with the sound of music. After that there was more drinking to be done, though, of course, dancing was not an option on the Sabbath! Perhaps all this was not particularly restful but it certainly knocked my bed in the forward lounge into a cocked hat!

But the *Caledonia*'s accident in the Kyles transformed the situation. No sooner were we displaced from our position as acting Arran ferry than we found ourselves increasingly reverting to our former role as Ayr cruise steamer, whenever our advertised timetable could be suspended without rousing too much complaint.

Day 10 *Monday 8 July*

Left Corrie on 6.30 bus with my pals and joined the *Graham* at Brodick. I quickly changed and resumed normal duties on the Death boat crossing. At Ardrossan we discharged our passengers and then moved over to Jerry's quay to allow the *Sannox* into the main pier while we took on fuel. We lay there, while much scrubbing and cleaning was carried out, until 11.45 when we proceeded blank to Rothesay. During this sail, I polished the ship's bell and brasses. Reaching Rothesay at 1.00, we lay off for a while until the skipper took us in close to the pier and we learned that a berth would be free at 1.30. On berthing, I went ashore and returned to the *Graham* at Gourock, courtesy of the *Duchess of Hamilton* on her 6.35 sailing from Rothesay. The B.T.C. inspectors were on board but I got past ticketless! The *Graham* had done her afternoon cruise Round Bute from Rothesay and Largs, where she picked up a good crowd, and then sailed blank to Gourock. Went off early to bed.

Commentary Day 10
Throughout this week we followed our advertised programme and cruising out of Ayr was suspended. Blank runs were frequent, giving me time to relax and enjoy the sail and scenery although I did take to polishing the ship's brasses on these occasions. I have always found polishing to be satisfying if rather messy on the hands. Certainly, the brasses on board presented quite a challenge. They were black and tarnished when I took the job on and required regular polishing to keep them presentable. Nothing could be done for the ship's siren, which had been painted black. Anyway, the pilot would have looked askance at my ascent of a ladder with implications for health and safety. Cleaning the brasses on a blank run also gave an excuse for going right up to the bow where you could lean over and watch the prow cutting through the water like a knife and occasionally sending a feather of spray up towards the anchor. It was *infra dig* to do this when passengers were aboard, but with the ship to ourselves we felt free to break loose!

Bow spray on the various members of the fleet when at speed was a hit or miss thing. The *Marchioness* threw up a feather of spray erratically, as was the case also with *Queen Mary* and *Talisman*. *Jeanie Deans* behaved likewise, though the feather which graced her bow was particularly fine. *Waverley* consistently achieved a bow spray, while the *Duchesses* invariably did so. *Jupiter*, of course, never managed one, whereas *Caledonia* acquired the ability late in her Clyde career. The old flyer *Saint Columba* never saw the need for such a frivolity in her later years and was content to send a long wave streaking down her bow to indicate her undoubted speed! Yet there is no doubt that bow sprays had a photogenic quality and gave a touch of class.

This was a quiet day and as such it had been designated by Donald as my day off. But I was again in no hurry to quit ship. When I did eventually join my parents ashore in Rothesay, my main business would be the exchange of soiled clothing for clean ones, and acquiring titbits like grapes and cakes to enhance my diet. More surprising was my return that night to rejoin the ship. Of course, I was delighting in my freedom to travel on various fleet vessels and get to know other assistants - but that bed in the fore saloon! Surely I would have been wiser to sleep at the Rothesay house and travel up to Gourock next morning. No doubt I feared to be seen as a slacker and Donald would certainly have subscribed to this view.

The B.T.C. inspectors must certainly have given me cause for alarm, novice that I was, and yet the diary entry makes light of the incident. In those days, snap visits by the Transport Commission's inspectors were quite common, but rare enough to excite interest and comment and to send a frisson through passengers and crew alike.

Caledonia, dressed overall, berths at Brodick.

Day 11 *Tuesday 9 July*

Very warm and sunny.

Was up at 8.30 since we did not start till after 12.00. Decks were well washed and I did some brass polishing to pass the time. At dinner the skipper kicked up a fuss about a bad potato and too little pudding (rather without cause) and called the steward and cook up to his room for an explanation. Then we left for Rothesay at 12.10 and passed the *Caley* limping up from Ayr for the Albert harbour in Greenock. She was at about half speed. She will be laid up till the Greenock Fair is over and will be replaced on Citizen Showboat runs by the *Montrose*. We'll probably be going to Ayr. There were about 212 on our Arran coast cruise from Rothesay, Largs and Millport although a lot got off at the intermediate piers. We sailed down from Corrie to Brodick with lots of time, as the coal was good and we steamed well. The *Montrose* drew away from us as we came out of Rothesay at 6.15. *Jupiter* did Dunagoil cruise while *Maid of Cumbrae* took the smaller numbers on the Cumbrae circle. Arrived at Gourock at 7.00 and I fished before going ashore. Turned in early.

Commentary Day 11

Fine weather did not stop me from taking a long lie in the hell-hole down forward. Rest was preferred even when comfort was lacking and I rose late at 8.30 to witness the morning ablutions - for the skipper was not one to encourage idle hands and he kept the crew fully employed. Perhaps it was consciousness of all this work going on around the ship that got me back to the spit and polish! Certainly idleness weighed heavy on the captain and this may well have prompted his barely justifiable attack on the steward and cook. But, as we remarked earlier, he was always ready to pick a quarrel with the steward, quite regardless of the state of the moon. The sight of the *Caledonia* limping past the Cloch light reminded us of the vacancy in our old station down river at Ayr but it would take the Kremlin some time to rearrange rosters and so we continued our advertised programme.

The comment on coal quality is significant. Given the proper size of fuel - the engineers called it doubles - we steamed well, so that a lengthy view of the Arran coast - even Brodick bay - was possible. But if the coal was unsuitable, a distant sighting of Corrie would be the norm. Binoculars were then advisable to confirm the sighting and a cruise to the Arran coast appeared a very flexible term! Good coal could enhance our performance, but I never was aware of the ship's engines being driven hard as happened on the other turbines. There was never that extra vibration to be noted on the *Graham*. The old chief saw to that!

And so back to Gourock, leaving Rothesay soon after 6.00, on a delightful blank run, with the sun sinking at our stern and lighting up the turbulent waters which fanned out from our screws. We were no match for the *Montrose* on her return from Inveraray and bound for Wemyss Bay, Dunoon and Gourock. We would reach Gourock first, but only by reason of taking a more direct route. There I had ample time to get the fishing lines which were stowed carefully away in the crew's quarters, grab some fish from the pantry to serve as bait and while away some of the time that would otherwise be spent expensively at Cleat's pub at the head of the pier. Fishing, whether alone or in company, was not unusual aboard the *Graham*. I had always enjoyed line fishing so that this was a happy discovery.

Duchess of Montrose speeds away from Bute with a fine bow spray.

Marchioness of Graham at Bridge Wharf, seen from the King George V Bridge.

All action! A BBC trailer inches over the planks at a mercifully favourable tide. Chief with his back to us, skipper facing, beside the other truck, and TV personnel watch worriedly on the pier. Coal is wheeled aboard over another plank!

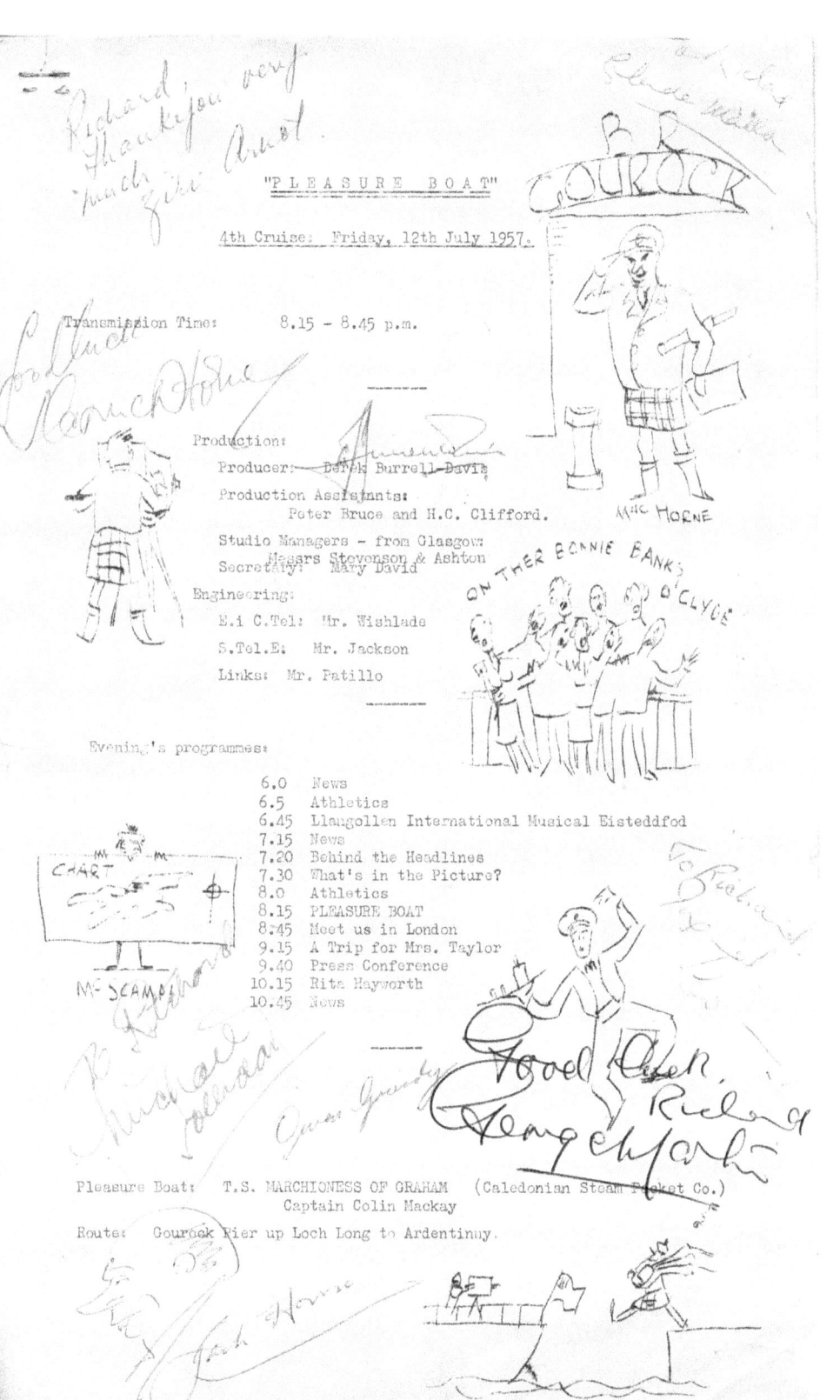

"PLEASURE BOAT"

4th Cruise: Friday, 12th July 1957.

Transmission Time: 8.15 - 8.45 p.m.

Production:
  Producer: Derek Burrell-Davis
  Production Assistants:
    Peter Bruce and H.C. Clifford.
  Studio Managers - from Glasgow:
    Messrs Stevenson & Ashton
  Secretary: Mary David

Engineering:
  E.i C.Tel: Mr. Wishlade
  S.Tel.E: Mr. Jackson
  Links: Mr. Patillo

Evening's programmes:

  6.0   News
  6.5   Athletics
  6.45 Llangollen International Musical Eisteddfod
  7.15 News
  7.20 Behind the Headlines
  7.30 What's in the Picture?
  8.0   Athletics
  8.15 PLEASURE BOAT
  8.45 Meet us in London
  9.15 A Trip for Mrs. Taylor
  9.40 Press Conference
  10.15 Rita Hayworth
  10.45 News

Pleasure Boat: T.S. MARCHIONESS OF GRAHAM (Caledonian Steam Packet Co.)
               Captain Colin Mackay
Route: Gourock Pier up Loch Long to Ardentinny.

Day 12 *Wednesday 10 July*

Fresh North wind. Very warm and sunny.

Up at 7.30, shaved and had breakfast. Went up on deck and borrowed Bridge Wharf destination board from *Hamilton* but had to return it at night. Left Gourock at 9.00 once coaling was complete and cruised from Largs to Rothesay, Dunoon, Gourock and Glasgow, arriving there at 1.50 as scheduled. Only 401 passengers sailed all the way to Glasgow and most of these came from Dunoon and Gourock. 440 passengers boarded for the return journey and we reached Largs 10 minutes late at 8.05. Dick left us at Gourock on the downward run. Mum and Dad were out on Rothesay pier to wave me past. On return to Gourock, I sorted tickets. There I was informed that I was to join the *Cowal* for tomorrow while the *Graham* rehearsed for her role as TV Pleasure boat. TV vans arrived after we docked and in no time our well-scrubbed decks were crammed with valuable equipment (including the barrows of coal for our stokeholds which were supplied by a local trader). I turned in early to prepare for an early start on the car ferry. Got a letter from one of my regular correspondents.

Commentary Day 12

This was our first appearance on the Upriver run to Glasgow which we were reviving this season after many years of disuse. As a tourist attraction, the Clyde at this time still had much to offer, what with the numerous busy, noisy shipyards to survey, the regular shipping movements well up river and near the city itself and the city bus tour to complete the learning curve linking Glasgow and its river. It had fallen to *Jupiter* to inaugurate the sailing on the previous week while we were standing in for the *Sannox* at Arran. Despite the weather, numbers carried were disappointing, although the evening sail downriver, termed delightfully an "evening breather", grew steadily more popular as the season progressed. Seeing me in action at the gangway still appeared something of a novelty for my parents. Thus they came down to the pier for no other reason than to offer support and solidarity - there was no parcel of food or clothing mentioned in the account! Our mighty mongrel dog was with them to bark his encouragement.

Nothing was left to chance for our involvement as TV Pleasure boat. We would be participating as one in a series of such seaborne entertainments aboard vessels around the country and we would be the Scottish representative. So trucks and trailers were trundled aboard over the planks in readiness for rehearsals and to permit an early start if anyone was so desirous. We even took on coal, our second coaling in one day! Finally, lest we got ideas above our station, Dick was given his day off while I was peremptorily dispatched to serve on the Gourock-Dunoon treadmill on rehearsal day. So much for signing on to work on the *Graham*!

Regular letters were exchanged between ship and shore during my time on the steamer. As noted above, there were two particularly reliable correspondents, my school mate Iain (Tubby) MacCormick and my local pal Highet Rodger and these enabled me to keep abreast of what was happening with my friends at home. They served a valuable function and their letters were keenly awaited, eagerly received and avidly read.

Events were to prove that Steamer Services took precedence over Pleasure boat and we headed off for Fair Saturday at Arran.

Day 13 *Thursday 11 July*

Cloudy with showers and strong Easterly wind in the evening.

Was up at 6.00, wakened by Hughie, the night watchman. Boarded *Cowal* 20 minutes before she left at 6.45 for Dunoon. There was not much traffic and between the 6.45 and 3.00 runs, when we tied up at Gourock, we carried about 1,800 passengers and 90 cars. My main employment was with the passengers but I also did a little cargo checking. The crew are a friendly bunch and the purser and his assistant were particularly pleasant. It turned out that the purser had been working on the *Caledonia* when I chartered her for the school in May. Tickets were cancelled in the car garage. Meals on *Cowal* are noticeably better than on the *Graham*. *Bute* replaced us at 3.00 but I did not join her and instead I headed for the *Graham*. TV men had been working since morning and two trial sailings into Loch Long had been made. She was littered with equipment. We were due to sail again at 4.00 but, owing to the strength of the wind, she could not get her bow off the pier and it was only by hauling her off on the wires (usually the preserve of the *Duchesses*) that we were able to get away at 5.00. A little more filming was done despite the worsening weather and I watched this inside on the screens. Returned to Gourock to find outer berths filled but we got in at length when *Bute* left at 7.05. There we berthed for a while buffeted by waves and on came the stars - Kenneth Horne, Jack House, the singers, etc. Our planned departure was delayed first by *Waverley*, then by *Maid of Cumbrae*, since each berthed in turn right at our bow and prevented us from moving off. Our signals were ignored.

Only the company's publicity manager sailed with us. The general manager and his depute seemed to find it chilly and went back ashore. The mate took us out at 8.40 while the captain was interviewed by Kenneth Horne. One TV man was left ashore to photograph the ship leaving and then leaped aboard once he had got his picture! We sailed up to Ardentinny amid mist and rain and, after the necessary filming, we turned back again at 9.15, all of us cold, wet and bored but kept going by plenty cups of tea. Tied up at Gourock in drenching rain and were drawn out on the wires. Thus endeth the day.

Commentary Day 13

The absence of a designated place for the cancellation of tickets came as the greatest surprise aboard *Cowal*. All the traditional steamers had appropriate provision, but here on the car ferries space was so tight that this fairly sensitive job had to be done in the car garage among noise and fumes from engines. To counteract the noxious effect of the diesel fumes, car ferry crews were provided with an allocation of milk every day. Guinness or whisky would have no doubt been preferred but this option was not on offer. The cheeriness aboard *Cowal* compensated a little for the early start though the Death boat at Arran had hardened me to such demands. It also made me aware that my ship was a less happy place of work.

The prospect of better food on the *Cowal* counted as nought when return to my little turbine, awash with media stars, was possible. I had been told to serve on the *Cowal* and followed the instruction slavishly. *Bute* had not been mentioned! Yet what a day it was for the rehearsals! The strong onshore wind and the lack of cooperation from other members of the fleet - no doubt they were envious of our selection as Pleasure boat - added to the discomfort occasioned by the heavy rain. Little wonder that Alex Stewart, the CSP manager, and his clerk, John Gunn, were ready to abandon ship and opted for shore comforts!

The behaviour of the *Maid* and the *Waverley* brings into sharp focus a shortcoming of turbines when placed in this situation. When lying at a long pier where there was no space ahead or astern to allow the possibility of swinging out bow or stern, there was a problem if the wind was blowing onshore. Paddlers could use their paddle box as a fulcrum, but turbine steamers had no such convenient pivot. Often the only policy was to drive the outer screw hard and so to ease the bow a little away from the pier. Then full ahead, bouncing along the pier until the helm took effect and the vessel sailed out. This manoeuvre required space both ahead and astern and both were denied us here. O for a bow thrust! So we just had to wait for the pier to clear and give us space, as use of the wires was not an option at the berth we occupied.

The demented posturing of the publicity manager as he dashed about causing confusion where there had been none added to the general feeling of dissatisfaction. This company agent was responsible for my being exiled to the car ferry for the day and so he was not popular with me! He was bald and noisy and something of a bull in a china shop. We returned to port cold, soaked, and disconsolate but overflowing with tea. Only our elevation to the status of being hauled off on the wires overnight gave us a boost. What would the morrow bring?

Day 14 *Friday 12 July*

The day started mild, dull and wet.

Was up at 7.30 and had shower. Stayed on board while *Marchioness* did practices and came up from the wires to the head of the pier. Then on the subtle "advice" of that baldy publicity manager, I joined *Bute* at 1.30. There I remained till 6.15, dealing chiefly with gangway work but occasionally I did a little cargo manifest work. Both the purser and his assistant were good fun to work with. I made a bold leap down on the *Graham*'s after deck as she left at 6.15 on a practice, and this annoyed some of the crew but no matter! After yet another practice, the big moment came at 8.18 when at last we went "on the air" for the TV. It was all over by 8.45. When we got to Gourock, I secured a copy of the programme and got it autographed by some of the stars. Jack House and Kenneth Horne sat with me to share some Black and White whisky. I had two tumblers and was quite dizzy. The relief mate also appeared inebriated as the night progressed, but fled for cover when I said that the skipper was approaching. We tied up for the night at 9.20 but there was much clearing to be done after that.

At Arran, *Glen Sannox* is causing a lot of problems. Her ramps regularly get out of alignment and the lift lurches alarmingly from one side to the other. The *Arran* has been down assisting with traffic - the old cargo boat *Kildonan* is sorely missed. *Waverley* stood in for us on the late crossing and other relief work. Apparently she had some bother getting into Ardrossan.

Commentary Day 14

Practices or TV rehearsals were very much the norm for the day. Any hopes that I entertained of remaining as part of these were dashed when the baldy one got his eye on me – foolishly, I had been all too visible even in the inclement weather. I was unceremoniously dispatched to assist on board *Bute* on the service run to Dunoon.

Of course it should more properly have been Friday 13 - then we would have known what to expect. Instead, I fled from *Bute*'s treadmill in the evening and threw myself spectacularly aboard the departing Pleasure boat lest I miss out on the excitement. No doubt the TV photographer of the previous day inspired me with his Killiecrankie-like leap aboard. I can well understand why the crew were cross, as the deck was wet and slippery, and the skipper would have been wild if he had witnessed the jump. I fancy his attention was elsewhere. Not that it did me any good.

Gradually, the news filtered around that the filming had been a failure and the programme was all too literally a washout. No images of the *Marchioness* or her celebrity cast made the national network.

Nonetheless, with my 14 page programme, buff-coloured and with the full banal script, I can revisit the occasion. It starts with production details and there follows the entire programme described minute by minute and the route to be taken by Pleasure boat *Marchioness of Graham* from Gourock up Loch Long to Ardentinny.

Sheet A
REHEARSALS

Wednesday 10 July
Evening: *Marchioness of Graham* at Gourock to load engineering equipment and props.

Thursday 11 July
10am-1pm: choir rehearsal at Selgrave Boys Club
10am
Engineering test runs and production rehearsal runs all day

Friday 12 July
10am All artists to be aboard.
10-12 Band call
10am-1pm Camera rehearsal
1-2pm Lunch
2 onwards: Rehearsals with artists and cameras
8.15-8.45pm TRANSMISSION

Sheet B
RUNNING ORDER

There follows here the summary of the 30 minute Programme broken up into contributions lasting from 15 seconds to 3 minutes and comprising action, interviews, songs, and commentaries on background and scenery.

Pages 1-11
Headed camera, vision and sound, this leads us through the exact programme in minute detail.

Camera 2 Pleasure boat lifebelt Music - *Roaming through the gloaming*
Kenneth Horne comes round corner of deckhouse singing *Roaming through the floaming with my lassie by my side.*
[that surely makes you wince a little - perhaps it was better after all that it was not transmitted with all the anglicisations, corny jokes and misprints!]
Horne now proceeds to give commands, then
Good evening - welcome aboard your Pleasure boat. We're all ready to cast off and sail towards the setting sun and the lochs and mountains. Yes, as you've probably guessed, you're in Scotland…..
Through that arch is the railway. You come off the train right on to the quay. Suddenly all the uniform caps have white tops, the buttons have anchors, you smell the sea and get this view….. [Well, what view? An unfortunate line in the circumstances, when mist and rain were obscuring the entire vista]
Slack away forward
Let go forward
(Kenneth Horne with Captain watching in a puzzled sort of way)
Dead slow astern
Slack away stern rope
Let go
Half speed ahead

(Captain approaches)
Not a bad bit of seamanship, what! Years of training, of course.
Captain: could have been worse for a first time - but it is as well you watched me and did as you were told…..
Horne: Ziki! Find able seaman Holliday and ask him to sing. Something appropriate - like a wee doch(sic) and bagpipes, or I'll be in Benghazi afore ye…..

So the "banter" goes on. Holliday sings Loch Lomond
Enter Glenda Mallon. She asks if she will sing "in the Gaelic".
Horne: In the Old Kent Road if you like, but sing in your native tongue.
She sings *Cockle Gatherers* and later *Eriskay Love*

```
Lilt. George Martin with Shrimpy and choir show a
chart and do some fillers. Jack House offers several
short commentaries on places of interest.
Holliday sings My Little Baby. Concludes with a
rendering of Ardentinny
Choir sings Pleasure boat song and Road to the
Isles.

Caption ends:
Next cruise
The Kyles of Bute
26 July
```

So ended that Pleasure boat fiasco. My programme, with a whole rogues' gallery of autographs, provides the evidence that it actually happened. Jack House scores highest in this section with a little caricature of his face adjoining his signature. Kenneth Horne offers a mere signature. I wonder if any film still survives in the TV archives.

I have my copy of the entire script for the programme but the above extract well illustrates the overall standard. Someday it could perhaps be the basis for a bad comedy!

Watching in the rain - Pleasure boat in the rain at Gourock with *Cowal* beyond. Note the loud hailer at the left, no doubt belonging to our baldy friend.

Day 15 *Saturday 13 July*

Cloudy but dry.

Beginning of Glasgow Fair Holiday and need for embarkation tickets on Arran run. We left Gourock at 7.15 with not a trace of TV equipment. Headed blank for Ardrossan and docked at 8.50. Did the usual Whiting Bay crossings with about 500 passengers on each crossing. *Glen Sannox* was running so late that she took over our normal last crossing to Brodick at 6.45. Heavy traffic, a slight sea swell and lift troubles caused the *Sannox* to run increasingly late. She was 3 hours late when she came to do the last run, leaving us free to proceed blank for Ayr. We kept reasonably well to timetable during the day, though we were 30 minutes late at 10.20, partly caused by train. Then the *Sannox* held us out for 20 minutes at 3.10 as her timings worsened. *Cowal* appeared for *Sannox*'s last crossing at 4.20, though of course *Sannox* was back later that evening at Ardrossan. Fate was against her that day. She lost 45 minutes when she had to leave and allow Burns Laird *Royal Ulsterman* out of the inner harbour, as her bow was blocking the Irish boat.

We're the first boat to sail out of Ayr since the *Caley* went off for repair, except for the *Hamilton*'s afternoon sailing round Ailsa Craig. I went ashore at 10.00 during which time Dick and I visited the 3 pubs nearest the boat and had rum, whisky, cider and Carlsberg Special. I was feeling a bit dizzy on the way back. Bruised and scraped my shins when I slipped on floor cleaner in the pantry. Bed about 11.15.

Commentary Day 15

Glasgow Fair Saturday seems not to have been much of a problem for us, to judge from passenger numbers. Even the embarkation tickets get only a cursory mention. Things were tougher on the *Sannox* and the erratic behaviour of her car lift, combined with the increase in car traffic, meant that she required assistance from the *Cowal*. We were not to become involved and were released early from Ardrossan to go down to Ayr when the *Sannox* took on the last run to Brodick for the day. At last, something was being done for the Ayr passengers and we were back in our old haunts, even for just a Sunday - though an important day for my weekly pay packet! Other days were to be added when it was thought we could be spared, as Ayr had a good reputation for turning out traffic.

So Ayr provided us with a new base and it is no wonder I was feeling dizzy after my visit to the harbour pubs. Apart from Corrie, this is the first indication that I was taking drink seriously. Perhaps I was testing the ground and unaware of the dangers of mixing drinks or more likely I was just experimenting to find the tastes I liked. At all events, I seem to have achieved the desired effect. Beer was still without favour (flavour too, in my unschooled opinion!) but the sweetness and strength of Carlsberg was already proving a temptation if not a delight. Note too the reference to pantry raids to supplement the ungenerous supper laid on for us at the end of the day. Such raids were often aided and abetted by the night watchman as a means of enlivening his night. I was now well into the business of learning bad habits!

Day 16 *Sunday 14 July*

Bright intervals. Strong Westerly wind.

Left Ayr at 11.15 with only 150 passengers aboard. Considerable swell on the water but it was chiefly on the return journey that we began to heave and take on water. Called at Troon (50 more) and Ardrossan (93) and then Largs (where it was very rough in the Westerly wind), Dunoon and the Gareloch. Donald was in a shocking mood today and was constantly narking, grumbling or interfering. Insisted on our doing stupid wee jobs for him but we used tickets as an excuse to avoid them. We were a little late on our arrival back at Ayr but Dick and I found time to go ashore and did a round of the cafes buying ice cream, chips, cherries and a coconut. The relief captain kept us merry at meal times and the greasy chop and potatoes at lunch were the worst of the day's meals. *Glen Sannox* spent weekend at Brodick. Turned in quite early.

Note: at night on Ayr sailings we used to print out in white chalk on a blackboard (kept specially on *Graham* for this purpose) details of next day's trip. The board was propped up against the funnel and was quite well used by the people. We also had a TOMORROW board among the destination boards and this was used as another way of advertising our sailings.

Commentary Day 16

The wily people of Ayr were not to be tempted out by our advertising boards. One look at the sea was enough! They probably remembered all too well the *Graham*'s lively antics when previously based at Ayr. Yet I well remember one tall, gaunt figure who often sailed with us and particularly favoured a stormy day. In our talks he told me how he came down river from Glasgow and found Ayr especially fresh and exhilarating. He also enjoyed the *Graham*'s lively performance and would take up his position towards the bow, swathed in a long gabardine, once black but now showing greenness with age, and with a worn black trilby pulled tightly down over his prominent nose. His nose was long and thin, and down its entire length there ran a prominent vein which attracted the eye like a magnet. He was by nature quite reticent but willing to be drawn and enjoyed reminiscing about former vessels on the Ayr station, especially G&SW's famous old paddler, *Juno*. This sturdy vessel of the Glasgow and South Western Railway fleet made quite a name for herself at the Ayr station. He liked the *Graham* for her unencumbered decks and lively performance. Thus he was certain to appear at a stormy weekend and particularly favoured his stance at the bow, regardless of the flying spray. He also frequented the *Montrose*'s Ailsa Craig excursions as being into open waters.

Donald did not share his fondness for a blow and would have preferred to be home at Gourock – not even extra Sunday money fully compensated for the fear of the ticket case being tumbled and tickets strewn on the deck. Many extra rope lashings were employed to reduce the risk to a minimum. Other "wee jobs" were also devised to spread the misery. But Dick and I were glad of the extra Sunday payment and glad to see the *Caledonia* indisposed. Certainly, I had lost my weekends at Corrie but now we had Ayr and the fairground and the chance to win a coconut!

Preparing the chalkboard could be seen as early preparation for my teaching days. The printing had to be legible, preferably eye-catching and also weather proof. This last was hard to achieve in wet weather and meant seeking out a place of shelter for the blackboard. Inevitably, a sheltered place was less visible to the public and I suspect that our standard destination boards, being white paint on varnish, were more effective in attracting passing trade.

Day 17 *Monday 15 July*

Dull, becoming bright.

Fairly strong Westerly wind made things rough for us at Ayr. Still, we left at 5am for Whiting Bay, Brodick and over to Ardrossan. Sailed blank but for 2 passengers with bikes to Gourock in 1 hour 40 minutes. *Hamilton* left late from Gourock at 9.30 with *Saint Columba* close behind. For Glasgow Fair, *Cowal* was assisting *Sannox* at Arran, *Montrose* with *Queen Mary* at Glasgow, and *Jupiter* at Dunoon and Wemyss Bay. We were mainly on extra sailings between Gourock and Rothesay and these were hardly necessary. At 10.40, we took 537 passengers from Gourock and returned from Rothesay with only 6 at 11.40. Word came too late that we should add a special relief from Wemyss Bay. We had already left for Gourock and so *Maid of Skelmorlie* took over. Our 12.40 relief out of Gourock was cancelled but we did sail at 2.40 for Dunoon and Rothesay with 567 on board. Our arrival at Rothesay was held up as the pier was full. *Saint Columba*, *Talisman*, *Maid of Cumbrae* and *Arran* were all there. This caused us to hold up the *Montrose* as she headed back from the Kyles to Glasgow. We took 250 back to Gourock and returned again to Rothesay with only one passenger! There 250 boarded us, acting as replacement for *Waverley* which was chartered by Evening Citizen for their evening Showboat charter. *Caledonia* was the original choice for the charter but was of course not available. Instead, *Waverley* was quickly dressed overall after her day's sail and proceeded at 6.25 for the Citizen cruise to Loch Long and Loch Goil. Back on the *Graham*, we had found a notice inscribed CANCELLATION TICKET OFFICE and put it above our door and cleaned it. We then tidied the office. Donald was in a better mood.

I left for my day off at Rothesay at 7.00. Talked with the crew of the car ferries at pier. Visitors at our wee flat on the front, so I went a walk out the shore with the assistant from the *Arran*. Got to bed at 12.00.

Commentary Day 17

All change again, as the Glasgow Fair Holiday sent a frisson through the Gourock Kremlin and vessels were dispatched in all directions on relief duties. Certainly, our Death boat sailing from Arran was unaffected and resulted in an extremely early departure for us out of Ayr with breakfast (and furtive shaving) on the crossing. But then we were put on unadvertised reliefs between Gourock and Rothesay in case there should be overcrowding on service runs, as this would have caused embarrassment for the management. We were rarely needed as the figures attest (never more than half filled and with six, in fact even *one* on our rostered sailings) and I suspect this was the case with other ships on relief work. Anyway, I enjoyed the relaxed sailing schedule.

But what of these two passengers waiting at Ardrossan with their bikes? How did they discover our secret service? The master generously took them aboard - he was not always so minded - and Donald was left with the task of finding a suitable fare for the passage amid his usual myriad of moans!

The Evening Citizen celebrated the first week of Glasgow Fair with a series of evening cruises out of downriver resorts designed to fit in with the regular day sailings. They were lively occasions with bands aboard and usually well supported. Larger vessels were preferred so that we were not selected. *Caledonia* was a natural from among the paddlers - *Waverley* had to act as substitute in *Caley*'s absence - and the *Duchesses*, though costlier than paddlers to charter, were much sought after.

My discovery of the CANCELLATION TICKET OFFICE sign while raking about in boxes was significant. It allowed us to serve notice of our special position to all and sundry. Unlike those assisting on the car ferries, we had our own designated room for sorting and cancelling tickets. So not only did we clean the board of excess varnish and grime, we even cleaned out the room! Now we could welcome visitors to our quarters. The designated sleeping accommodation below provided neither space nor privacy and our circle of assistant purser friends and communicants was ever increasing.

CANCELLATION TICKET OFFICE

My sole souvenir from the ship! The Notice for the Cancellation Office which of course served as my cabin at night..

Day 18 *Tuesday 16 July*

Cloud at times but mainly sunny. Very warm.

All three relief runs were done today and each was reasonably busy. At 4.00, the *Graham* took over the *Talisman*'s run to Largs via Kilchattan Bay and Millport and again was well filled. *Talisman* was thus free for Craigendoran where she picked up *Waverley*'s passengers and the latter proceeded to Gourock to get ready for being Citizen Showboat. *Talisman* was 30 minutes late out of Craigendoran and ran late all the way to Rothesay. She was 10 minutes late on the return from Rothesay to Craigendoran and was further delayed at Innellan when her warning horn signalled a fault in her steering gear. This was quickly rectified and she proceeded. The *Graham* came up from the last Millport run and reached Gourock just behind the *Talisman* which then sailed to Craigendoran before heading back to Millport. *Saint Columba* received a freshener for the Glasgow Fair and was looking well. She, like all the steamers today, was well filled. *Jupiter* again took over the busy Dunagoil cruise from the little *Maid of Cumbrae* which in turn did the Cumbrae circle.

My day off today was spent largely in bed at Rothesay and I joined *Talisman* for Gourock at 7.10. Thence to the *Graham* and I turned in after a walk with two other assistant pursers.

Commentary Day 18

A base at Rothesay in these days gave an interesting view of steamer activity, even when much of the time was devoted to bed! Hence the running commentary on ship movements. The day's diary is even more detailed and expansive so that I have cut it a little. Trust MacBrayne's to have the *Saint* freshened up with a coat of paint on the funnels! I do find it surprising that I was not out and about. This was not typical, as I often took the bike out to watch steamers in less familiar locations. Why was I not at Kilchattan watching the quite unusual sight of my *Marchioness* circling the bay? Or viewing the *Jupiter* and seeing how far from Dunagoil she was when she terminated her cruise? Speed was not her strong point and she must have turned early! This must remain a mystery. But at least I was on the spot to witness the excitement, however short-lived, when the warning siren sounded steering problems on board *Talisman*.

By now I was into my third week afloat and was getting to know quite a number of the other assistant pursers. Gourock was the best chance to meet several at one time and I took advantage of the opportunity when offered that evening.

The *Graham* graces Troon and shows her attractive view from the rear.

A view up on the after deck on a day when both upper decks are open to the public – with supervision by yours truly!

Day 19 *Wednesday 17 July*

Dull and showery. Varying winds but NE wind rose in evening.

Left at 10.40 with 460 on board for Rothesay but only 2 on the return trip. The next relief return sailing was cancelled and we left again at 2.40 for Dunoon and Rothesay. The captain seemed to forget Dunoon and we were past the Cloch light when a seaman, emboldened by approaches from 65 anxious Dunoon passengers, reminded him. The skipper declared that of course he knew he was to call but he did not think there was anyone wanting to land. Later he revised his story and said he had extended the sailing and gone a cruise round the sunken Norwegian ship off the Gantocks. There was some delay when we did make our call at Dunoon, as we had to coax an unwilling horse aboard before proceeding to Rothesay. There we circled the bay till the pier was clear and then left again at 5.05 for Gourock. As weather cancelled the *Jupiter*'s Rothesay Advertising Association charter, we were not required back at Wemyss Bay later and we finished at Gourock at 6.00. *Duchess of Hamilton* was chartered as Citizen Showboat tonight for Largs and Round Bute and was running well ahead of schedule on her service run. Dick and also Donald were on day off today and we also had a relief chief steward. He arranged for me to get a new mattress from Gourock. In preparation, I scrubbed out the cancellation office and this is now my bedroom! There was little to do in Gourock so I toured the cafes and turned in early. Found and bought a copy of ABC of Clyde Steamers at 3/6.

Commentary Day 19

The Fair reliefs were proving increasingly poorly supported and quite unnecessary. Some were cancelled, a fate shared by *Jupiter*'s charter by Rothesay Advertising. The Citizen could do better by appealing to its wider readership and so the *Duchess* hurried her sailings so as to be ready for her evening charter.

The captain's minor blunder at Dunoon had us all fascinated, the more so when he came up with implausible excuses. How could he know or not know where his passengers were travelling and how could he play ducks and drakes with his roster anyway? What if people were waiting for us at Dunoon and he chose to miss the call? OK, perhaps there was only a horse waiting, and an unwilling horse at that, but he had a schedule to follow. It may be that on reflection the skipper realised that this explanation was weak and he raked about for another one. It was even worse. A short cruise round the Gantocks! Why? We would be sailing out this way on our route to Rothesay - but of course the Dunoon passengers would have lost out. So that was why he fitted in a little extra cruise. Of course, that explains it all. No! One has to ask if it was merely amnesia or was the moon influencing things?

My new bedroom plan was the other event of the day. I timed the move when neither Donald nor Dick was present and when there was a tame and sober chief steward to hand! The recent cleaning had been with a single end in view. By making the cancellation office serve also as my bedroom, I would escape the squalor and unruly squabbles in the stuffy forward lounge. Dick had his cabin below and I would have mine above! The need to move the bedding each morning was more than compensated for by a better sleep. A new mattress was now on order and I contented myself that night with a skimpy offering brought out of store. I blessed the relief steward for his enthusiastic support and prepared for an improved life style.

Day 20 *Thursday 18 July*

Cloudy but cleared in afternoon.

Had a very good sleep in my new bed in the cancellation office, so I'll be sleeping here from now on. Will keep all my bedding here as well. Left at 9.20 bound for Campbeltown, as *Hamilton* is acting for *Jupiter* (on tender to *Carinthia*). The *Duchess* needs to be available at Wemyss Bay at 6.30 as Showboat, sailing to Holy Loch, Loch Long and Gareloch. So *Jupiter*'s roster suits.

We lost 45 minutes on the outward journey (only 15 minutes late at Keppel) and were 30 minutes late at Rothesay on return. *Waverley* was waiting for us and we sped out together. She overtook us just past Toward light. With her call at Innellan, she still caught up and tied up just ahead of us at Gourock. The assistant purser from the *Hamilton* sailed with us all day but Donald clung to him all the way. On getting back to Gourock, we escaped from Donald and did a round of the cafes etc together. Plenty talk. I did most of the tickets while Dick addressed the passenger log.

Commentary Day 20

Once again we found ourselves at Campbeltown, but we were more used to its demands and the *Graham* performed reasonably. 45 minutes late at Campbeltown was an improvement of 20 minutes on our last effort! The race down Kilbrannan Sound proved, as ever, beyond our capability. There was the usual transfer of the cumbersome, great mahogany ticket case from one ship to the other and more deckchairs were borrowed in the unlikely event of a crowd. The relief purser had made no preparations and no doubt Donald groaned loud and long as we prepared ourselves for the long haul. Poor weather favoured us since fewer travelled, so enabling us to put up a creditable performance. Don't forget that we had not been slipped to clean our hull for the summer season and so we were inevitably a bit sluggish. And that, I have no doubt, explains how the *Waverley* could show us a clean pair of paddles as we passed Craigmore bound for Toward light. That and the old chief's unwillingness to push his precious engines!

Dick was obviously freewheeling when he took on the log and left me with the ticket cancellation and sorting. Tallying the total of passengers carried was certainly less time consuming than the tickets, but I had the assistance of the *Hamilton*'s student purser at such times as he managed to escape Donald's clutches. He had been sent to assist, as the run was familiar to him and no doubt Donald had insisted at Gourock that this should happen. His own job thus became that bit easier, as he could leave him to get on with booking, a duty rarely entrusted to Dick for all his seniority. Come Gourock at night, we were able to converse without interruption. Incidentally, for café substitute pub, as usually applies in this account.

But the entry of the day must surely be my delight in my new bedroom. Scrubbed clean and with my temporary mattress spread over the table top, it was just what the doctor ordered. The cancellation office was up on deck and so was quite airy. The only disadvantage was that I was exposed to the noise of the hosing of the decks early each morning, but that was a small price to pay for such luxurious surroundings!

Day 21 *Friday 19 July*

Cloudy and showery early but cleared and stayed dry.

Woke at 7.20 and went early for breakfast. Donald was in a terrible mood all day and narking at us both. Again, we released *Hamilton* for Showboat and went to Campbeltown. Left Gourock at 9.20 and were 35 minutes late by Lochranza. Yet we managed to keep to anticipated timings and reached Campbeltown, 35 minutes late, at 2.15. We left again at 3.15 to the annoyance and disgust of our 349 passengers. Reached Keppel with a bang and removed a large splinter from the pier. Rothesay pier and bay was busy with five ships around but we managed away at 7.05, 30 minutes behind. *Maid of Skelmorlie* took over the evening run to Tighnabruaich, as there were too many for the *Countess of Breadalbane*. So we cleared the pier and made an extra call at Innellan. Clashed with Donald on occasion at meal table and the chief kept his customary silence. Food was reasonable today. A rush to the bank at Campbeltown for £37 change was a novelty. *Skelmorlie*'s assistant purser sailed with us from Rothesay to Gourock. We had a scene at Dunoon on the evening call when Donald shouted at me for loose gangway lashings and for not having three counters available - his office happened to be locked! - and he also turned on the big seaman from the *Caledonia*. Large crowd waiting to land at Gourock and I ignored Donald's order for one gangway and hurried them ashore with two. He never put in an appearance and the skipper sided with me. I entrusted our tickets to the assistant on the *Montrose*. Then time for café/pub and wrote to some of my friends at home when I got back aboard.

Commentary Day 21

Another day for us at Campbeltown since the *Hamilton* was on charter as Showboat. Timings were similar to yesterday although we were commandeered at night to take over the 7.00 roster to Gourock as well as our own, as the *Skelmorlie* was needed for Tighnabruaich; the wee *Countess* was far too small for the task. This meant an extra call for us at Innellan. The *Hamilton*'s assistant was off, so that he did not sail with us in the morning and that may account in part for Donald's moodiness. He always liked extra help and regarded the Campbeltown sailing as a major imposition. Or to put it another way, he was simply scared stiff by the increased responsibility! This was big time involvement, giving scope for big time mistakes. So he took out his temper on Dick and me whenever he had a chance. He got nowhere squabbling at the meal table, as the old chief kept up his guard and refused to be drawn into argument, particularly on trivial matters. The incident at Dunoon was different and I can accept blame for slack lashings. I was still a rookie! No doubt the seaman took my side as he was a pal and sympathetic to my plight. He came on loan to us from the *Caledonia* for the duration of her absence. He was a great ox of a fellow and Donald backed off and sought out a fresh gripe. His next point of attack was the lack of extra enumerators to count on at the gangway. Here again he was foiled when it was revealed that his office had been locked, making it impossible to get spare enumerators. He liked to slip away for a doze between piers and this could have explained his absence. Again, he felt that he had been worsted. His parting shot was to insist that only one gangway should be used at Gourock and off he flounced. I am sure he had no thought of possible damage to the deck, with only a single protective mat, nor of ensuring a more accurate count. He just wanted to throw his weight about to compensate for his bad day. And of course, he was foiled again when the skipper decreed that two gangways should be used. It was just not Donald's day! Nor for that matter was it a good day for passengers wanting more time ashore at Campbeltown. You can't please everyone! Come to think of it, Keppel pier had a bad day too with us knocking lumps out of it. Had it been Dunoon, the pier master would have been there immediately with an on the spot assessment of damages. Keppel was much more relaxed and took it on the chin, so to speak!

Day 22 *Saturday 20 July*

Mostly cloudy and rain followed at night.

Left Gourock at 7.20 blank for Ardrossan and I did a little brass polishing to maintain standards. We were back on the Whiting Bay run with two return sailings and the last run at 6.45 from Ardrossan to Brodick. At night we headed blank for Ayr with 7 passengers and a motorbike. The skipper brought the ship back in again at Ardrossan this morning to take aboard 8 passengers who came up late. We were berthed round in the inner harbour and returned to the Railway pier since the *Sannox* had left. We were ahead of time on all crossings and even the *Sannox* was running to time. *Lairds Isle* was well filled this morning. There was a slight swell off Ayr. Carried only 909 passengers over the day. Some High school friends sailed with us today. Donald tried to keep us busy with amending ledgers but the excuse of arranging tickets numerically was invaluable in avoiding his "wee jobs". Got an informative letter from one of my friends at home. By the time we reached Ayr, it was too late for the pictures and too late to take a walk, so my evening was spent reading in bed.

Donald's closing remarks:

"Here now, you know these signs that came on? Well, you'll need to get them in out the rain for they're away out forward and the bills will be coming off. Well, you'll need to get up early tomorrow for these signs will need to go back out again. You'll need to be on your toes."

The bills in question were Q HERE notices intended to separate ticket and non-ticket holders at Ayr.

Commentary Day 22

Here we were, back in familiar waters at last and the coal was good so that we kept well to time. I'd like to think that we could have kept closer to timetable on the Campbeltown run if only the coal was up to standard but I have my doubts. The schedule was tight and, without a slipping over the winter to clean the hull, we were certainly at a disadvantage. And then, of course, there was the old chief!

The attractions of my newly acquired bedroom are obvious. Normally our first thoughts on reaching Ayr at night were a visit to a hostelry. Granted the nights were already drawing in, but going to bed this early? I ask you! Yet, the room was attractive, being bright and airy, and the night was wet and a threat to the billboards, as Donald was quick to emphasise.

AMENDED PLEASURE SAILINGS
from
AYR and TROON
until 9th August, 1957

NOTE :— For sailings after 9th August see separate announcements.

MONDAYS

To BRODICK (Arran) and DUNOON on 22nd July only

OUTWARD	a.m.	RETURN	p.m.
Ayr Harbour	Leave 10 0	Dunoon leave	3 0
Troon Harbour	,, 10 40	Largs ,,	3 45
Brodick	arrive 11 55	Brodick ,,	5 0
	p.m.	Troon arrive	6 15
Largs	,, 1 15	Ayr ,,	7 0
Dunoon	,, 2 0		

Fares from Ayr or Troon to

Brodick 7/-   Largs 8/6   Dunoon 12/-

To BRODICK (Arran) and ROTHESAY (Bute)
(Outward via Brodick and Kyles of Bute and returning via Garroch Head)
on 29th July only

OUTWARD	a.m.	RETURN	p.m.
Ayr Harbour	leave 10 0	Rothesay leave	3 30
Troon Harbour	,, 10 40	Brodick ,,	5 0
Brodick	arrive 11 55	Troon arrive	6 15
	p.m.	Ayr ,,	7 0
Rothesay	,, 2 15		

Fares from Ayr or Troon to

Brodick 7/-   Rothesay 12/-

TUESDAYS

To MILLPORT, LARGS, DUNOON and LOCH GOIL
on 23rd July and 6th August

OUTWARD	a.m.	RETURN	p.m.
Ayr Harbour	leave 10 0	Dunoon leave	3 30
Troon Harbour	,, 10 40	Largs ,,	4 15
Millport (Old Pier)	arrive 12 20	Millport ,,	4 40
Largs	,, 12 45	Troon arrive	6 15
Dunoon	,, 1 30	Ayr ,,	7 0
thence cruise			

Fares from Ayr or Troon to

Millport and Largs 8/6   Dunoon 11/-   Loch Goil 12/-

To LARGS, ROTHESAY and KYLES OF BUTE (Tighnabruaich)
on 30th July only

OUTWARD	a.m.	RETURN	p.m.
Ayr Harbour	leave 10 0	Tighnabruaich leave	3 5
Troon Harbour	,, 10 40	Rothesay ,,	3 55
Largs	arrive 12 30	Largs ,,	4 30
Rothesay	,, 1 5	Troon arrive	6 15
Tighnabruaich	,, 2 0	Ayr ,,	7 0

Fares from Ayr or Troon to

Largs 8/6   Rothesay 11/-   Tighnabruaich 12/-

SAILINGS TO AYR AND TROON (continued)

THURSDAYS

To WHITING BAY (Isle of Arran) and CAMPBELTOWN (Kintyre)
on 8th August only

OUTWARD	a.m.	RETURN	p.m.
Ayr Harbour	leave 10 0	Campbeltown	leave 3 15
Troon Harbour	,, 10 40	Whiting Bay	,, 5 0
Whiting Bay	arrive 11 55	Troon Harbour	arrive 6 15
	p.m.		
Campbeltown	,, 1 45	Ayr Harbour	,, 7 5

Fares from Ayr or Troon to
Whiting Bay 7/-   Campbeltown 12/-

FRIDAYS

To ARRAN COAST AND ROUND HOLY ISLE
on 26th July and 2nd and 9th August

Leaving Ayr at 1.45 p.m.—arriving back at 4 p.m.
Cruise 4/6 fare

SUNDAYS

To ROTHESAY and LOCH RIDDON
on 21st July and 4th August

OUTWARD	a.m.	RETURN	p.m.
Ayr Harbour	leave 11 15	Rothesay	leave 4 5
Troon Harbour	,, 11 55	Largs	,, 4 45
	p.m.		
Largs	arrive 1 45	Troon	arrive 6 35
Rothesay	,, 2 25	Ayr	,, 7 15
thence cruise			

Fares from Ayr or Troon to
Rothesay 11/-   Loch Riddon 12/-

To DUNOON and GARE LOCH
on 28th July only

OUTWARD	a.m.	RETURN	p.m.
Ayr Harbour	leave 11 15	Dunoon	leave 4 0
Troon Harbour	,, 11 55	Largs	,, 4 45
	p.m.	Troon	arrive 6 35
Largs	arrive 1 45	Ayr	,, 7 15
Dunoon	,, 2 30		
thence cruise			

Fares from Ayr or Troon to
Largs 8/6   Dunoon 11/-   Gare Loch 12/-

BUS CONNECTIONS BETWEEN PRESTWICK AND AYR AND AYR HARBOUR AND ALSO BETWEEN TROON AND TROON HARBOUR.

The Western S.M.T. Company's buses will run between Prestwick and Ayr Stations and Ayr Harbour also between Troon Cross and Troon Harbour in connection with these sailings. Bus fare additional to those shown.

CONNECTING TRAIN SERVICES FROM GIRVAN AND MAYBOLE:—
On Monday, Tuesday and Thursday
OUTWARD—Leave Girvan 8.47 a.m. Maybole 9.7 a.m.
RETURN —Leave Ayr 7.38 p.m. arriving Maybole 7.55 p.m. and Girvan 8.18 p.m.

The tickets are valid on the dates for which issued.

**LUNCHEONS AND HIGH TEAS SERVED IN THE DINING SALOON.
SELF-SERVICE CAFETERIA. REFRESHMENTS.**

NOTICE AS TO CONDITIONS—Tickets are issued subject to the Conditions and Regulations contained in the Bills and Notices of or applicable to The Caledonian Steam Packet Company Limited or to any other body, company or person upon whose services the tickets may be available.

B.R. 35001 B. 22198—QU—JULY, 1957.   Printed in Great Britain by Hugh Paton & Sons Ltd.

The new mattress, laid out on top of the mahogany desk where the tickets were spread out by day, was inviting on such a night. The light for reading too was excellent in my elevated position atop the desk.

Our chalk written notice advising of next day's sailing programme was equally vulnerable to rain and there were also the little handbills which were appearing like a rash around the town and up at the railway station. The first batch was printed in lurid red and detailed our programme of Ayr sailings from Sunday 21 July to Thursday 8 August. It was headed AMENDED PLEASURE SAILINGS FROM AYR AND TROON and sailings on Monday, Tuesday, and Thursday were programmed whenever we were available. Thus we sailed to Dunoon via Brodick and Largs on Monday 22nd and to Rothesay via Brodick on 29th. The fare for the full distance was the same, 12/-, in each case. Tuesday 23rd and 6th August had us at Loch Goil via Millport, Largs and Dunoon while on 30th July we made for Tighnabruaich by Largs and Rothesay. Once again the fare for the full trip was 12/-. Thursdays saw us at Whiting Bay and Campbeltown, Sundays at Rothesay and Loch Riddon on 21st and 4th August or Dunoon and Loch Goil on 28th. In all cases the fare for the full trip was 12/-. Oddly enough, though we also called at Ardrossan each way on Sundays and Tuesdays, the amended programme neglected to mention this! The *Hamilton*'s Friday sailings round Holy Isle were also listed at 4/6d for the afternoon trip. Evening cruises out of Ayr were abandoned. So we were clearly identified now as Ayr steamer except on Upriver Wednesdays, and on Fridays and Saturdays when we were resting or involved with Arran sailings to Whiting Bay. How long this would continue lay in the lap of the *Caledonia*!

The skipper was clearly in one of his obliging moods. First, there was his return to the main pier at Ardrossan after departure to pick up a group of 8 passengers. Then, even more remarkable, our supposedly blank run over to Ayr at night was enhanced by the arrival of 7 passengers and also a motorbike. He never did things by halves and was totally unpredictable! *Glen Sannox* was behaving better on the run and any cars that appeared, whether at Ardrossan or Whiting Bay, were pointed in her direction. We were now mainly a passenger ship - unless it suited the skipper otherwise!

Previous pages Red Handbill, with AMENDED PLEASURE SAILINGS FROM AYR AND TROON TILL 9TH AUGUST when *Caledonia* was expected to be back.
Whatever happened to Ardrossan? - for we did call there!
I imagine the second page should have read FROM rather than TO Ayr and Troon- signs of a rushed job!

Day 23 *Sunday 21 July*

Very wet at 7.00am then dull. Beautiful by 1.00.

Despite the unsettled weather to start, 260 passengers boarded at Ayr and we carried some 1,700 passengers over the day. The ship refused to swing round at Ardrossan when moving astern. We merely went to and fro off the pier until we got a rope ashore and were ignominiously pulled in. Again, the skipper ordered us to put out the gangway for 11 passengers who appeared late at Ardrossan and yet, despite these delays, we kept good time all the way via Troon, Ardrossan, Largs and Rothesay to Loch Riddon and back. On the return to Ayr we took a wee while to turn around in the harbour but it was a remarkable performance. The skipper turned us around with only yards to spare at bow and stern without any bow rudder or using a rope to swing us round. It was quite a leisurely day and I spent my birthday quietly and told no-one of the occasion. Mum and Dad recognised it by coming down to the pier at Rothesay as we called and we exchanged greetings. Dad seems to be getting on quite well with the old chief, to my surprise. They usually confer at the engine room opening. Wrote a post card to Grandpa and Grannie at Clarkston.

Commentary Day 23

This was very much the skipper's day: timekeeping was good, he was again sympathetic to latecomers and the morning problem getting alongside Ardrossan was more than made good by his masterly showing at Ayr harbour in the evening. Some of the steamers were notoriously fickle at piers and sometimes their masters made things worse. The captain of the *Sannox* depended heavily on nylon ropes for bringing his mighty charge alongside piers. If it was windy, you had to be quick, as her high superstructure acted like a sail and the skipper seemed unsure of how to use her considerable propeller power! The *Caledonia* too was notorious for doing her own thing at piers and totally disregarding the helm. *Waverley* also has long had a reputation for behaving unexpectedly, although the grounding at the Gantocks in 1977 was not entirely the fault of the ship's erratic behaviour. Then there was the *Jupiter*. Her captain liked to take almost the full length of Rothesay pier before settling back into berth 3 and was quite oblivious to the public's perception of the manoeuvre. Considered against these other performances, our captain's showing was indeed masterly.

The camaraderie, which was developing between my father and the lugubrious chief, certainly surprised and fascinated me. The old chief liked to lean on the rail outside his engine room but with a morose and forbidding look, calculated to keep the public at bay. He preferred his Stygian solitude and brooked no interruption. So, witnessing his readiness to drop guard when my father approached him was really surprising. On occasion, he would even venture a fleeting smile. It was uncanny!

You will note that I kept the occasion of my birthday to myself. Not that there was any fear of being given the bumps or tossed in a blanket as could have happened at school. Rather, I was more anxious to conceal my comparative youth, especially as I was gaining recognition for my incipient achievements where drink was concerned. It would never do to reveal a potential chink in the armour!

Marchioness lies low at the end of lengthy Whiting Bay pier.

Coming into Rothesay with a good crowd from the Ayr sailings.

Day 24 *Monday 22 July*

A fine, fresh morning, with SW wind rising later.

Left Ayr at back of 4.00am for Whiting Bay and I got up about 5.15. Started our Death run at 6.25 and the skipper insisted on removing the gangway though there were 3 passengers running up the long pier and only a little distant. He would not let them on and so they had to go and take a taxi for our departure from Brodick at 7.05. At least they had that choice! *Empress of Scotland* sailed up at 6.30 and came back down river in the late afternoon. We then made for Ayr, leaving at 10.00 with 447 aboard for Troon, Brodick, Largs and Dunoon. The *Sannox* held us up at Brodick for 35 minutes and we crept up almost alongside but achieved nothing. Her skipper was not for allowing us alongside! The result was only 30 minutes ashore at Dunoon and a lot of grumbling. The gangway was off when 3 elderly people came running up. A younger man and wife jumped on but the elder group did not dare. They were joined by a frantic stout man who shrieked up at the captain "Stop, stop, sir! Ayr, Ayr!" The captain was unbending and later declared "I told them 3.00. I was fouling the *Montrose*'s bow in berth 1"- which was nonsense! The other passengers gave us a hard time but we had no power to help. Down river, we met the naval depot ship *Adamant* and a frigate exercising off Arran. A signal from the *Adamant* caused us to swing hard a port and a submarine surfaced immediately ahead of our former course. Seeing a dredger in the River Ayr, the skipper remarked that its captain was trying to worry him as he knew the *Graham* was only on the run for a few days. Still, he tied up at Ayr without bother and in good time. Two photographers whom I had first met on the *Sannox* on 29 June were waiting on the pier and I showed them some of my steamer photos. We went ashore in Ayr from 8 till 10.

Commentary Day 24

Today the skipper was a very different beast and it certainly was not his day! Gone was his willingness of previous days to return to pick up latecomers. The 4.00 start had perhaps ruffled his feathers although **he** at least might put in for overtime. Whatever the cause, the passengers left on the pier at Whiting Bay were first to suffer and had to endure not one but two runs along the hugely long, wooden pier. Appeals to the purpling, square face under the white topped cap scowling down from the bridge were in vain and off we went. But at least they could catch us up again at Brodick with the help of waiting taxis.

It was a different matter for those left at Dunoon. Granted they had been given only half the expected time ashore because of the *Sannox* holding us out of Brodick. But we all know that time and tide wait for no man and the captain respected that maxim on this occasion. As at Whiting Bay, so now at Dunoon, he was quite unbending: if you were late, you had to face the consequences. The young couple who had hurled themselves aboard were ignored, to my amazement. I would not have been surprised if he had gone back and put them off again! Down at the gangway, it was we who got all the flack. He was well away from it, up there in his lofty eyrie, thinking up excuses for the inexcusable. "He told them!"- nothing of the kind! That was the job of the assistants and we certainly had performed it. "Fouling the *Montrose*'s bow!" Again nonsense. She was in no hurry, as she was performing the relief programme we had been doing last week and no doubt would have been doing now, had the *Caledonia*'s mishap not changed everything. No, it must have been that moon again!

The same paranoia must have influenced his attack on the captain of the dredger *Carrick* who was only carrying out his duties. There was nothing sinister about it. Nor was the submarine's sudden appearance in our path to be explained by some fell plot. Was the delay caused by the *Sannox* at Brodick to be put down to some undisclosed scheme? Perhaps he thought so. At all events, all these incidents added up to a bad day for our captain.

Day 25 *Tuesday 23 July*

Mild and bright but not much sun. Fresh SW wind.

Up at 8.am to the ringing of the breakfast bell. In my haste to put away the blankets, I covered the tray of yesterday's tickets and it was only when sorting the day's tickets at Dunoon that we missed the tray. A search followed and it was found with its contents. Quickly put away yesterday's tickets and turned to the new! We left Ayr at 10.00 with 445 on board and called at Troon and Ardrossan which took us nearly 100 above complement. 262 got off at Millport and a few more at Largs. We passed *Cowal* and *Maid of Argyll* on a 2.40 Fair relief from Gourock to Rothesay as we passed Innellan. They were not particularly busy looking, Dunoon landed 474 passengers, so that we sailed into Loch Goil with under 400 aboard - well within our limits and a comfortable number for the cruise. We kept excellent time all day but, at the entrance to Loch Goil, naval MFV 1186 blocked our path. We went alongside and were told we were limited to 45 minutes in the Loch as submarines were exercising. On our return to Dunoon, after yesterday's fiasco, the captain was clearly wrestling with his conscience and was for leaving no one. He even ordered Donald to let on the Ayr passengers though we had returned early to Dunoon - "in case people begin to complain"!

Returning ahead of time, we went into Millport ahead of *Jupiter* though she was timetabled to arrive just before us from the Dunagoil Bay cruise. Instead, we went straight in after *Maid of Cumbrae* which was on *Jupiter*'s normal roster. We reached Ardrossan at 5.30 just ahead of the *Sannox* and, ignoring the porters' shouts from Jerry's quay, the skipper made straight for the main pier. So the *Sannox* had to wait for us to come out astern and then she in turn crossed and stopped before our bow, causing us to stop and swing round her. The *Sannox* ignored our derisive blasts on the horn and went in astern to the pier. Our tally of figures for the return trip was a bit confused and a lot of changes had to be made. Went to see "The Incredible Shrinking Man" at the Gaumont cinema in Ayr with Dick. This was a stupid sort of thing but the accompanying film about Redcoats versus Indians was more to our liking. Had supper with mate, 2nd engineer and relief captain from the *Caledonia* who joined us this evening. Earlier in the day, our own skipper spoke over dinner about buses going right past people at the stops and remarked in all seriousness "What kind of hearts have men like these got?"

Queen Mary left 200 at Glasgow this morning and was so crowded that she allowed no passengers to come aboard at Rothesay, even after many went ashore.

Commentary Day 25

Well, there is no doubt that I was finding my bed in the cancellation office comfortable, when I could sleep through all the racket occasioned by the early cleaning of the decks and not waken till 8.00. I had no time for a shave before breakfast and little wonder that the tickets were swept away unnoticed in the mad dash to get organised. At least they turned up again as the day progressed!

Again, the captain was a wonder to watch. First of all, he had his ship full to the gunwhales - he liked that! But it made our job harder as we tried to make seats available and keep our public happy. Then he had his little brush with authority at Loch Goil. This certainly seemed to have an effect on him. Passengers were welcomed on early at Dunoon and there was no recurrence of people coming late. I wonder how any latecomers would have been treated on this day of the month! If his remarks at table can be given any significance, surely he would have waited? Or did that only apply to bus drivers? I wonder who brought the conversation round to this? Most likely it would be the old chief. He would have enjoyed the situation and revelled in the skipper's comment.

After that, there was no stopping our man. Down the river he rushed, ahead of time and jumping in ahead of the *Jupiter* at Millport. Strictly speaking, both ships were scheduled for the same arrival time but our skipper seized the advantage. His behaviour at Ardrossan was even less responsible. There he ignored direct instructions and went straight into the main pier. Our passengers may have been grateful, as they avoided the difficult walk round from Jerry's quay, but the *Sannox*'s captain was furious and showed this by his manoeuvres as we tried to leave. But this was all grist to our captain's mill. He clearly enjoyed sparring with other colleagues. And he knew he had come off best on this occasion.

The steamers did well for traffic that day, as our captain's contempt for complement attested. I don't know if the *Queen Mary*'s skipper was as cavalier about numbers, but his refusal to take on any passengers suggests he was already above his numbers and reluctant to make things worse! It was always maintained that skippers hailing from the north side at Craigendoran were much more observant of the regulations than their Gourock affiliated counterparts.

Day 26 *Wednesday 24 July*

Dry before 9.00 but then rained, almost without a break, for the rest of the day.

Came up blank from Ayr and waited off Largs till 9.40 when the *Talisman* left. My two photographer friends joined us unexpectedly at Largs and took snaps on the cruise. They brought with them colour transparencies of the various ships and crews. Despite weather, we had 339 on upward cruise to Glasgow and 406 on way back - a remarkable success. Sold about 100 brochures on river and got 4 shillings commission. I even sold one to the chief engineer! We were 25 minutes late at Glasgow since the relief captain was extremely cautious and went half speed all the way, almost stopping at times. It was the same on the return. The baldy traffic manager was hopping around everywhere between Gourock and Glasgow on his wee car. I went ashore and managed to get a copy of *Clyde Steamers at a Glance* at Fisher's in Hope Street although long out of print. Donald's son, the skipper's wife and lots of other relations of the crew were aboard today and so there were lots of free passes to inspect. I jumped ship at Rothesay on return trip and was met by Mum and Dad. Went back to our wee flat next Victoria hotel which is now finished. Read Agatha Christie book. *Jupiter* did Rothesay Advertising cruise despite the rain. *Waverley* lay out in the bay from 6.00 till after 10.00 while men climbed up and down at her anchor and hung over the bow. It appears she broke down on her return from Round the Lochs at 6.00 when her paddles stopped turning just opposite the *Gay Queen* slip. The *Countess* ferried her 200 passengers ashore where they boarded *Duchess of Montrose* from Lochranza and Campbeltown. The *Waverley*'s engineers worked on her till they got her going again at 10.10 and she headed off for Gourock.

Commentary Day 26

Selling brochures on the Glasgow run was a useful way of supplementing our meagre pay. It was particularly lucrative for the assistant on *Queen Mary* where passenger numbers were high - her complement out of Glasgow was a staggering 1,820 souls. The brochures were little river guides which opened out to display sections of the river with a descriptive text. They cost sixpence, with a halfpenny commission going to the seller. For me to sell 100 on a wet day was certainly good going and provided invaluable supplementary beer money!

Captains varied greatly in their attitude to the river run. Some took the Dead Slow signs literally and, if no obvious indication was given how far the notice applied, they played very safe rather than risk a fine for speeding and causing damage to the river bank or ships moored at the quay-side. Our relief captain on this day was one of the cautious breed, unlike our regular master. Progress was slow and sometimes we appeared to be drifting with the current. Fortunately, there was enough time allowed at Glasgow to take account of late arrivals and the city bus tour was unaffected.

Clyde Steamers at a Glance was a little booklet designed to help steamer spotters recognise the vessels in the fleet. It provided black and white profiles of each ship with a descriptive text highlighting points of difference. *Waverley* was the newest entry and the *Maids* and car ferries were still in the future. So, obtaining a copy for the record was something of a scoop, as it was long out of print. Naturally, I had no need of its aid for steamer identification but it deserved a place in my collection of steamer books.

My arrival on the pier at Rothesay must have come as a surprise to my parents and our large, barking dog. But next day was my day off and I was becoming less frenzied in my desire to sail extra hours. The novelty was waning, I suppose. Anyway, I was eager to see around our new flat, located next the Victoria hotel on the sea front. This was now furnished and painted. Being a top flat, it had a low ceiling but its position offered excellent views of the pier and ships at close hand. It was quite easy to see a steamer approach and be down on the pier in time to board her. Perhaps there was not the panorama across the bay afforded by my grandparents' old house up on Chapelhill, but for convenience it was unsurpassed and became a favoured haunt for winter weekend jaunts by me and my student pals. The taller ones just had to watch their heads, especially after drink! On this first evening, I was able to enjoy an undisturbed view of work progressing on the immobilised *Waverley*. *Gay Queen* was a little motor ship run by a local family. Her cruises usually lasted two or three hours and her boarding slip was just opposite the Pavilion on the sea front. At this time "gay" simply meant merry or light hearted and had none of its modern connotation. Gay Queen today would certainly seem an interesting juxtaposition. A rival ship, owned by another local operator, sailed from the inner harbour and was named, more sedately, *Maid of Bute*.

Mention of the two photographers reminds me how few regular travellers we attracted to the *Graham*. Naturally, we were visited by members of the River Steamer Club as they did their rounds of the fleet, but they were hardly regulars. The *Duchesses* certainly attracted their own following of worshippers, especially the *Hamilton*. Of the paddlers, probably the *Waverley* came closest to having a following. *Queen Mary* too attracted her own team of distinctive followers on her Glasgow sailings. Was it largely because of the sailing schedules? *Jeanie Deans* was much more spacious than *Waverley* and just as fast if called on. But she was daily Round Bute that season and enjoyed none of the variety available on *Waverley*. Our Ayr cruises should have attracted a following but perhaps our distant base put us out of the running. There was of course that lean, gabardine-clad ancient with the veined nose whom we met earlier and who appeared from time to time to blow away the cobwebs. Ayr was his favoured base - nothing much was said about the steamer, though he did like our uncluttered decks. So, you see, the photographers were something of an anomaly. One was a doctor who travelled to the Clyde from his home in Preston each summer to join forces with his Kilmarnock pal. The pair of them travelled the river together and recorded their activities on colour slides and black and white photographs. Their arrival on board was always a real pleasure and gave me a chance to show my own photographic efforts.

Opposite: Three popular booklets:
CLYDE STEAMERS -Banks (1947) - My first booklet covering *King Edward* to launch of *Waverley*. Ends with thoughts of nationalisation.
CLYDE STEAMERS AT A GLANCE - Marshall (1948) -18 traditional ships in profile, both broadside and head on with tips for recognition.
ABC CLYDE STEAMERS - Milne (1956) - Best of the bunch, crammed with helpful information.

Day 27 *Thursday 25 July*

Rained almost continuously and a Southerly wind arose in the night to heighten the effect.

The result of this was that I spent my day-off indoors, reading *ABC of Clyde Steamers* and then Agatha Christie's *The Labours of Hercules*. Occasionally I ventured out briefly to buy a film for my old Kodak camera, or to obtain a plastic cap cover as a better protection against the droppings of sea gulls, or to view the *Marchioness* on her calls at the pier. This was the next TV effort. These TV folk seem very unlucky with the weather! Kenneth Horne appeared aboard at 7.10 in the evening (the *Arran* was 20 minutes late) and everything was held up accordingly. *Waverley* was back as large as life (I am told she actually had one short stop again) but traffic was light and holidaymakers were wet and miserable. *Graham* called from the Kyles at 1.00 and again at around 5.30 when she lay for an hour before moving into the bay to make room for other steamers. Returning at 7.00, she lay between berths 1 and 2 and delayed *Arran* till she moved forward to berth 1. She did one more run into the Kyles before finally leaving for Gourock at 9.35. I had an uncomfortable bath.

Commentary Day 27

This was typical Glasgow Fair weather - what a misnomer that use of Fair often is! It was also coming to be seen as typical TV Pleasure boat weather. For this was the run up to our next TV appearance and we were based this time at Rothesay instead of Gourock. We were to sail up the Kyles and into Loch Riddon. As before, she had several practice runs to perform on the day before actual screening. These she performed, shrouded in rain, and full dress rehearsals were postponed till the following day when the weather might improve. But then, it was still Glasgow Fair and the Kyles were ever a good place to look for rain. The omens were not good!

The weather prevented any plans to move around the island and instead I was able to carry out a few necessary tasks. There was very little free time ashore from the *Graham* to allow me to do such personal errands. When it came to photography, I favoured black and white for reasons of economy. The old Kodak camera was expensive for colour pictures. The following year I bought a 35 mm camera and colour followed naturally. I frequently wish that I had changed over to 35mm for 1957, as I would have taken many more photographs aboard the *Marchioness*. The white top on my cap seemed to attract seagull fire like a target and cloth covers were difficult to clean quickly and looked the better for being ironed. The obvious solution was a readily washable plastic cover and there was a shop in Rothesay which supplied these - perhaps a throw back to the days when the navy used Rothesay as a submarine base.

As to the uncomfortable bath - this can be explained by its limited dimensions. After all, the house was tiny and so were its kitchenette and bathroom. We were in fact lucky to have a bath at all, given the restricted space available. But at all events, I was escaping the baneful scowl of the lugubrious chief as he considered the loss of his precious steam and the threat to the ship's stability whenever I ventured to suggest a bath aboard. It was a wise move.

Preparation for TV Pleasure boat Round 2 - out of Rothesay this time, still in the rain and oilskins!

Fraternising- from left to right, TV engineer, our waitress Jean, Dick and myself- I am now sporting a less lumpy plastic white top!

Day 28 *Friday 26 July*

Very wet again all day. Gale force 8 wind rose from North in course of the day.

I had time to read in the morning as the *Graham* did not appear till 1.30 from the Kyles. I also had both breakfast and dinner at home. Talked to assistants on *Bute* and *Countess* while I waited for *Graham* to call. Our photographer friends were on the pier and snapped the *Graham* moving astern from berth 3 and along the pier. She had unusually come to berth 3 with her bow facing south to Albert pier. We sailed at 2.10 - because we were not at Gourock, there was no attempt to shift mere assistants to other vessels - and were overtaken in the Kyles by *Queen Mary*. Then we anchored in Loch Riddon for two hours, returning to Rothesay at 5.30. At this point, Donald left us for his home in Gourock and was replaced by the baldy publicity agent. Not a word was said about our not being away working on car ferries! Left again at 6.25 and sailed up to Loch Riddon to await the real thing. Surf riders were ready for action in the bay and only the weather seemed unwilling to cooperate. Dick and I went forward to the bow in an effort to get in the cameras at the Narrows after we left for the start of the programme at 8.00 but we failed. A little later, I walked up the deck in full view of the camera, all unaware, but it was to no avail. There had been no sound and after 8.18 there was no picture either. The programme was abandoned. The surf riding continued, pipe bands played and the crowds cheered dutifully - until they learned that it was all off. The Buteman reported that Kenneth Horne alone appeared oblivious to the weather. " While the others were encased in oilskins or waterproofs, he came ashore hatless and in a pullover. The deck of the *Graham* was covered by TV equipment, cameras, vans, etc., while aerials decorated the masts." So the ship too had some measure of protection! There followed much confusion when the pipe band insisted they get transport to Gourock after the provost got off at Rothesay. In the end they had to jump aboard as we set off for Gourock. An attempt was made by the producer to have a repeat performance tomorrow but, after much debate within the Kremlin, this was refused. Up until this decision was announced, the TV stars sang and danced in the saloon. The wind caused problems and we took two attempts at berthing at Gourock and finally had to bring the bow right against the pier. Clearing of the TV equipment went on till the early hours.

Commentary Day 28

Another Pleasure boat fiasco! They should have steered clear of the Glasgow Fair. Indeed, if they had done so, they might have persuaded Gourock to give them another chance. As it was, the Kremlin folk were too nervous about traffic numbers to risk losing a ship for the Saturday.

Dick and I certainly enjoyed ourselves, though we failed to secure the public notice which we courted. The baldy marketeer for the Company passed no comment on our being aboard - no doubt he had other things buzzing about in his baldy cranium as he bustled breathlessly about ship. Had we been sailing out of Gourock, we might have got his attention and been redirected but here out of sight meant out of mind. I might even have succeeded in reaching the national screens if vision had not failed. Instead, I managed to secure only a copy of the programme summary, not the full script this time - and no autographs! Once again, Kenneth Horne did the talking, Jack House passed comment on places of interest and singing was provided by Glenda Mallon (*Kishmul's Galley* and *Rothesay Bay*), Michael Holliday (*We Will Make Love* and *I've Got Bluebirds in my Heart* - surely a quaint selection this!) and Grace O'Connor (*I'm Having the Time of my Life* and *Enough of your Blarney, Barney*). The provost of Rothesay was the main guest of the evening and such others as George Martin and Shrimpy made up the score. But all to no avail! Weather and transmission problems combined to frustrate the enterprise and Pleasure boat on the Clyde passed into history just as if it had never happened. And yet, how I would love to know if copies of the Pleasure boat films taken still exist in BBC archives. They might be good for a laugh!

The local newspaper carried a slightly flippant article on the abandonment of the cruise. It described how first skipper Horne and then the provost were seen by viewers - but not heard. There followed the familiar caption "Normal service will be resumed as soon as possible" and then 15 minutes of music and apologies as fill in before the abandonment was formally announced. Later, the provost expressed his disappointment and praised the excellence of the film he had seen on the monitor screen. The TV producer was quoted as saying it would be sometime before they got over the breakdown, which had been a thousand-to-one chance, and he hoped to make amends for this sad experience - but sadly this never happened! On this occasion, the timing was the root of the problem. The Kremlin could never countenance release of one of their units on a Saturday, no matter what the weather or the potential publicity if the televising had worked. Pleasure was denied and we were back to being the Whiting Bay relief.

Coming up from Ayr. A typical busy scene at Largs. The skipper would have cleared the pier if at all possible!

Loading cars on planks on to *Talisman* - a familiar if scary scene on the Graham.

Day 29 *Saturday 27 July*

Sunny with occasional cloud. Fresh NW winds rose all day and sea became quite rough.

Up at 7.30 for leaving Gourock. *Arran* left Rothesay for Ardrossan and we sailed ahead of her all the way, going by Portencross, while the *Arran* went by Garroch Head. The General Manager featured glumly on the pier, while we faced the usual grumbling about the need for embarkation tickets. The *Sannox* was more or less on time till her 6.00 out of Brodick when she was running 90 minutes late. We were busy on the morning crossings in both directions, carrying upwards of 700 passengers, but later crossings were quieter. Toilet rolls among the rigging, streamers, tomatoes, pennies and lots of people attended the Whiting Bay departures. There was also plenty cargo. The ship was rolling very heavily towards evening and the waves were getting huge. I got soaked at one point. On 6.45 sailing, I took shelter on the bridge deck but the spray reached me there too. *Empress of Scotland* sailed up and back down and we saw the *Montrose* rolling her way back from Ailsa Craig. The new lightship *Hesperus* and a coaster were sheltering in Brodick bay. We had to wait till 8.20 for the *Sannox* to leave, two hours late, with 40 cars. All our crew were cursing since we'd be late in Ayr for the pubs. Heavy seas running and when we swung round off Ayr and took the sea broadside instead of semi-stern, we really rolled over. Once again I watched the show from the bridge deck. In Ayr harbour, the wind was a real problem and we turned our bow in, striking the harbour wall, and dropped anchor - quite a good effort considering the wild weather. We finally tied up at 9.55 and all rushed ashore for refreshments.

Commentary Day 29

This marked the end of the Glasgow Fair and the beginning of a new fortnight. Hence traffic was heavy and the *Arran* was down to assist the *Sannox*. Ticket collection was complicated and the requirement of the large blue embarkation tickets added to the complexity. These were issued to people of all ages, including infants, and quickly filled hands and pockets for the ticket collector at the gamgway. Embarkation tickets featured on the four busiest days of the summer: 29 June, 13 and 27 July and 3 August. However, we got off lightly. They were only required on the 10.20 Brodick crossing and we received them from passengers who decided to change route and make for Whiting Bay.

The *Sannox* had a bad night. Deserted by the *Arran*, plagued by steep gangways, ill served at low tide by the painfully slow car lift for a full load of cars, and with a skipper whose ship handling was often abysmal, she was two hours late leaving and kept us out in the bay for an hour, where we lay along with the other ships seeking shelter from the storm.

This was an excellent day to watch the *Graham*'s lively performance in heavy seas. The observation deck below the bridge was a particularly pleasing place to stand and view the show, as it offered a solid rail to duck down behind when the spray rose high. She did all the pitch and toss imaginable on that blank run over to Ayr. She could also manage a double roll over on occasion, before pulling herself up again and this was scary stuff! Nowhere was safe from the surges of spray flying up as she bucked and kicked with propellers racing in the trough of larger billows. Yet our skipper was quite unperturbed. He could have sailed straight in and turned on the ropes at the quayside that night or next morning. But oh no! He performed a masterly manoeuvre inside the breakwater with the help of the anchor and took only a glancing blow on the bow as he swung her round. But of course, he had all the time in the world. Pubs meant nothing to him! Needless to say, he was not one of the gang who dashed up town once we were berthed!

Day 30 *Sunday 28 July*

Dry and strong N wind all day. Some bright periods.

Up at 7.30 and cleaned out cancellation office with strong soap solution provided by stewards. Spent some time polishing ship's bell and plate as well as compass brass in wheelhouse. At 11.15 we set off, with 242 from Ayr, via Troon, Ardrossan, Largs and Dunoon for cruise to Gareloch. Very blustery. Skipper hit Troon pier both calls with the bow cutting into the cement and also struck Dunoon so hard that he took off the corner pile and its metal retaining cover. The ever-officious pier master was quick to assess the damage at £50. We again left a group of three on the pier at Dunoon on the return and others made a jump for it. We were 5 minutes late at that but kept good time all the way. We were 10 minutes ahead at Ayr but lost this in getting alongside. The ship refused to swing round and we ended up on the opposite side of the river! Once ashore at our proper berth, I bought chips, apple and seedless grapes. Then walked out on the breakwater, climbed down the rocks and walked a bit along the shore - the tide was low. Tore off one of my soles at the toe in the sand. Read for a while on return and shared a delicious pineapple with Dick which he got yesterday. The photographer friend from Preston came down this morning to let me know he was finished his annual holiday and going home.

Commentary Day 30

A late departure, it being Sunday and all that, meant I was at a loose end and seeking useful, if not gainful, employment until sailing time. So it was that I got busy with the Brasso after a thorough clean out of my bedroom/office. You can be sure the skipper was absent from the bridge it I dared to shine up brass inside the wheelhouse! The wind proved troublesome and first of all we gave Troon a hefty clout but got the worst of it, as the pier there was concrete. Still, we left our mark in the concrete and came back at night for a second shot. We made a better job at Dunoon and ripped the metal protector from the corner pile. The piermaster, with grim scowl and heavy jowl, was efficiency itself and delivered an on the spot damage estimate of £ 50 - which seemed on the low side to me!

Dunoon was becoming our skipper's bane, so that it was natural that he should complete his visit by leaving passengers behind again. These were of a less histrionic disposition than on the previous occasion and they watched our passing with resignation! They recognised that they were late and would need to make alternative arrangements. Ayr concluded a bad day for the skipper. His usual dexterity in the harbour mouth failed him and he took 30 minutes to get alongside on the right bank of the river. Surely it was the *Graham*'s way of getting her own back for these hefty knocks at the piers.

The day ended pleasantly enough for us, the assistants. We had a sensible diet of varied fruits to supplement the menu aboard ship. Fresh fruit never featured there. Tearing the toe off my shoe was a nuisance as I had no spare shoes and this must have resulted in awkward walking till they were repaired. But the desire to exercise was commendable and the damage relatively slight.

Day 31 *Monday 29 July*

Occasional misty patches but mainly fine. Fresh NW wind.

Up at 5.30 as we were on the usual Death boat run out of Whiting Bay and Brodick. We refused 2 cars owing to the state of tide (very low). 401 made the crossing and two school pals were among them. I talked with them on the sail. Both have summer jobs and have just finished holidays. Sea still choppy but not causing much motion. Seems that rough weather caused problems for *Waverley* turning in Ardrossan harbour on Friday night and she was over 30 minutes late. We were away on Pleasure boat. We reached Ayr again at 9.25 for our 10.00 departure after a 75 minute blank run down from Ardrossan. 275 passengers out of Ayr and another 175 from Troon. We left about 30 who ran up late at Ayr but waited for 10 latecomers at Troon. Then off to Brodick and Rothesay via the Kyles. *Sannox* caused us less delay than last week and we were leaving Brodick bay as the *Waverley* entered on her Arran via Kyles sailing. Rothesay pier was very busy - we lay at berth 2 while *Saint Columba*, *Queen Mary* and *Talisman* appeared around us, followed by the Wemyss Bay car ferry and *Maid of Cumbrae*. I slipped ashore for 10 minutes to see the folks and drop off clothes for washing. Tide was very high at Rothesay so that our fender was almost level with the pier. *Caledonia*'s chief is relieving our 2nd engineer for a long weekend. He is very affable. I went to see Twelve Angry Men with Dick and our mate after a brief call at a pub. This was a very skilfully arranged film. *Hamilton* was on a specially time tabled Upriver run to Glasgow today to compensate for our absence on Wednesday. She was evidently well patronised.

Commentary Day 31

It is worth noting that we occasionally took cars on our sailings out of Whiting Bay even when the new car ferry had taken over at Brodick. After all, it was not so long since we had been Arran's sole steamer and taking cars as a matter of course. But what a procedure! Creeping along these two narrow wooden planks must have been an ordeal for drivers and indeed there were stories of crew members taking over from drivers who baulked at the challenge. Our skipper was never one to turn away such trade unless conditions were really bad, as on this occasion at low tide. I do wish that I had dared to photograph some of these breathtaking moments! But I was too afeared of that square jawed, purple hued face that leaned over from the high eyrie overhead and no photograph was ever taken.

If he was always ready to take cars, his attitude to passengers was more ambivalent. Ayr, like Largs or indeed Glasgow Bridge Wharf, was one of these piers where people were always apt to show up, ready to sail if the ship was waiting. The timetable had no meaning for them, anymore than the chalk written blackboard or liberally scattered amended sailing leaflets. No! It was the sight of the ship which drew them like a lure. Inevitably, some turned up too late but 30 is a surprisingly large number to have shown up too late at Ayr. On a different occasion, our man would certainly have turned back for them as he did that same morning at Troon - and for a lesser number. There was just no way of predicting his moods and decisions.

You can be sure that the *Hamilton*'s unusual appearance on the Upriver run would draw a crowd. There would be her own fan club in the first instance but these would be supplemented by the River Steamer Club and other enthusiasts, eager to participate in any departure from normal timetabling.

Day 32 *Tuesday 30 July*

Bright and dry with Westerly wind later.

Up at 7.40 and shaved before breakfast. Left Ayr with 763 passengers - we normally allowed a maximum of 621 out of Ayr to leave space at the other piers. A few hundred more joined at Troon and Ardrossan and this took us over our down river complement of 891. More still followed at Largs. This was not so bad, as we were permitted 1,300 passengers upriver. However, by this time Dick and I had panicked and approached the skipper. He was wild with us for mentioning figures and informed us that the numbers were not our concern. Moreover, he would sack either of us who ever mentioned numbers again to him. So that was an end of it! Donald's accounts were, as usual, a bit short at the end of the day. The visit from the audit officer at Rothesay confirmed this deficiency. There was a lot of cash about and the decks were crammed. All meals were fully booked before we left Ardrossan. The nervous twitching of the chief steward can be imagined. We ran a little late after Rothesay on the outward, as we took ten minutes there to get our bow into the pier and then had to move out at Tighnabruaich to allow the *Saint Columba* to call. We reached Ardrossan after the *Sannox* and had to use Jerry's quay. Overcrowding caused frayed tempers all round today, from the master down. There were heaps of tickets to be sorted in numerical order and the calculation of the passenger log proved chaotic and required a lot of adjustment. Skipper made a good job of coming into Ayr and Dick and I went ashore to the pubs to lick our wounds when the tickets were finished. Among the ship's mail, I got a letter from one of my regular correspondents from home.

Commentary Day 32

Ayr and Glasgow, at either end of the Clyde ports of call, always responded well to a run of settled weather and the crowds appeared. This was just such an occasion at Ayr and the first when we became seriously concerned about possible overcrowding. But we should have known better than go to "himself". The mate would have been a much wiser choice as a first resort. But nerves got the better of us and we confronted our lord and master in his eyrie. The response was unequivocal. "Just listen you to me, Mac. Numbers are not your business. I'll sack you if you speak to me of numbers again." Well, that was clear enough and our hearts and loins froze as we listened. This was a move never to be repeated.

That day surpassed the bedlam normally associated with our

Campbeltown sailings. Meals sold out, deckchairs sold out, planks were used as extra seating, the balance failed to balance, and the chief steward lost his nerve. Taking on our full complement was no light matter for the purser. Most of the passengers had to be booked aboard and, when you added meals and deckchairs, this was a substantial burden. Up at Glasgow, *Queen Mary* had a similar situation but to assist the purser there were two junior pursers booking tickets as well as one assistant who might occasionally be called on to issue tickets. Big Donald may have faced smaller numbers down river but he had poor support by comparison. One assistant was not trusted and the other was still viewed as a novice! The arrival of the company auditor at Rothesay added to the general confusion and confirmed Donald's fears for the balance. Even the log let us down and all collected tickets had to be sorted numerically. It was one of these days and tensions ran high. Little wonder we took to drink that night!

The Evening Citizen that night chose to picture the *Graham* arriving at Ayr under the caption "The Gay Ship that goes out to play" and showing me smiling at the gangway. Certainly the ship is crowded and the passengers look happy but, of course, the picture was taken on a different day. There is no evidence of the tension or the overcrowding which made this particular day so memorable. Reference to the ship as being "Gay" would also have raised eyebrows today as we noticed earlier. Times change as does language use.

Day 33 *Wednesday 31 July*

Showery most of day but broke up and cleared around 6.00 into a lovely sunny evening.

Up at 8.00 and after breakfast went up town with Donald to bank and then to station. Dick and I completed sorting and tying yesterday's tickets and wrapped them in a long, coffin-shaped bundle. After that we did a few odd jobs for Donald. We had dinner before leaving Ayr at about 1.00. Plenty folk came to see if we were doing a cruise and it seemed a wasted opportunity. Crossed blank to Whiting Bay and anchored there till *Hamilton* left for Garroch Head and up river at 2.30. During this interval at anchor, the captain, the seaman from the *Caledonia* and I took turns fishing at the bow. We were rather far out and the tide was strong - that was our excuse for catching nothing. Donald was busy most of the day with the month end figures and we kept at a distance. We carried 273 and ten barrow loads of cases and trunks out of Whiting Bay at 3.50 on our single timetabled crossing. I went off at Ardrossan and walked to South Beach station where I got a privilege ticket to Largs for one shilling and two pence return. *Montrose* was running late from Campbeltown and so I hurried down to the pier and got aboard before she left for Rothesay, thus saving the bus fare to Wemyss Bay. Several assistant pursers were aboard - I brought the number up to five. *Countess* was crammed for Tighnabruaich tonight and I made a return trip over on the *Bute* to Wemyss Bay.

Commentary Day 33

Our only sailing today was a special crossing according to timetable at 3.50 from Whiting Bay. We would have been more profitably occupied on our usual Upriver run but this was not timetabled and the *Hamilton* in fact had done a specially advertised Upriver run on Monday as if to compensate. This was one of only three days that we missed the Upriver run this season. The others were when *Jupiter* stood in for us early in the month when we were serving as Arran steamer and later when we were on Glasgow Fair reliefs on 17 July. But on that latter occasion there was no spare *Duchess* available for a Monday special!

We used the extra time at Ayr that morning to replenish our stocks of change by visiting the bank. The other regular job to be done was a call at the station to collect the ship's mail and any other items. This was far preferable to doing other wee jobs for Donald and it also allowed us to display our seagoing credentials to the citizenry of bonnie Ayr toon!

Normally, this job had to be rushed and fitted in prior to a morning departure.

Thereafter, we repaired to the cancellation office to finish off the tickets and kept well clear of big Donald as he sweated over the month end returns. We had time on our hands and this explains our endeavour to create a coffin shape with the ticket parcel to keep the Kremlin girls at Gourock entertained when and if they did their double check on the collection. Similarly, we found alternative occupation at Whiting Bay. I seized the chance to fish along with the captain who was being approachable. Fishing seemed an occupation where he could comfortably climb down a bit and mix with his men! Bait was got out of the galley and the fishing lines were at the ready in the crew's quarters forward. The fish refused to bite and passenger trade was little better, although admittedly there was no lack of cargo on our crossing. No mention is made of who did the cargo check, though I fancy Dick took it under his wing. I was never enthusiastic about this chore.

I felt it a wasted day and was glad to make off at Ardrossan for my day off on the following day. The *Montrose* was obligingly late at Largs, so that I crossed with her to Rothesay and compared notes with the cluster of other assistants I found on board. Then there was time to glut myself with a return trip to Wemyss Bay and a blether with her pursers before joining my parents at the Rothesay flat.

Day 34 *Thursday 1 August*

Beautiful, blue sky with bright sun and little cloud all day - a perfect first of the month.

Up about 9.00 and handed in shoes to cobbler for repair and put in a film for developing. After dinner, with Dad's own bike and one borrowed from the cobbler, Dad and I set out for Ettrick Bay while Mum went on the bus with Vic, the dog. We sunbathed and Dad and I swam - Mum paddled. Returned at 6.30 and later I met a pal of Mum's in town and took her up to see Mum in the flat. She was impressed by its location. Had a bath and went to bed about 11.00. All the steamers were very busy and no exceptions. Even the Campbeltown sailing was busy! *Jupiter* carried capacity crowds from midday on and *Saint Columba* was comfortably filled. *Waverley* arrived at 7.10pm, 45 minutes late. This was because of record breaking numbers to Arrochar. Pier officer confirmed that last week's advertised sailings by the *Marchioness* to the Arran coast and Round Bute were cancelled.

Commentary Day 34

I chose a good day to take off as the weather was perfect. We kept one bike at the flat for occasional use such as this and had a remedy available if two were needed: the friendly cobbler had another ancient bike which could be borrowed for the price of a half hour blether. He loved to talk and this was a small sacrifice for the loan of a bike. Anyway, some of his yarns were quite funny and had not always been already heard before! Then there was that shoe with the sole ripped off on the beach at Ayr. It all fell beautifully into place! When the family went to Ettrick, we favoured the stretch of shore at Glecknabae, a mile or two North. This was quieter and, though the shore was stony, there was a fine stretch of sand out in the water. A perfect place for dog, swim and picnic. Besides these undoubted attractions, there were also some sites of archaeological interest nearby to complete the picture.

The crowded steamers were what one might expect in fine weather. The drift abroad to sunnier climes than Costa Clyde was still in its early days and August was always a good time for English visitors. Not that the *Graham* enjoyed any share of the day's bonanza. She was again scheduled to squander another opportunity for profit on a poorly supported single crossing from Ardrossan to Whiting Bay at 10.10. Had she been sailing out of Ayr that day, she would certainly have been stowed out and I would not have been given the day off!

Day 35 *Friday 2 August*

Another scorcher from morning till night.

Up at 7.00 for *Jupiter* over to Wemyss Bay, then bus to Largs, 9.00 train to South Beach and a walk to the harbour for around 9.45. Ship was all bustle - *Sannox* had broken down at Brodick (later learned it was the lift again) and we were to take over with assistance from car ferry *Bute*. Delay followed, as there was no sign yet of the skipper. Donald too was missing. Orders were given for the mate to take charge. Meanwhile, the queues were forming on the pier. Then word came at 10.15 that the *Sannox* was on her way over. A last minute decision put the passengers on her with a 11.00 departure while the *Bute* arrived soon after to take all the cars. It was a great relief for us but not so good for *Sannox*'s passengers from Brodick. They found no engine on their train and it was 1.00 before they reached Glasgow St Enoch. Furious protests! Meanwhile, *Sannox* had her lift repaired and *Bute* returned up river. Painting and washing proceeded on our boat and I polished the brasses. It was all so peaceful! Dick had his day off. Brasses done, I sunbathed on the upper deck and watched the *Lady of Man* call, then move out for *Mona's Queen* to depart, before coming back in again astern. I photographed both of them. Saw my photo today in Wednesday's Citizen while on gangway duty. Our only crossing of the day was at 7.05 to Brodick and Whiting Bay and we then returned blank to Ardrossan. Got fresh linen bedding today and wrote grandpa and my local correspondent pal in my leisure time. It was very hot aboard ship today. The mate won £50 on the horses this week. He is always studying form and this time it paid off. *Sannox* received her ship postcards today and so I bought one. The evening newspaper version of the day was: *Sannox* broke down at Brodick; *Marchioness* was needed but it was her crew's day off and she could not come out and so the *Cowal* was sent to Brodick; soon after, the *Sannox* was repaired and took over - well, at least they got it right about the *Sannox*!

Commentary Day 35

I found all this rather disappointing. We should have been getting a share of the action and good days were few and far between this summer. The idea of returning as Arran steamer for the day was appealing and certainly preferable in my view to idling away the day at Ardrossan until our one late crossing. It was not to be. The *Sannox* could not take the waiting cars but there were far too many for us and so the *Bute*, summoned from upriver, filled in and we remained inactive. The newspaper reference to the crew having a day off was not so wide of the mark! Bless the Isle of Man steamers! They provided something worthwhile in the way of shipping activity beyond the routine sailings by *Bute* and *Glen Sannox*.

I certainly had a leisurely day, rather like that first Sunday at Ardrossan after working my first day on the then brand new *Glen Sannox*. And though we had been denied the blaze of publicity, which the TV Pleasure boat might have offered had the two efforts not failed so miserably, at least my appearance in the Evening Citizen earlier in the week at the gangway afforded some form of recognition. So I treasured that item and have kept it safe to this day. Such is fame. *Carpe diem*.

Mona's Queen leaving Ardrossan viewed from *Graham* at Jerry's Quay

Day 36 *Saturday 3 August*

Would have been another scorcher had it not been for the heavy heat haze which weakened the sun and shrouded the scenery. Sea like a millpond.

Up at 7.45 and shaved quickly as breakfast bell had been rung. Went over to our side berth about 9.00 and *Sannox* came in along front at Winton pier almost on time. Huge number of cars waiting. We took some 600 passengers on 10.20 to Whiting Bay and there was the usual fuss over embarkation tickets. General Manager was down watching this morning. Quite busy all day and plenty friends from home and school were among them to keep me interested. We also had flag sellers on board for several runs. *Sannox* was about 45 minutes late on all her crossings from the mainland. Fewer toilet rolls were in evidence today as we left Arran. Skipper was in a touchy mood. Thus he threatened Dick with sacking for asking a man to bring his bike up the wooden planks laid out for barrows. The gangway was roped as we were ahead of sailing time. Dick saw the planks as the obvious alternative. The skipper took up his position at the gangway end and said to Dick "Do you know what I'm going to do with you now?" No answer, of course. "I'll sack you for that. I could be in trouble for it." His mood later improved so much that he called back for a motorbike and rider left on the pier. Then on the last run over to Arran, he met a large naval supply ship. He decided against going round her stern as expected and instead headed straight for her and cut engines when very close. He then continued on his way. En route for Ayr at the end of the day, we lost speed for some time when a flow pipe blocked and the engines seized. The reason given was lack of winter overhaul. But the chief was off the weekend and the ship was being harder driven - we were ahead of time all day - and so that could have explained the incident. At all events, it resulted in a slow passage to Ayr and our time off was reduced. But the most colourful moment of the day came at our last Ardrossan call, as we prepared to leave at 6.45 with 93 passengers and a princely 5 cars. The 2nd steward had collected supplies from the baker's van on the pier head. When the bag was passed aboard, the captain asked to see in it. The steward replied that the bag belonged to a galley boy and he alone should open it. Up came the galley boy and the steward laid down the parcels and began opening the bag. Thereupon the skipper exclaimed "No, No! I don't want to see in it!" The steward asked for an apology or he would phone Gourock and lodge a complaint. Then the skipper cried "Away with you, away with you and your apologics. I know everything that goes on in this ship. Go and complain to the captain of the *Queen Mary*!"- this last reference was understood by no-one. Further words were exchanged and at last the skipper shouted "Go right up and sign off now" and off he swept. The chief steward tried to calm the situation and went to see him only to be ordered out. End of round one!

Commentary Day 36

This was a really busy Arran Saturday when even embarkation tickets could be justified! There were also significant numbers of friends making the crossing and this was a pleasing feature of the Arran run in summer. There were always likely to be pals from school appearing unheralded, mainly of secondary school vintage but some even dating back to primary. The General Manager's arrival was not so welcome, although his attention was taken up entirely by the *Sannox*. He wore the usual dark suit and waistcoat and black Homburg hat as well. But, in deference to the heat, he had doffed his coat.

This was of course a red letter day for the captain and his antics. It started with the cyclist who was made to "walk the plank" and perhaps the threatened sacking of Dick caught the captain's fancy and put him in the mood for blood. Anyway, the incident with the 2nd steward was a full scale onslaught. Catering staff were always liable to be viewed with suspicion by other members of the crew. After all, they handled food and money, both of which were thought to offer the possibility of venality.

Monday's Bulletin carried a banner headline "12 THREATEN TO WALK OFF CLYDE SHIP" The account began with a reference to the 500 meals served aboard next day out of Ayr and then revealed the row. The steward explained that he had been carrying a case belonging to a galley boy and the captain asked him to open it He had refused and the boy explained that the case contained two shirts. He was then told by the skipper to watch himself and, on asking for an explanation, he was ordered to sign off. This he did under protest. The other catering staff supported the steward and would walk off if he were not reinstated. The captain's comment was that in his view there was nothing in this and any enquiries should go to Gourock office.

The repercussions of this incident were to continue. They had an immediate effect on the captain: when he saw the naval vessel in his path on the run across to Brodick, he uncharacteristically ignored the rules of the sea and headed straight for her, making no attempt to give her space. Instead, he went into reverse on drawing close and then continued on his way. He was certainly making a point of some kind!

Meeting the *Queen Mary* off Greenock as our ship returns from Upriver sailing.

In familiar waters approaching Brodick.

Day 37 *Sunday 4 August*

Beautiful, warm day with little wind.

Up at usual time and took a cold bath after breakfast. Polished brasses. Queues started in Ayr at 9.45 and we let them on at 10.00. Took on 693 at Ayr for cruise to Loch Riddon via Troon and Ardrossan where we picked up over 500, putting us well over down river complement. Another 101 at Largs and we were nearing our up river complement too so that any late arrivals were left for the *Talisman* coming over behind us to Rothesay. We were 5 minutes late on arrival at Rothesay, as we were packed. Passed Dick's uncle on his motorboat as we sailed up the Kyles. *Maid of Ashton* was relieving on Largs /Millport crossing. Dad, along with my sister, was on the pier to watch our return to Rothesay. 2nd steward came aboard at Troon and resumed normal duties. Skipper did not address him directly but said to Donald "I see we have a passenger on board. I hope he's got a ticket." We think he is serious. It was a beautiful cruise and we were well filled, like the other steamers too. *Maid of Cumbrae* was on relief from Bridge Wharf. On the morning call, we turned round inside Troon harbour in case the dolphin obstructed our leaving the harbour with the wind on the pier, but it took time and was not repeated in the evening. Dick and I went for a bathe along the shore on tying up at Ayr. Pretty cold as the sun was sinking fast. Then supper and cancelled remaining tickets.

Couple of blunders:

At Rothesay Dick was told he had Ardrishaig, not Ardrossan, on his fan board and quickly changed it.

At Largs the pierman shouted that he had put up Kirn for Troon. Dick thought he was joking until another pier hand repeated it. He was horrified.

Commentary Day 37

So the 2nd steward returned to duty without the skipper's blessing. No doubt, he had received a frantic call from the chief steward when the crowds piled aboard and his help was clearly needed. Of course, the captain did not see it this way and treated him as a non-person. But it was a battle between the two of them and we certainly were not expecting him to show a ticket, whatever the captain's wishes.

The fine weather on a Sunday had the usual effect on the crowds and we spent a busy day. Of course, nothing was said to the captain this time about numbers. We had been well warned! No doubt he was sorry to leave any passengers at Largs for *Talisman* to carry. High numbers were in fact unlikely to have caused our lateness at Rothesay. More likely, it was a display of some caution after yesterday's engine seizure or unsuitable coal was the reason.

The reference to the cold bath in the morning takes me back to late teens and student days. The Sunday Post doctor had pronounced that a cold bath every morning would ward off colds and flu. I took him at his word and for some years I religiously followed this harsh regimen regardless of season. On another occasion, the Sunday Post doctor recommended the taking of malt and our family dutifully obeyed - once we could get a supply, as the shelves in Boots the Chemist were cleared. Such was the power of the Post! Anyway, a daily bath was not so easy on the *Graham* when there was the old Welsh chief to contend with. Certainly, the bath was always there, filled with cold water to ensure our stability, as the chief imagined. But it would require emptying and refilling and that might have proved risky. So my cold baths were less frequent that summer. But I made up for this by other forms of masochism! An evening bathe at Ayr on an August evening once the passengers were ashore must have provided a suitably chilling experience. Only the dog walkers could have witnessed this cool ritual - the day trippers would have long gone and the shore was left largely to ourselves.

The changing of the fan boards showing our ports of call was usually one of Dick's tasks. If we were short of fan boards, some would be moved from one side to the other according to which side the pier was on - just like the mats were moved to protect the deck below the gangway. In the general excitement, it was relatively easy to make mistakes but two on one day was good going!

Day 38 *Monday 5 August*

Shock for all - wet and windy despite yesterday's settled outlook.

Up about 5.00, as we were doing Death run and left Ayr shortly after. Only 265 travelled from the two Arran piers including a few friends, most notably my pals with the house in Corrie. Big headlines on bill posters "Strike on Ayr steamer"; "Clyde Steamer Strike" etc. Daily Express has a column telling steward's version and quoting skipper "Don't ask the catering department! I am the master." The report continues that if the steward is not reinstated by tomorrow the strike will go ahead. Several company officials came on at Ardrossan as soon as we docked and went up to the chart room on the bridge. The rest of us waited anxiously, particularly the chief steward, and before we sailed again, the deputation departed in their chauffeur driven Humber. Rumour has it that the skipper has to accept the steward back. This was confirmed later - a climb down. Our special 10.10 run to Whiting Bay was delayed a little while passengers and cargo came round to Jerry's quay. Skipper waved *Sannox* out first and we followed, turning in the harbour. On our 3 crossings of the day, we carried only 432 passengers and the ticket bundle was tiny. Anchored in the Bay from 11.45 till 2.30 and did a spot of fishing. Again, no luck since we had no proper bait. We left Ardrossan for Ayr at 5.00. Took just under the hour so I went for a bathe. Rain cut it shorter than I intended. It turned out to be a shower so I went up town for grapes and then walked round the fair. Answered some questions at the gangway while putting up next day's sailing on the blackboard.

Commentary Day 38

The saga over the steward continued and the press delighted in a change of headlines. But it did not last long and the ending was almost inevitable. The captain's behaviour was considered unreasonable and the steward was reinstated. All the big guns from Gourock had made an appearance and it was left for the press to embellish the account. "I am the master" in the Express certainly had an authentic ring about it!

This was one of a half dozen days set aside that summer for the *Graham* to make a special sailing to and from Whiting Bay, but at least we had the normal Death run also to fill up our day. Traffic certainly did not justify this incursion into our regular programme and fishing was no more successful. On this occasion the captain did not make an appearance. Mixing with the men after his recent climb down had no attraction for him. But at least it passed the time for us as there was little to do. It also allowed us an early arrival at Ayr and tempted me to go swimming until I was rained off. The fair was always an entertaining end to the day when we lay at Ayr. The side stalls provided some relief. But you certainly would not expect to meet the captain in such a venue and on this particular day he must have been preoccupied and licking his wounds!

The open nature of our terminal at Ayr encouraged regular meetings with passers-by. You never felt alone! And so it was I had ample scope for honing my customer service skills while engaged in setting up the display boards for the morning.

The *Graham* having a quiet smoke at Brodick pier.

THE CALEDONIAN STEAM PACKET COMPANY LIMITED

AMENDED
PLEASURE SAILINGS

From AYR HARBOUR by T.S. "MARCHIONESS OF GRAHAM"

WITH CONNECTING TRAIN SERVICES
FROM
GIRVAN and MAYBOLE

UNTIL 22nd AUGUST

DAYS	TO	Through Rail and Steamer Fares (Second Class Rail) from	
		GIRVAN	MAYBOLE
MONDAY 12th August	BRODICK (Arran)	11/-	8/9
	ROTHESAY (via Kyles of Bute)	16/-	13/9
MONDAY 12th August	BRODICK (Arran)	11/-	8/9
	DUNOON (via Largs)	16/-	13/9
TUESDAY 13th August	LARGS	12/6	10/3
	ROTHESAY	15/-	12/9
	KYLES OF BUTE (Tighnabruaich)	16/-	13/9
TUESDAY 20th August	MILLPORT	12/6	10/3
	DUNOON	15/-	12/9
	CRUISE TO LOCH GOIL	16/-	13/9
THURSDAYS 15th and 22nd August	WHITING BAY (Arran)	11/-	8/9
	CAMPBELTOWN (Kintyre)	16/-	13/9

CONNECTING TRAIN SERVICE from GIRVAN and MAYBOLE

OUTWARD		RETURN	
	a.m.		p.m.
GIRVAN - Train leaves	8 47	AYR - Train leaves	7 38
MAYBOLE ,, ,,	9 7	MAYBOLE ,, arrives	7 55
AYR ,, arrives	9 21	GIRVAN ,, ,,	8 18

NOTE—The Western S.M.T. Company Limited will provide connecting 'bus services between Ayr Station and Ayr Harbour in each direction, 'bus fare additional.

STEAMER LEAVES AYR HARBOUR AT 10 a.m. AND ARRIVES BACK at 7.0 p.m. ON EACH OF ABOVE DATES

The tickets are valid on the dates for which issued.

LUNCHEONS AND HIGH TEAS SERVED IN THE DINING SALOON. SELF-SERVICE CAFETERIA. REFRESHMENTS.

NOTICE AS TO CONDITIONS—Tickets are issued subject to the Conditions and Regulations contained in the Bills and Notices of or applicable to The Caledonian Steam Packet Company Limited or to any other body, company or person upon whose services the tickets may be available.

Day 39 *Tuesday 6 August*

Dull and misty till 3.00 and then bright and sunny.

Up at 7.45 and after breakfast walked up town to bank with chief steward. We were each laden with money! He related yesterday's interview with the Kremlites and told how skipper had rushed to Donald at high pitch asking for a letter which was intended for the General Manager and in which he attacked the catering staff. When he showed this to the deputation, they told him to repudiate its claims or else carry on and see where this got him. In the event, the 2nd steward was reinstated. Locked our money in the night safe at the bank, placed an order for fish for the galley and returned to find crowds already boarding. Took on 736 at Ayr and left over 150 who had not prebooked tickets. Another 100 at Troon and left as many non ticket holders - similar picture at Ardrossan. Thus again we were over subscribed downriver but fortunately 268 went ashore at Millport, making room for another crowd at Largs. Of course Donald had assured us that "thousands would come out from Millport and Largs as this was a popular cruise and we couldn't turn them away". In fact, just over 700 sailed with us from Dunoon for Loch Goil cruise and of these only 170 boarded at the piers in question! Met *Waverley* on return as she entered Loch Goil and exchanged blasts on the horn. A short delay for two *Maids* at Dunoon allowed the *Sannox* to get into Ardrossan first and we had to use Jerry's quay. *Jupiter* had decided to take no risks and gone to Keppel on returning from Dunagoil cruise and left Millport Old Pier for our exclusive use. No delay there! Once again I had a bathe when we reached Ayr and then visited the fair - but the old chief was back and the bath aboard was again under observation.

Lairds Isle made her last crossing today and *Irish Coast* replaces her. This BTC (British Transport Commission) decision has lost Burns Laird their Irish day trippers as the replacement is too slow to allow time ashore. *Caledonia*'s boiler test this morning must have hit a snag, since she will not be out before next weekend and we continue out of Ayr next week. There has to be an enquiry tomorrow by the Kremlin over the sacking and the high degree of publicity in the media. Donald and skipper are to attend and the 2nd steward may be in trouble for encouraging press interest.

Commentary Day 39
Poor weather at the start did nothing to dampen the enthusiasm of our following. Perhaps Monday's cancellation of Ayr sailings to allow

Opposite: AMENDED SAILINGS – GIRVAN AND MAYBOLE.
The blue Handbill of Amended Sailings from Ayr and Troon till 23rd August was issued around this time.

us to while away the day at Whiting Bay acted as an incentive. Perhaps media publicity over the sacking incident had roused public interest. Whatever the reason, we were very much in business and only ticket holders were taken on board. The two queue procedure separating ticket and non ticket holders worked effectively and saved us from any major confrontation with the master. Naturally, I took delight in accompanying the chief steward up town first thing so as to get the low down on the sacking and the outcome. This was more for my own fascination than for the real purpose - to bank the weekend takings at the night safe as the bank was not yet open for business. We were intended to offer each other mutual protection against attack and this very suspect security system was fortunately never put to the test. But this system was commonplace around the steamers and considerable sums of money used to be carried by one or sometimes two assistants through busy streets.

You may wonder at the cryptic comment about the *Jupiter*. The fact was that the Dunagoil cruise boat was timetabled to call at Millport Old Pier on its return at 4.40. We were scheduled to call at exactly the same time from our Loch Goil cruise. But Millport was shielded by several islands and the *Jupiter*'s captain was clearly uncomfortable about bringing his expansive charge among these islands, especially at low tide. So he opted instead for Keppel pier, just 15 minute walk round from Millport Bay and the usual arrival point of the turbine steamers. Our master felt no such qualms about Millport Old! After all, he had been master of the old *Duchess of Fife* and *Talisman* on this route for several years. He knew his depths perfectly and in he went, turbine or no turbine. Thus both masters saved time and worry and I had some extra time to enjoy a quick bathe in the gloaming on reaching Ayr.

News of *Caledonia*'s extended absence resulted in the immediate preparation of a new handbill and poster. The earlier red printed sheet applied till 9th August and now a further notice of amended sailings, largely a repetition of the first, appeared in blue print. This was to operate till 23 August, allowing plenty margin for possible problems with *Caledonia*. Neither handbill made any mention of a specific ship by name.

Day 40 *Wednesday 7 August*

Very similar to yesterday but cleared a little earlier. E wind rose in evening.

Sailed up from Ayr to Largs with our new Bridge Wharf board on show. Good numbers all the way, especially from Dunoon. Mum and Dad joined us at Rothesay. The bald publicity agent for the company was much in evidence, shouting and cavorting on Gourock pier. Took 618 up to Glasgow and 856 back down. Sold about £5 worth of brochures on the river section. Saw *Queen Mary* passing each way and *Lairds Isle* laid up with *Kildonan* in Albert Harbour at Greenock. *Caledonia* was also there. Lost 25 minutes on way up river as relief captain is cautious. Our departure was a little delayed for two coaches returning late from the city tour. A lot of shipping activity on river but the highlight was the shouts and jeers of shipyard workers "Come on the VP boat", "Come on with the whisky", " Good on the 2nd steward" and the like. Reached Rothesay at 7.50 and had to wait while *Jupiter* left, bedecked with flags, loud with bands and laden with passengers, on the Rothesay Advertising Association Mystery cruise. We were then held at Rothesay for 40 minutes to pick up an acute appendicitis case for Largs. The young lad was rushed off at Largs, looking very poorly. Then blank to Ayr, arriving 10.35 after a further delay caused by a Kelly boat ahead of us. A cheap night and straight to bed.

Enquiry into sacking meant relief skipper, purser and steward as well as additional catering assistance. All our men from the enquiry rejoined us at Gourock on the downward sailing with the exception of the skipper. Got a letter from my regular local correspondent.

Commentary Day 40

So now we were the proud possessor of our own Glasgow Bridge Wharf board. No more scrounging from other ships for a day's loan nor attempting to make a scarcely legible chalk entry on the thickly varnished blank boards which we carried. This was a belated step forward! The continuing spell of fine weather boosted numbers on the Upriver sailing. Our relief purser was being made to work for his money!

It was the day of the enquiry and several of our regular officers were summoned away. Not that this made any difference to the shore batteries! The workers in the yards lining the river were obviously well read and were watching out for us. They must also have known our timetable and had formed their own opinion of what might have been in the now notorious bag. Hence the barrage of cat calls as we made our cautious passage upriver. They clearly felt certain that it was a matter of illicit drink smuggling and the enquiry could decide whatever it wanted! But it fell to the relief skipper to take the bows and plaudits. Goodness knows what the regal *Queen Mary* must have thought as she sailed grandly on the river which she had made her own! She was resplendent this season with single funnel and looking every inch a queen! I had witnessed the conversion from two funnels to one in Barclay Curle's yard and wondered if she would really recover from her ruinous condition without boiler, funnels, decking and foremast but recover she did, with speed enhanced and looks updated. So it was, for this one season, Glasgow was served by two one-funnel turbine steamers, *Queen Mary* downriver to Rothesay and the Kyles and my *Marchioness* on the upriver from Largs.

What with the disciplinary hearing, the appendicitis case, the delay occasioned by the Kelly boat at Ayr, this was a long day and I needed my bed!

The *Marchioness* meets up with the *Duchess of Hamilton* at Campbeltown.

Our ship heads off blank from Rothesay to Gourock.

Day 41 *Thursday 8 August*

Dull and showery - a dismal outlook. Strong E wind rose later.

Despite the weather, we took on 881 at Ayr and another 205 at Troon. This took us over complement and it was as well that we did not call at Ardrossan. With Dick off, Donald lectured to me much of the day and "encouraged" me to be a better assistant and not to follow Dick's "bad" example. We cruised to Whiting Bay and Campbeltown, landing similar numbers at each. The *Hamilton* beat us to Campbeltown and chose the berth down the side, leaving the front of the pier for us. Chatted with her assistant for a time until *Hamilton* left first at 3.15. Our departure time was the same and we backed into the berth she had left and followed her out. A pretty stormy crossing, particularly on the way to Pladda island. We went down side of pier at Whiting Bay owing to the weather - a most unusual occurrence. Will need to wait till tomorrow morning to leave for my day off. Today, I began to keep a closer watch on ticket collection at the gangway and so did the luggage man. This proved quite successful. Late arrival in Ayr, despite a lovely bit of canting into the pier by the relief skipper. It was pouring cats and dogs when the passengers started to go ashore. I wrote myself a Privilege ticket for the morning, arranged my luggage and turned in early.

Commentary Day 41

As was often the case, poor weather, so long as it was relatively calm, did nothing to deter the good people of Ayr this day and down they flocked. This was the first time we had been available this season to perform this particular cruise and it may be that the chance to round the south of Arran had a special appeal. At any rate, we were well filled, rain or no rain. Our lack of deck cover or a comfortable lounge proved a real pain and discomfort in these crowded and wet conditions. With the best part of 1,000 passengers on board, it was verging on vile. Add the later stormy seas and surf sweeping the open decks and you have a fair picture of Hell afloat! At least in winter, when the *Graham* was the regular Arran boat, numbers were invariably small and the limited accommodation sufficed when the deck was best avoided by all but masochists, people like me!

Still, none of this deflected big Donald from his mission of improvement. The season was fast coming to an end and he was anxious to save me for better things. With Dick on his day off, conditions were ideal. And he clearly had some success! This must have prompted my increased vigilance over ticket collection and my approach to the luggage man. He and I normally shared the same gangway at piers and so it made sense that we should both try out our new procedure. Though unwilling to wear his spectacles and so damage appearances, he was very willing to get in on the act and we made a fine team. The diary entry shows clearly that we were pleased by the results and those without tickets or tendering old tickets were our obvious target.

Meeting the *Hamilton* at Campbeltown was a bonus. Our timings at the pier were very similar so that there was ample time to meet with her assistant and exchange news. Our news must have been the more sought after, as we were only one day on from the hearing over the sacking and we were certainly the talk of the steamers! Had we been quieter, I might have been allowed to go up to Rothesay on the *Hamilton* but with Dick off and no shortage of disgruntled passengers, big Donald would certainly not have agreed. Using the side of the pier to facilitate departure from Campbeltown was a sensible way of getting the bow clear of the pier. Whereas, going down the side at Whiting Bay was exceptional and required a good knowledge of depth of water. Our man would have been in his element here but the relief was no slouch, as he proved again on arrival in stormy conditions at Ayr. I am sure most of the passengers were glad to escape from the ship!

Be sure to note that I wrote my own Privilege ticket for the morning. I was clearly developing confidence with my increasing experience!

Day 42 *Friday 9 August*

Dull and wet but the strong E wind dropped as the day progressed and the sea became calmer.

Up at 6.45 to catch the train to Paisley. There I got the Wemyss Bay train and joined the *Hamilton*. A small gathering of steamer fanatics were already aboard. Weather kept the steamers quiet. High wind caused *Jupiter* to drop anchor off Berth 1 before she backed along to Berth 3. I collected some negatives at Sweet, the photographers, and thought them quite good. Stayed indoors all morning watching the bay and then walked in the afternoon. Called on a pal at his house and, after doing some messages with him, we decided to go to the baths. Though busy, the baths were enjoyable and we spent an hour in the pool. I was seized by cramp only in the last few minutes. We then walked out Ardbeg shore and, deciding not to swim in the sea, we bought chips and ice cream and went our separate ways.

Commentary Day 42

This was my day off and clearly a day for ducks. I had made myself out a Privilege ticket form for the train. How clever I was becoming! But it was an obvious move, as this would work out at about a quarter of the normal fare and was another perk of the post. At Wemyss Bay, I would travel without the need for a ticket to Rothesay. This free passage expectation was standard practice for assistants, whatever the vessel involved. On this occasion, it was my old friend, the *Hamilton*, and already her claque of supporters was in evidence. The captain of the *Jupiter* put on a special performance to delight us at Rothesay. Not only did he bring his charge up to berth 1 before reversing back the length of the pier to berth 3 as was his wont, but he even dropped anchor to enhance the effect. Standing there on the bridge in full oilskin attire and wellington boots, he made a fine advert for Clyde cruising!

At this time, I was the proud possessor of an old Kodak camera and used black and white film. Before taking prints, I would examine the negatives to assess their quality before lashing out on the final product! Hence the reference to negatives at Sweets. On board the *Graham*, I was wary about appearing with a camera to take pictures as I was unsure how the captain would regard this activity. I felt sure that he would disapprove and I certainly was not going to risk his wrath. This explains why I have no photographs at all of cars being loaded on board. Yet, how much I would have liked to record this! We represented the end of an era. Now, when nothing can be done, I greatly regret the absence of such photographs recording our diverse activities or the truly spartan conditions below deck or the plank seats created for busy cruises or the toilet rolls accompanying the end of a holiday fortnight at Whiting Bay – the list is endless! What a pity too that I did not ask for an old flag bearing her name before we parted. Good ideas often come too late.

But what an end to the day! A visit to the baths when the weather is poor is easily understood but what is the significance of the cramp "only" in the last moments? Was this a regular problem at this time? Was it a comment on our staying in so long? No explanation is offered, but our skin must have been shrivelled like a prune at the end of such a lengthy saturation! And after all that, the idea of an additional sea bathe was still considered a distinct possibility. Surely our brains must have been addled by their extended immersion! Then comes ice cream and chips as a substitute for a splash in the sea, and not a mention of a pub! Curiouser and curiouser!

Day 43 *Saturday 10 August*

Back to mild, bright weather. Very hot at midday but showery later.

Mum left for a golf match on the early boat and I followed at 7.45 on the *Jupiter*. Took bus along to Largs where I hurried to catch train to Ardrossan. No sign of relief purser so Dick was in sole command of the office till he appeared. Our average for the crossings was 300 with the busiest at 10.20 and few on the last run over to Brodick. Met a couple of local pals at Whiting Bay and they almost persuaded me to join them for a swim. The skipper is noticeably quieter today and the relief mate is suitably relieved! Sea was very calm all day. Took a photo of the funnel from the bridge at a quiet time. Also wrote a letter home to my correspondent pal. Snaffled last week's sailing instructions for my collection of *memorabilia*. Got a change of bed linen supplied today. We carried 9 knowing people across on the late run blank from Brodick to Ayr. It was dark when we arrived and so no point in putting up our information board for tomorrow's cruise. Went off early to bed.

Commentary Day 43

By this time I naturally had the bus service from Wemyss Bay to Largs well taped, as this was my most direct way of reaching the ship at Ardrossan. This entailed a brisk walk from the station at Ardrossan South Beach to the pier but I have always relished a walk and the sea air added to its appeal. We were certainly not busy on the Whiting Bay service that weekend and I can't blame the relief purser for not hurrying to join us. But if it was because he imagined the office was in capable hands - well, in that case he was mistaken and open to blame! But Dick had a brief spell of glory and revelled in that solitary status.

As the skipper was in a subdued mood, I made so bold as to go up to the bridge for a good photo view of the funnel. Most of my funnel shots were taken at deck level to avoid the captain's attentions and this freedom of movement was too good to miss. You may be sure that I had been watching carefully for him to leave the bridge before I ventured aloft! Funnels and paddle sponsons have always appealed to me and the *Graham*'s funnel was particularly attractive and photogenic. Some steamer *cognoscenti* apparently see sexual connotations in these vital steamer accoutrements but I am not of that number. A funnel is just a funnel, though some certainly are more attractive than others. Of the older vessels, *Caledonia* and *Talisman* seemed to me not particularly favoured in this regard. Seen from the stern, when funnels take on a new significance, *Caledonia* verged on hideous, thanks in no small measure to that ugly funnel. The *Duchesses* too were anything but beautiful viewed from the stern but the wee *Graham* was quite attractive from this angle, as was *Queen Mary*. Most of the paddlers too were quite presentable when seen from the rear, provided always that we exclude *Caledonia*. But then came *Glen Sannox* and the later and greater car ferries, and even *Caledonia* fared better in comparison! The *Sannox* was abominable when viewed from the stern and the later car ferries like *Iona* or *Isle of Mull* are no better. Anyway, that is another story!

The arrival of the weekly sailing instructions, a sheaf of A4 papers issued to all fleet vessels and detailing changes in the roster which affected any of the ships in the week ahead, was always a high point and requiring careful study. For a ship like *Queen Mary* where the roster changed little if at all over the season, the instructions must have been a yawn but for the *Graham*, with her regularly revised roster, the expectation of change was high and rarely disappointed. It was natural that I was determined to keep a sample of these instructions for my collection of steamer items.

Reference to the change of linen is pleasing. You might have thought that I would have been overlooked when I moved my abode to the cancellation office on deck but no! An officer is an officer wherever stationed and I was well served. The stewards were always punctilious about even handed justice for all!

That nine people should have turned up for the blank run over to Ayr was something of a record as well as a mystery. Obviously our movements were noticed and people used to appear in the off chance that they would be taken. We were under no obligation but our master rarely turned unexpected travellers away. People who were already booked were not always so sympathetically treated!

And you will have noticed yet another thought of a swim, this time while lying at Whiting Bay. I clearly was obsessed!

Day 44 *Sunday 11 August*

Dull and wet till noon when it gradually cleared into a beautiful evening. Little wind.

New flags up all over ship today. Left Ayr at 11.15 for Gareloch cruise. Unusually, we picked up scarcely 300 passengers from Ayr, Troon and Ardrossan, probably owing to the threatening sky. Another 300 joined us at Largs and Dunoon. *Maid of Ashton* was as usual relieving *Ashton* and *Leven* on the Largs to Millport run and delayed us a little. Still, we kept ahead of time all day. With the relaxed relief purser aboard, Dick and I had a fine easy time of it and there were not many tickets to deal with at the end of the day. Wore shorts ashore at Ayr tonight and enjoyed a bathe although the water was rather brown. Took supper with relief purser and old chief and, just as we were finishing, the lights were switched off. The chief roared "Put on these bloody lights!" and the command was promptly obeyed. Moments later, the skipper, clad in civvies, crept down the stairs with a sheepish grin and explained that he thought that he must have left them on after supper. The chief was highly amused - after he had gone! I turned in quite early.

Commentary Day 44

Sunday marked an extension to our time on the Ayr station and the new blue handbills took effect from that day. The Amended Sailings were effective till 23 August although *Caledonia* in fact reappeared before that date.

As an antidote to the gloomy weather, we put up fresh flags at the mastheads as well as at bow and stern. These were likely to be the last for this season. As I have said above, it is a matter of great regret that I did not ask for an old name flag before it was torn up for dusters. Just think of the number of letters in her name! The Caledonian lion rampant which I later acquired from *Queen Mary* had no lettering and I also kept the specially created High School flag flown from *Caledonia*'s masthead on our charter earlier in the season bearing only the letters SURSUM SEMPER - the Latin meaning "Always Higher" seemed particularly apposite on a masthead! Still, fresh flags did nothing to tempt out the canny people of Ayr on this day. Our numbers were a little disappointing, particularly when compared with the crowd which presented itself for Whiting Bay and Campbeltown on the previous Thursday. Perhaps reports had got around the town about that stormy passage.

The diary records that I was already into wearing shorts at this time.

I have always favoured them, though I did wear the kilt in upper school and university. Shorts are fine for climbing and walking, except perhaps in winter, and it is no surprise to find that I had shorts with me on the boat. The bathing obsession continued, even when the river Ayr was in spate thanks to the heavy rains and caused the sea near the outflow to be brackish.

The supper incident made the day. The captain was still clearly unmanned by his skirmish with authority over his sacking escapade and took the chief's onslaught on the chin and without demur. Obviously, the old chief was delighted by the occasion and must have thought his unwonted bellow well rewarded. No doubt he was expecting some lesser light such as the night watchman to be the culprit, not the master himself!

Day 45 *Monday 12 August*

Dull, wet and windy - a real dirty day.

Left early from Ayr to cross to Whiting Bay and do the Death boat run. I shaved on the crossing. After making my bed, I finished yesterday's tickets. Did not appear at Whiting Bay but took gangway at Brodick. My school pal, Colin from Corrie, sailed with us and reported on the *Waverley*'s problems on Friday 26 when she took our evening run from Ardrossan. There was plenty of other news to share as well. We then proceeded blank to Ayr. Left with just over 200 for Troon and cruise to Brodick and Rothesay. Sea was choppy around Arran in the E wind. Despite this and a delay caused by *Sannox*, we were on time at Rothesay where Dad was waiting. Went up to the house for a break and had dinner. Returned to watch *Talisman* arrive and then took the gangway. A little late leaving, as captain was engrossed in discussion with *Talisman*'s captain. Even at that, a man jumped aboard late as we left. The skipper ignored the incident though he saw it clearly. *Saint Columba* was coming up behind as we turned away down river for Garroch Head where we passed *Waverley* on way back to Rothesay. Put up signs and blackboard on reaching Ayr and had a pint with Dick at the Marine. Then we met up with our sole remaining photographer friend from Kilmarnock and his girl friend at the Academy café. He drove us around Ayrshire through Kilwinning, Irvine, Stevenston and Saltcoats, with intermittent stops for further refreshments. Needless to say, we returned to the ship in the best of spirits.

News came that *Caledonia* has passed boiler tests.

Commentary Day 45

It is easy to see that the relief purser was still aboard when I could choose not to appear at the gangway at Whiting Bay. Instead, I got on with domestic and other chores in the cancellation office, leaving the ever-faithful luggage man to attend to gangway duty single-handed. It is unclear who was in the main ticket office. Dick could have been there if the relief had not yet surfaced or it might have been the other way round. One thing is certain. I hardly touched issue of tickets and left this task to those with more experience - writing Privilege tickets was quite bold enough for me at this stage! Anyway, Dick loved booking tickets, though Donald saw to it that he had little opportunity to satisfy his craving.

As often, I used the lying time at Rothesay to good effect and went up to visit the folks. Dad saw to it that I would not forget, by coming down to meet our arrival. I note that I took dinner. Of course, I had earlier had dinner on the *Graham*. Either it is a reflection on the meal served aboard or, more probably, it is just an aspect of youthful appetite.

As we left Rothesay our timings were similar to those of *Saint Columba* and she gave chase. It was no contest and a merciful turn away down river for Brodick saved us from total embarrassment. As we sailed off down the firth, we left the fine old three funneller cleaving the waters with her knife edge bow on the way to Toward Point. As for the mad leaper as we left the pier, what can you do? There is no stopping them in mid-flight and who was I to criticise when I had done the same when the ship left Gourock on Pleasure boat business? I suppose we could have gone back and landed the offending passenger as punishment. But that would have made us late and the skipper had no time for that! No, the Nelsonian eye was the preferred course of action.

The news of *Caledonia* was significant and alerted us that the end of our Ayr flutter was in sight. Soon we would return to our leisurely cruising programme upriver and let *Caledonia* return to her rightful station at Ayr. So we did well to enjoy a night out round Ayrshire with our photographer friend. His associate had now gone south after his holiday and he must have been keen to continue his steamer associations. We were happy to oblige.

Day 46 *Tuesday 13 August*

Dull and showery with S wind rising later.

Up at 7.40 and had breakfast. Then walked to bank and station with relief purser who was still smelling of drink. This smell freshened as we approached Ardrossan and the end of his weekend relief. 390 boarded at Ayr, 88 at Troon and 120 at Ardrossan, not bad considering the weather. Donald rejoined us at Ardrossan and we proceeded to Largs where we lay off to allow *Talisman* to make her call. Here, I agreed to allow an English couple to store luggage in my office as they wanted freedom to move about and go ashore. Over 100 went ashore at Rothesay but the majority sailed to the Kyles. Reached Tighnabruaich at 2.00 and moved out for *Saint Columba* at 2.30. However she was late and *Queen Mary* nipped in first, making the *Saint* even later. She eventually left, 30 minutes late, at 3.10. We then called, picked up our passengers and hurried to Rothesay. We were late all the way from there and arrived at Troon to find the Railway pier occupied by the *Thelma*. We crossed over and landed our passengers at the Ballast quay. We then moved astern with the assistance of the Troon pilot in a noisy but powerful motor boat. We arrived late at Ayr and I did the tickets, as Dick had left at Largs along with his parents who had sailed on the cruise with us.

Commentary Day 46

Note how I have by now claimed exclusive ownership of the cancellation office -"my office"! Dick no doubt took advantage of my claim by avoiding ticket duties whenever possible. But against that, I had an airy bedroom, a place for friends to stow luggage or have a talk and a means of supplementary income on the odd occasions when I made it available as a safe repository for left luggage. It is a wonder that I did not make a point of developing this potential source of further income. All that was needed was an advert on the door of the cancellation office and there would have been no end to the possibilities!

The relief purser was a delightful fellow and a pleasure beside the grumpy Donald with all his wee jobs and constant narking. He smoked like a chimney and his clothes bore many a cigarette burn. But then, he had little interest in his appearance and it was alcohol which claimed his attention. He popped in and out of the ship's bar without attempting to conceal his uniform and got on terribly well with the chief steward. They were two of a kind. You can imagine the skipper's feelings towards the two of them! We were sad to see his weekend stint over and big Donald hovering at Ardrossan to take over.

This was a day for pier movement. At Tighnabruaich we had to contend with first *Queen Mary* and then *Saint Columba*. From an arrival ahead of time, the activities of the two big turbines ensured that we were late when we eventually set off on our return down river. The situation at Troon made things worse. No doubt *Thelma* would have occupied the berth even had we been exactly on time. So the skipper was forced to take evasive action. By landing on the far shore, he gave himself an impossible task when it came to reversing out again. We had no bow rudder. Indeed, only *Queen Mary* and *Duchess of Hamilton* were so equipped, the former for river manoeuvres and the latter for Ayr harbour - the *Hamilton* was originally intended as Ayr steamer and it was recognised then that a bow rudder would be invaluable on this station. Neither the *Caledonia* nor the *Graham* were so endowed and so our captain had to humble himself and request the aid of the Troon pilot to provide him with a much needed tow into open waters. Yet again, I chose an early night rather than go ashore with others of the crew. Money must have been tight!

We meet *Flying Merlin* towing *Bardic Ferry* while *Hopper no 9* lies ahead.

To the rear, *Chieftain* tows *Joseph Lykes* past *Bardic Ferry*. Busy times indeed upriver!

Day 47 *Wednesday 14 August*

Dull with heavy showers. Some bright spells.

Left Ayr about 8.00 as usual for Largs and Upriver run. Considerable southerly swell running and we were prancing about to some tune, so that the deck chair piles were tossed all over the place. Transferred ticket cases with Donald - Dick had his day off - and made up a special board for the cruise. As often, we waited for the *Talisman* to clear the pier and then went into Largs where we took aboard 117 passengers, despite dreadful weather. 60 boarded at Rothesay, including Dad, and 200 at Dunoon. Another 100 were waiting at Gourock. Held up on the river by shipping as we approached King George V dock - we were given advance warning at Bowling control point. First came *Joseph Lykes* and attendant tug *Chieftain*. No sooner did we manage to squeeze past her than we met *Clan MacRae* coming down with tugs *Strongbow* ahead and *Brigadier* astern. *Bardic Ferry*, a new ship heading down river for trials, turned ahead of us at KGV dock with assistance from tug *Flying Merlin* and followed behind the Clan ship. Next appeared *City of Lichfield*, delayed by *Bardic Ferry*, and she passed with *Warrior* leading and *Forger* behind. Further up we found *Stirlingshire* with *Brigadier* ahead and *Cruiser* and *Wrestler* astern. In dock were *Sunrose* and *Rhodesian Star* attended by *Flying Spitfire* ahead and *Flying Tempest* and *Meteor* behind. We pushed through all this activity and caught up with *Hopper No.9* and the puffer *Starlight* ahead. It was near 2.30 when we docked, full 40 minutes late. We hurried along to the bank for change while the bus trips hurried their intending passengers aboard for the curtailed city tour. It was all quite hectic! The tide was with us down river so that we were 15 minutes early at Gourock. At Rothesay we were met by Mum and our barking dog, waiting for Dad to return. After Largs we headed off for Ayr. Our 2nd last cruise out of Ayr is tomorrow. *Caledonia* is due out on Saturday and our last Ayr sailing is on Monday. *Caley* takes the Sunday cruise but does a sheep run from Arran on Monday. I did some booking at the window today and also made over 4 shillings on brochure sales. It was a busy day. Nly gale was blowing off Portencross and there was a heavy sea running behind us. Fortunately, it was not broadside on or we would have had a wild journey! Reached harbour entrance at Ayr at 9.40 and swung into outer harbour to turn. There we dropped anchor and were quickly blown round. Shifted anchor again to get nearer quay and put ropes ashore. Alongside by 9.55 with winds rising rapidly and whistling in the rigging. Started coaling at once and I turned in for bed soon after.

Commentary Day 47

These were comfortable numbers for the *Graham*, even in poor weather. We could handle anything up to 600 fairly well but on the occasions we passed the 900 mark things became unpleasant. The problems for us on this particular day were caused by external factors. Heavy seas were one significant feature but these affected us most on our blank sailings to and from Ayr. The lively leaps and rolls which were our forte must have caused headaches for the staff in the dining room as they struggled to keep the tables set for action. We had only the deckchairs spilling around the decks to concern us and the occasional fear of a ticket case moving, although we roped these tightly in position. On the way back blank from Largs to Ayr, the full force of the sea took us from behind so that we plunged our nose into the troughs and sent out great swathes of green sea and white foam as the waves rolled past. For our passengers, any problem that day was chiefly occasioned by the state of the upper river. Certainly the waters in the Clyde were sheltered - but we were carried up on the flow and, as high tide approached, it was inevitable that we should find the big ships seizing their chance to leave the upper river. No other Upriver day this season came close to this for the amount of shipping movements, but this was dictated by the state of the tide. At least it was plain sailing when we set off down river with the ebb tide to carry us along.

It is noteworthy that big Donald was increasingly using me for new tasks. Dick's absence had much to do with this. Otherwise, he would have been alone and unaided! Thus, I was called on to assist with the transfer of ticket cases from below, substituting the upriver stock for our usual Arran and Ayr stock. Then there was the preparation of the special advertising board designed to woo Largs folk aboard for the sailing - a vital part of our marketing practice! Finally and most significant was the introduction to ticket booking and sole control of the office, enabling Donald to leave for lunch, or more often for a snooze. I could now be entrusted with greater responsibility. And despite all these heavy commitments, I still found time to sell brochures for my personal gain and managed time to appear at Rothesay to give an encouraging wave to my doting mother, as well as tending to the needs of my father who was making a quick run up to Glasgow with us. No doubt, he was also well received by the old chief.

But the end of the Ayr programme was now fast approaching and *Caledonia* was around to confirm this.

Day 48 *Thursday 15 August*

Gale force Nly winds and continuing. Cloudy early but brightened in afternoon and delightful.

Only 300 from Ayr and Troon for the cruise to Whiting Bay and Campbeltown. Went up to bank and station in fish delivery van. Dick rejoined us about 9.15 and we sailed at 10.00, once we had got the bow off the pier in the wind. Further wind delay at Troon and 15 minutes late at Arran. But the chief delay was weather. Pretty stormy crossing and we took our share of water aboard! Wrote up some of Donald's books on crossing to Arran but after dinner I went on bridge deck as we rounded Pladda. Fair scud on the water but not so many big rollers as on run to Arran. Plenty spray to duck from and a lot sick around deck. *Hamilton* beat us in again and, after passengers went ashore, I changed into civvies. Both ships were along the front of the pier, bow to bow. Joined *Hamilton* with her two assistants and we left first. *Graham* had to swing her bow round once we left. Not so rough on the run up the Sound to Lochranza. Saw the *Stirlingshire* heading off downriver. Friends of family aboard and I spoke to them till they left at Largs. *Hamilton* was late all the way back and further delayed by a *Maid* at Largs. She lay at side but we risked waves and came along front when she left. *Waverley* was close behind as we came into Rothesay Bay and *Caledonia* exercising on far shore. Mum and Dad at golf, so I walked with my pal over Loch Fad and on to the hills on the West side of Bute. There we gazed at the scenery for ages, stumbled home by Barone hill and joined the Straad road into the back of Rothesay, passing the old cotton mill. Reached front, tired, muddy but content and was home just after 11.00.

Commentary Day 48

This was a much calmer day on the nerves than yesterday although the sea was anything but calm. My expedition up town on the fish van was a real novelty and one to be savoured. Clearly, the stewards had seen a window of opportunity opening before them and were quick to take advantage. As we normally accompanied them up town, we were not forgotten and so it was that opportunity knocked!

Notice that I had allowed myself to be inveigled into helping Donald with his ledgers. This was no great hardship provided you could close your ears to his flood of expletives whenever his calculations or copying went awry. Anyway, this was not entered on lightly: there was a *quid pro quo*! It had been agreed that I should start my day off early by joining the

Hamilton for Rothesay at Campbeltown and I was keeping Donald sweet and smoothing the passage for myself.

But there was no smooth passage for my *Marchioness*. First, she was battered by the seas as she left Troon for Arran. These she took at an angle and pranced about, as was her wont. Occasionally, a larger wave would lift the screws out the water and the turbines would race and the whole ship would give a judder. Then came the next instalment as we rounded the south of Arran. Here the waves were choppier and we threw the spray about as we cavorted towards the shelter of Davaar island and Campbeltown. I greatly enjoyed these antics but it must have been a nightmare for anybody prone to nausea. The saving grace was that we were relatively quiet, unlike the previous occasion a week past. Perhaps the people had been warned!

Thereafter, it was out of uniform and aboard the waiting *Duchess*. The relative calm in Kilbrannan Sound must have been a disappointment. I had always thought of these waters as the stormiest in the river but now I had discovered that the south of Arran could surpass them.

On arriving at Rothesay in the calm of the evening, I was able to take to the hills above Loch Fad with my friend and from there to view the tranquil beauty of the firth as the sun set over Arran and Kintyre, bathing all the landscape with its fading grandeur. Another day lay ahead and back we tramped in the gloaming, stumbling through muddy fields as darkness closed in. Altogether memorable!

If Arran rightly claims to serve the climber with its challenging peaks, Bute is the place for walkers, with marvellous views around the river. The south end is wild and scenic with fine views of Arran but certainly more accessible than the north end, which requires a lot of determination to get through the undergrowth and marshland. Still, there is offered the compensation of interesting views across to Tighnabruaich. The hills above Loch Fad too offer a magnificent vista.

Landing passengers at Gourock from Upriver run, with *Maid of Argyll* beyond.

Duchess of Hamilton takes the last Sunday run out of Rothesay with what appears to be an impressive overload.

Day 49 *Friday 16 August*

My day off and a lovely morning, but it worsened and was wet by evening.

Rose around 9.00 and went about various messages. I needed razor blades and toothpaste for the boat and also required new sandshoes. These I acquired after a lengthy search for my size. Mum and dog went by bus. Dad and I had a bathe - very cold though fine out the water! Went to Regal cinema with my friend and saw The James Brothers - a reasonable Western. *Montrose*, *Queen Mary* and *Saint Columba* were all running late today.

Commentary Day 49
Both the *Graham* and I enjoyed a relaxing day. My time was spent on Bute with my parents. After essential tasks, - purchase of sandshoes was clearly necessary after the loss of my sole on Ayr beach had shown the need for alternative footwear and, of course, my developing beard required increasingly regular attention - I borrowed the bike from our garrulous cobbler friend and set off with Dad for Ettrick where, naturally, we had a bathe. Rain or cold rarely deterred us from our purpose though the dog was unimpressed and kept a discreet distance lest it be dragged in also! As many another hardy Scottish bather has discovered, this was an occasion when coming ashore was far preferable to being in the water!

Further downriver at Jerry's quay in Ardrossan, the *Marchioness* was relaxing, while coal was brought aboard and the decks were scrubbed in readiness for her only service sail of the day, the 7.05 to Brodick and Whiting Bay. Then it was blank back to Ardrossan for the night.

This was, for the most part, a particularly uneventful day, as the short diary entry emphasises.

Day 50 *Saturday 17 August*

Showery with occasional bright spells. Nly wind rose later.

Up before 7.00 and caught *Jupiter* for Wemyss Bay. Only one assistant on her as the other has gone to the *Bute*. Largs bus was late and I missed 9.00 train. Had to pay 1/6d for Coast Bus Service. Travelled with our pilot and relief chief steward. On arrival, was told I have to work on *Caledonia* and her assistant would be on *Marchioness* - strange! Also that we're on *Talisman*'s run tomorrow since *Jeanie Deans* has broken down. *Caledonia* around today and appeared behind us at Brodick at 7.45 on an evening sail from Ayr. Only the 1.25 sailing from Whiting Bay was busy and toilet paper and streamers were plentiful. Our photographer friend left some photos for me. Spent an easy day. Skipper had an argument with a family who had waited to join our blank sailing up to Gourock. Eventually, we took them. *Empress of Scotland* sailed up in morning and down again in late afternoon. We began to heave a little as day progressed and wind rose. Left Brodick at 7.50 for Gourock after discharging 4 cars. Quite dark when we got there at 9.50 and illuminations looking lovely. Came up river with a beautiful sunset and red tinted clouds - quite magnificent, with Cowal hills tipped with red and the sea ablaze round Toward light. *Talisman* did the late Saturday run up from Rothesay at 9.00, as she replaces *Jeanie Deans* tomorrow while *Jeanie* gets her paddles repaired. Had a few drinks with some assistants on board *Talisman* when she berthed at 10.30.

Commentary Day 50

Caledonia was at last back in harness with an Ailsa Craig afternoon cruise and an evening cruise to Brodick. These Saturday Ayr cruises had been cancelled during our period of substitution, as we were otherwise employed. But with our Ayr programme about to end, it was fortuitous that *Jeanie* chose to take time off for paddle repairs. Her replacement by *Talisman* caused us to undertake the Millport roster and so I secured another Sunday salary!

You can imagine my annoyance at missing the train at Largs thanks to a delay in the bus arrival. I could not put the blame on *Jupiter* for her painfully slow crossing to Wemyss Bay - it was entirely the fault of the bus to Largs. I grudged the payment, unlike the pilot and steward who would think nothing of the fare and no doubt preferred the convenience of the bus as involving less of a walk.

The master was in one of his funny moods. There was no problem about taking 4 cars across on the last run to the island and that though the *Sannox* was the recognised car ferry. But a family on the blank run up to Gourock was altogether different and he needed to be persuaded to agree. You could never assume anything with the master! They would certainly have paid for the privilege and got tickets, once Donald had moaned about the inconvenience of it all. Perhaps, the toilet rolls aimed at the bridge or funnel top had unsettled him on the earlier crossing.

This was another of these memorable nights on the river, just like the other night on the Bute hills. With the sun behind us, the wash from our screws fanned out in a red tinted flurry of turbulence behind and the place to be was at the ship's stern. On other occasions, in calm seas, the very tip of the bow was the coveted spot, from where you could watch the water parting as the *Graham*'s sharp prow cut its way through and a graceful spray rose fitfully on either side.

The mysterious entry about the *Caledonia*'s assistant was later explained. It transpired that he was actually absent in Glasgow to sit a Latin prelim exam, not transferring to the *Graham*, and so I was needed to deputise aboard *Caledonia*. This suited the *Graham*'s needs as she was to be on charter and the company agent at Ayr was asked to sail with her. I would have been superfluous to requirements! As the season was drawing to a close, movement among assistants was proving necessary. *Bute* had lost her assistant and one of the two was therefore transferred from the *Jupiter*.

Time to relax on a blank run down to Ayr off Skelmorlie. The pilot sits under the bridge - his favoured spot - having a smoke before going up to take the wheel.

Day 51 *Sunday 18 August*

Bright intervals with some early showers. Fresh Sly wind.

Up about 8.00 and walked around the ships. At 9.37 the catering superintendent took off the gangway and cast off the ropes and we left for Wemyss Bay. *Jupiter* set off, just as we arrived, on her blank run to Glasgow for the afternoon sailing to Lochgoilhead. Carried a few hundred over to Rothesay on the 10.40 crossing before proceeding, almost blank, to Fairlie to take the 12.10 sailing to Millport, just ahead of the *Hamilton*'s call for Keppel. Walked round Millport with Dick before doing our main afternoon sailing to Largs (where we took on 500), Rothesay and Tighnabruaich. Met *Caley* from Ayr in the Kyles and then *Talisman*, being driven to maintain *Waverley*'s timings for Tighnabruaich. Next came *Waverley* on the *Jeanie*'s cruise to Skipness and Round Bute. *Jeanie* is now at Lamont's yard for repair and is expected to return to service tomorrow. No sign of the folks at Rothesay but various friends and acquaintances were aboard or at piers. Two girls we know were on board for the cruise. The skipper continues to behave peculiarly. At Largs, we loaded 3 cars for Millport after opening the railing all along and made history for Sunday cruise steamers! We were a bit late into Millport and found a huge queue waiting. We took on 430 passengers and another 3 cars for the record and crossed to Fairlie. The *Sannox* spent her weekend anchored off Cumbrae opposite Fairlie. We proceeded blank for Gourock, passing *Hamilton* with a huge crowd from Rothesay on the last Wemyss Bay crossing. Reaching Gourock at 8.30, we went ashore to the Bay hotel where we signed the travellers' book and drank till 11.00.

Notes: warning of a mine in the Kilbrannan Sound. A naval launch was sent out to scour the area and destroy it.

Duncan MacRae was among a group of celebrities who crossed on the 12.10 from Fairlie. After they had tea, I spoke to Duncan for about 15 minutes, discussing the decline of the steamers, and his summer job on the old *Columba*, where he took turns working as a bootblack, clothes sewer and other odd jobs. He recalled drinking sprees from the remains left by charter parties and finally discussed the need for Arts graduates in the modern world.

Commentary Day 51

So after a long interval, we returned to our overnight berth at Gourock - our Ayr based programme was at an end. Now I again had the chance to take stock of the other members of the fleet and to glean the latest news from other assistants. As the day progressed, it became clear how cut off we had been down at Ayr. Every member of the older fleet was sighted or noted in the diary. So this is what a day was like for the assistant on the *Talisman*!

But our skipper made sure that we bettered the *Talisman*'s performance. Just as at Ardrossan the previous night and as had been required of him at the start of the season when substituting for *Glen Sannox*, he was determined to demonstrate our dual capability. Unlike other steamers, we showed our readiness to take cars both to and from Cumbrae - and that though we were supposedly engaged in Sunday cruising! We really were an anomaly by this time on the river. Before the advent of the car ferries, the paddlers had all taken their share of loading cars by that alarming system of crossing planks at a suitable tide. But the *Talisman* rarely carried cars to Cumbrae when there were now agreed times for carriage by the ferries, and certainly never on Sundays! Indeed, you can only wonder at the efficiency of the bush telegraph when cars turned up for both sailings that evening. How on earth did they know we were likely to be a soft touch, particularly with our unpredictable skipper? And Largs seems such an unlikely place to expect cars on the pier! The actor Duncan MacRae should have been there to witness it. He had always been one of my pantomime gods when he performed in the Alhambra theatre in Glasgow and here he was now on my *Marchioness* sharing stories of his own involvement as a student on the old *Columba*. His had clearly been a funny *factotum* post on that renowned MacBrayne's paddler. Boot blacking and sewing clothes seemed unimaginable work for a student on the steamers. He clearly approved both my summer employment and my intention to follow an Arts course. He seemed smaller than he appeared on the stage and his accent was more of the cultured Kelvinside variety than I had imagined, but it was a memorable moment and one to be treasured. 15 minutes seemed to last for ever!

I celebrated the encounter in the evening when I went for refreshments at the Bay hotel. I signed in as a *bona fide* traveller coming from Millport, for these were the days when Sunday drinking was strictly controlled. You had to sign your name and travel details in an official visitors' book before acceptance. Even then it was said you could be limited to a single drink but I rarely recall this being enforced. It was usually far too busy for the hotelier to have time to consider it and the premises were usually awash with drink. We certainly paid no regard to such a restriction.

Reference to the two girls on the cruise is as interesting as it is unusual. The entry is brief and uninformative. Girls rarely feature in my account of the day's activities on the *Graham* and it seems as if these two had taken to our white tops and were not strangers to the ship. But no more information is offered.

A sheep run on *Waverley* - our skipper preferred to see the sheep at the bow!

Here we act as tender to the Cunarder *Sylvania* at the end of August.

Day 52 *Monday 19 August*

Continual drizzle and SW gale.

Left Gourock for Ayr at 7.00. Had a pretty rough ride and tables cleared themselves on the run. Spray billowed over us and the wind shrieked. One particularly violent wave struck the bow and stove in one of the plates, causing a soaking in one area of the lounge seats. Fought our way into Ayr, using the anchor to assist, and were met by the company agent at the head of a huddle of some 40 hopeful passengers. The *Caledonia*'s one assistant was also there with tickets for the sailing, as we had transferred our stock to the paddler when she resumed the service. The agent, full of efficiency, had decided to cancel the sailing and got approval from Gourock. The skipper acquiesced and added that he had best get away below for tea before they killed him. So the two of us assistants whiled away the day, hooking debris from the river with ropes, when we could have enjoyed our last run on the Ayr station and experienced a real battering on the sail over to Brodick. *Caley* arrived at Ayr about 3.00, having completed her special sheep run from Whiting Bay to Ardrossan. I took my necessary belongings on board her before the *Graham* left for Ardrossan. Even Dick got up from his sleep to wave farewell! My new assistant pal changed out of uniform and we went up town to the Odeon to see The Admirable Crichton, which was excellent, and The Phantom Stagecoach. Returned to *Caley* and had a chat with her mate. He had been aboard at the time of the school charter in May and is very approachable. Turned in thereafter.

Commentary Day 52

This was a wild and unrewarding day. It was intended as our last sailing out of Ayr, as *Caledonia* was employed taking sheep over to the mainland from Arran. The poor beasts must have wondered what had hit them! For ourselves, we took a pounding for the best part of three hours in the teeth of a SW gale as we headed for Ayr. The damage to crockery would have been considerable and the air in the dining saloon must have been blue! Just as we neared the breakwater, that nasty wave got under our guard and crashed against the bow, damaging a plate at the bow and sending water into the forward lounge. I suppose there is a lesson in this. A few similarly directed waves could have done real damage.

As it was, blissfully disregarding the dangers, I thrilled to our tempestuous conduct and marvelled at the chaos caused below deck. Undeterred, a few stalwarts were there at Ayr to greet us and come aboard.

But the Company agent was fearful and worrying about our fitness for next day's charter. He cancelled the sailing, although from his remark I suspect our skipper would have sailed regardless of the storm. Had the agent known about our storm damaged plate, he would certainly not have allowed us to sail and so it was all for the best. Despite the many stormy days we experienced this summer, this was the only day when weather stopped us from sailing and that decision was not taken by the captain.

I was one of the few to gain from the arrangement. When *Caley* appeared in mid afternoon from her sheep run, we were there to meet her and I transferred my belongings to her for the next day. Only then did the *Marchioness* proceed for Ardrossan in readiness for next day's charter. Dick went with her but he would be given his day off on the charter day while I experienced life on one of my most favoured ships. Leaving the seamen to clean the filth still remaining after the sea had done its best to clear the decks, the pair of us, assistants both, went up town to the cinema.

The *Graham* cants in Ayr Harbour at the end of a quiet day.

Day 53 *Tuesday 20 August*

Mainly fine though some dull spells. Wind veered NW but still strong.

Up at 7.30 and went to station and travel agency about bookings and mails after breakfast. Arrived in time to take over gangway on *Caledonia* before wee Donald, the purser, returned from bank. Took over mate's enumerator since he had started counting on. Took 218 from Ayr, 81 at Troon and 221 at Ardrossan. Very few joined us from Millport, Largs and Dunoon for Loch Goil cruise. Considerable swell running but less movement on *Caley*. Didn't hear either bells or engine change at Troon and had to rush out as we came alongside, change boards round from Ayr side and get to gangway - mighty big rush. Plenty to talk to wee Donald about concerning his big namesake - he was fascinated! He tells me he's heading for Gaiety theatre in Ayr tonight - a favoured spot of his. Did a sort of ticket check, as wee Donald aptly described it. But what a difference all round from the *Marchioness*! Much cheerier and relaxed and coffee at cafeteria! Followed *Jupiter* up to Dunoon on Hunter's Quay cruise and saw well filled *Queen Mary* en route. *Caley*'s other assistant is doing Latin prelim at Glasgow. *Graham* on charter to Brodick with 481 ladies - also the baldy publicity agent from Gourock and his Ayr based underling. We went into Jerry's quay at Ardrossan and I left there to join *Graham* on her return at 6.40. She had been kept late out of Brodick owing to a broken down bus.

Our skipper was all for leaving 9 busloads at Ardrossan this morning. They came late and it took all the agent's wiles to dissuade him from going without them. Welders were waiting for us at Gourock to repair the plate damaged in yesterday's gale. Had a returning party first ashore and then aboard. Dick and I downed half bottle whisky, some Carlsberg special and other beers. Ended up blotto - as was becoming a regular state!

Commentary Day 53

Made it to *Caledonia* at last, even if for only a day! I was the obvious substitute while her assistant sat his Latin exam, as I was now well versed in procedures for Ayr. The fact that the *Graham* was on charter made it perfect - the baldy headed company agent would not want assistant pursers swanning about the decks among all these women, whatever their age!

Caledonia was very different. For a start, everyone was very friendly and approachable. There was none of the backbiting and constant edginess which typified life on the *Graham*. The small, ginger haired purser, much given to expletives, was at first sight a rough diamond but proved to be a positive jewel. Once you had mastered his quick, often indistinct speech, he was a delight to confer with. Then, there was the cafeteria. The *Marchioness* knew no such institution and her tearoom, guarded by the strict old stewardess, was certainly not welcoming. Here on the *Caley*, visits to the cafeteria by pursers were not only expected but encouraged and in these far off days no encouragement was necessary! So here was a whole new dimension not dreamed of. Of course, it was disconcerting that you heard neither telegraph nor engine change in the ticket office as you approached piers. Instead, you looked out the window in time to see the pier adjacent and a mad dash ensued. But I could cope with that and I much enjoyed my day. I was sorry when it came to leaving at Ardrossan. Still, I soon donned my party mood and forgot the *Caley* when I went ashore with Dick. Whether he or I was categorised as blotto is unclear - no doubt we both made the grade. The skipper's plan to leave 9 busloads of the charter party delighted us. It must have made a fine scene with the baldy one remonstrating with him at Ardrossan, trying to persuade him that the customer had priority. At least all the party eventually got aboard. I wonder that he was persuaded to wait for the passengers on the broken down bus in Arran on the late crossing. I would not be surprised if his threat in the morning had just been a ploy to upset and test the baldy agent. At night, the decision was his and his alone!

I find it strange that the diary has so little to say about meals. Sometimes they are mentioned as being good or bad, and generally worse on the *Graham* than on other vessels. Yet, they were certainly not so bad as to be inedible. Far from it! One supper of tripe and onion is firmly fixed in my mind. It was on one of these late trips back from Arran to Ayr - suppers were served when we were involved in late sailing, say after 8.00pm. The tripe was more glutinous than when served at home with milk and potatoes, but it came as an enjoyable change. Therein lies the point - change of diet or choice was the real issue. If not sailing late, a rather unenterprising supper of sandwiches and cakes was set out, with a pot of tea, in the lower tearoom, to be taken when it suited. Otherwise, all meals, breakfast, lunch and tea, were served over two sittings when we were sailing and we ate in an alcove aside from the main saloon. The atmosphere was usually stiff and the level of discussion banal. The barely concealed hostility between chief and skipper made matters worse. The carpeting of cook or steward by the captain might almost be viewed as a diversion!

Breakfast was rarely served to passengers except on crossings like the Death boat, when any diversion was pleasing. We in the crew had the usual offering of porridge, ham and egg, boiled egg and sometimes fish, like smoked haddock or kipper, always accompanied by a generous supply of toast and butter. Lunch was normally available to passengers only on our cruises out of Ayr, Upriver or to Campbeltown. On such days, an improved range was on offer - soup, cold salmon salad or a hot meat dish, followed by ice cream and jelly, apple tart and custard or the like. The crew would share in this enhanced range on cruise days but otherwise Hobson's choice prevailed and you took what you got! High Tea, when on offer, provided fried fish or ham and egg, together with an unending supply of bread and jam as well as a selection of cakes. Once again, the fare was likely to be better on cruises. Visits to car ferries or to *Caledonia* made me aware that perhaps we were not best served in the food department. Even when the quality was good, presentation and cooking might leave something to be desired! Still, for a hungry student purser, things did not seem at all bad!

Day 54 *Wednesday 21 August*

Bright with some showers. Fresh NW wind.

Up early and no serious after effects from last night. Dick suffering and we were both exhausted. Usual sort of numbers for Upriver, with 555 to Glasgow. While at Largs pier, the new plate fitted yesterday at the bow was painted. Donald came on at Gourock where the relief purser left. He had said nothing about bottles and beer glasses lying in the ticket office and some of our happiness left with him. Dad at Rothesay pier and he gave me his camera to try and I bought a spool in Glasgow. 676 sailed down from Glasgow. Wrote a letter to my Glasgow pal and posted it in the city. Publicity agent was loose on Gourock pier calling on us with his loud hailer. Turned out well and we sunbathed on after deck for a while, sheltered from the wind. *Queen Mary* passed looking well filled. *Bardic Ferry* from Denny's yard was out on trial. *Jupiter*'s bow touched the bottom at Millport Old - *Maid of Skelmorlie* has also done this recently, leaving a nice bow print in the sand.

Commentary Day 54

Uneventful day and the river was quiet, in sharp contrast to the shipping activity of last week. We were a bit off colour too and that would influence our thinking. We were surprised that the mess we left after our binge of the previous night was largely ignored by the relief purser. Imagine what big Donald would have said! But when the cat's away…We were sad to see the relief go ashore at Gourock. There, he would again encounter that baldy headed one fitted out with his newest toy in the shape of a loud hailer. This he used to hail the ships as they approached the pier and he quickly made himself unpopular and a figure to be avoided. Clyde captains did not like this public airing of news and views! It was definitely demeaning.

Drink definitely debilitates! The excesses of the previous night proved this and the feeling was as yet unfamiliar. But the season was rushing to a close and Dick would soon be leaving, so that our night out was surely justifiable. The inevitable consequence was that it suited us that next day to keep a low profile. Indeed, the sun tempted us up to our private sundeck behind the funnel - a sort of secret garden! This was not strictly open to the public though we did make exceptions on a few very busy days as I have indicated. Normally, we reserved this secluded area for our exclusive use! We both felt the need for some escape on this particular day. Dad was experimenting with an Agfa camera and was keen to let me try it rather than my ancient Kodak. Sadly, his camera was not a 35mm and so pictures remained limited in number.

The speed with which repairs were made to the damaged plate at the bow was impressive. Monday saw the incident occur as we approached Ayr in the morning. The plate was repaired when we reached Gourock the following evening, while the final paint to conceal the evidence was applied at Largs on Wednesday morning. Obviously, the Kremlin wanted the damage to be put to rights with all speed and acted accordingly!

Jupiter's slight grounding at Millport Old pier must have confirmed her skipper's dislike for berthing there and strengthened his resolve to use Keppel whenever possible. However it was a blessing there was sand for a soft landing and the same applied upriver at Craigendoran where groundings were commonplace.

MacBrayne's *Loch Frisa* and *Loch Ard* at Kingston Dock, Glasgow.

Lying at Berth 1 in Rothesay the morning after Smart's Circus sailing, with the *Countess* adjacent in Berth 1A. The diary has it wrong, saying the *Graham* berthed at 1A.

Day 55 *Thursday 22 August*

Dull and showery. Fresh W wind.

Up at 7.00 and soon after breakfast we set out from Gourock, sporting the Cunard house flag, as tender to *Sylvania* at the Tail of the Bank. Came alongside smoothly and then shuffled about to get positioned opposite her landing door. We put up our gangway and a posse of officials went aboard. Delay followed as customs check proceeded and luggage was carried aboard by numerous stewards. Left about 10.00 and landed 331 passengers at Princes Pier. *Sylvania* set sail and we proceeded to Gourock where we lay till after midday. During this time, I put tickets ashore and chatted with the office girls, talked to the assistant on the *Cowal* and had dinner. Along to Rothesay next and picked up 150 for the cruise after a brief exchange with assistants on *Jupiter*. Over 200 came on at Largs and then we sailed for Millport and Arran Coast. Before this, Dick took his final leave of us at Largs, laden with three cases and various parcels. Wearing his fawn duffel coat, suede shoes and dark glasses, he cut a dapper figure! His pay off was £6. We had an emotional parting and I'm now alone at Donald's mercy. Several wee jobs were devised in the course of the cruise. We were steaming well and went in close at Corrie before going as far as Brodick bay. When we reached Rothesay, I changed and went off rather than do the blank run up to Gourock. It was a grand evening and I went fishing with a pal at Port Bannatyne. Caught two respectable fish. Found our cobbler friend and his wife at our house and walked them home with the dog.

Commentary Day 55

This is what life would have been like that summer, if the *Caledonia* had not gone AWOL. We would have been spare vessel most weekdays, with only the Upriver run as a serious commitment and the fairly light Arran schedule at weekends. Short afternoon cruises would have been our normal employment and a base at Gourock would have made us available for tender work to such visiting liners as *Sylvania* and *Empress of Scotland*. But it was now late in the season and we had had little opportunity to act as tender. It was quite a novelty! The disembarkation opening in the liner's vast hull was tiny, so that getting us in the right position was a delicate manoeuvre. Then a steep gangway was raised from our deck and up went the officialdom. Customs ran the show. However, if you were a bit forward, it was always possible to obtain a menu or sailing card from the liner before she left.

Without such tenders to occupy us, we would have spent the morning around Gourock pier, chatting up the girls and doing wee jobs for our cheery senior! That the season was coming to an end was signalled by Dick's departure. Several other assistants had already left. Indeed, from mid August there was a steady trickle of departures and seldom were there replacements. Instead, the number of assistants on the larger ships would drop from two to one and people would be transferred to assist on busier crossings. Had Dick not left at this time, one of us would certainly have been moved to a busier route. But we had the best of all worlds this summer when *Caley* decided to take to the rocks in the Kyles of Bute and leave the Ayr station without its steamer. We started quietly once *Glen Sannox* took up her rightful run, proceeded to replace the *Caledonia* at Ayr with a great increase in blank running and variety of cruises, and then slipped back to a leisurely conclusion to our summer programme.

As for Dick, he never returned to pursering on the Clyde. Perhaps his niggardly pay off was the deciding factor. It certainly would not have funded a decent holiday. Perhaps he took a supply of Privilege tickets to support him but these would quickly become invalid. He was a good mate and I would miss him though big Donald certainly would not! Still, that night went easily as my day off was Friday and, as usual, I was allowed to jump ship at Rothesay. Fishing completed the day and we even made a catch, although the type is not identified. I never once recorded a catch when fishing from the *Graham*. Perhaps our elevated position at the bow made us all too visible to the fish or else they did not care for the bait provided from the galley. Perhaps, like me, they were frightened by the skipper! Whatever the reason, none of us were ever successful.

Day 56 *Friday 23 August*

Torrential rain and gale force winds. Bright spells later.

Steamers almost empty, even *Queen Mary*! *Waverley* on Round Bute and kept ahead of time. *Saint Columba* came round back of the bay to enter berth 2 for an easier departure in the gale. *Montrose* was late back from Campbeltown. The annual Fancy Dress Parade went ahead, following a late change of heart and improving weather. Though dry, it seemed a very small parade. Had a long lie and went out to the baths where I took a hot soak. On return walk home, I got thoroughly drenched! Mum had visitors so I went over to my pal's house. Pier man reported that 50 passengers left the *Hamilton* at Ayr and made their way back by bus. The seas were wild.

Commentary Day 56

This was clearly not a day for sailing unless, like me, you were a masochist and enjoyed the feeling of the ship as she tossed and turned in heavy seas. Things had to be bad when even *Queen Mary* was quiet! She had the reputation for being constantly crowded out on the Glasgow run. The passengers on the *Duchess* to Ayr were not of my persuasion, preferring the security of a bus on *terra firma* to the return trip by sea. No doubt the *Marchioness* maintained her standards and did a good bucking performance on the evening run from Ardrossan. But in any case, I was not sailing as it was my day off. I chose a long lie to celebrate the occasion. But I still wanted to get wet, so that a visit to the baths was an obvious move and there was the added opportunity of a soaking in the wind and rain. I was successful in my mission!

The show must go on. In these days, Rothesay was still running its programme of evening cruises during the Fair if the weather was at all favourable. Another feature was the end of season Fancy Dress Parade. In days gone by, this had also included a Carnival Queen, but these highlights were fading fast. Rothesay too was once famed for its annual illuminations which led to a striking gathering of steamers in the Bay to view the spectacle, with the flickering lights from innumerable lamps burning all around the shore and a dazzling display of fireworks to finish off the spectacle. Sadly, spiralling costs put an end to these glory days at Rothesay, leaving only Millport to continue the proud tradition of the illuminations these days.

Day 57 *Saturday 24 August*

Mainly dull and wet but some bright spells in the morning. Wly gale gave way to Sly gale in afternoon.

Took *Jupiter* over to Wemyss Bay and talked to her assistants. *Talisman* even later this week but Largs must have been desperate. Managed to catch 9.00 train from Largs and joined *Graham* at Ardrossan. *Irish Coast* failed to get out inner berth but Isle of Man boat managed. Considerable swell even inside harbour but first *Sannox*, then our boat went out to face the seas at 10.25. Stormy crossing to Whiting Bay and arrived at 12.00. Four Kelly boats, MacBrayne's *Loch Frisa* and two other coasters were in the bay sheltering. Our first attempt at the pier failed when the one and only rope at the bow snapped. The second time, we came down the side and then swung along the front. We took 25 minutes to get positioned. At 1.25, with 339 aboard, we were just casting off when an elderly man took a severe shock - he was paralysed down right side and lost power of speech. His wife and daughter were appalled. Doctor was called at Lamlash and, when she arrived at length, she gave the patient an injection before moving him to the hospital. An hour later, we again set off for Ardrossan. *Sannox* wired us that she had managed into the harbour and we did likewise. Over again to Whiting Bay, leaving Ardrossan at 3.20. Our next sailing from Whiting Bay was 5.10 and we were lashed by wind and rain. This time our consultation with the *Sannox* (though she had again managed into Ardrossan) determined that we would make for Fairlie and the *Sannox* made for the same pier on her last run. We reached Fairlie at 6.40 where we then had to wait for our passengers to come along by rail from Ardrossan and we finally left Fairlie at 7.20. Buses awaited our late arrival at Brodick at 8.45, so I hopped aboard and off I went to Corrie. Had a few drinks before going to the dance which was very quiet. There followed a rowdy party with whisky and much else till 2.00am.

Got news that ferry *Arran* crashed into Dunoon pier and was taken out of service.

Commentary Day 57

Wild weather again lashed the river, upsetting steamer services. On days like these, in a westerly gale, Ardrossan was a really difficult pier to use while Largs and Wemyss Bay were also very exposed. So it is no surprise that the bulky *Irish Coast* made no attempt to sail. The Isle of Man steamer, typically, took a different tack and set out regardless. I always thought that the IOM steamers put services before all else and it took a lot to rein them in. If she could sail, then so could we and first the *Sannox* and then our little turbine poked their bows into the breakers which awaited them as soon as they cleared the harbour light. I will not attempt to describe the crossing. You have already had plenty descriptions earlier of our lively antics in stormy seas. Suffice to say that the plates at the bow held firm! The main incident at Whiting Bay, after we were in the lee of the island and among the many vessels sheltering in the bay, was when we attempted to berth. Only the bow rope was successfully thrown, but our attempt to hang on with this till the engines pushed us in was foiled when it snapped with a mighty crack. By this time, the *Sannox* was equipped with nylon ropes for such situations as they were much stronger, but they were also far more expensive and the other members of the fleet were not so equipped. Our manoeuvre down the side of the pier proved effective and we tied up a full hour late.

We were on time for our 1.25 departure but the shock patient put us back another hour while the doctor took the necessary actions. The *Sannox* too was running late but not so late as we were, for a change! Thus she signalled to us that Ardrossan, rather surprisingly, was still accessible for our afternoon call and later again advised us to make our final run from the Bay to Fairlie. We complied and this, of course, meant that our passengers for the late run over to Brodick had to be redirected from Ardrossan to join us at Fairlie. We did amazingly well to leave Fairlie at 7.20, only 15 minutes after our scheduled sailing time from Ardrossan! I mentioned above that Ardrossan was difficult in stormy conditions. At this time Fairlie was available as an alternative harbour, but it added 20 minutes to the crossing. For this reason it was not favoured by the islanders when these two piers were being considered as a permanent mainland terminal for the Arran ferry. Ardrossan won the contest, although busier and more expensive with its hefty pier dues as well as often inaccessible in heavy seas. Fairlie on the other hand was a railway pier and offering sheltered moorings.

That concluded a hectic day and I sped off for Corrie to recover my land legs and resume the Sunday breaks there, which had been interrupted by our extended stay on the Ayr programme. Any plans I may have had for treading the light fantastic were dashed by the poor attendance at the dance. The weather dampened the ardour and instead we resorted to the demon drink - again!

Day 58 *Sunday 25 August*

Very wet morning but sunny by afternoon. Nly gale whipped the sea to foam all day. We were not feeling in a condition for church. After breakfast, played Monopoly till the weather cleared. Went down for a bathe at the diving board - water not bad though very rough. Did not stay there long but walked to Sannox and followed the shore till we reached the post marking the Measured Mile. Remained blustery and we prepared tea after 6.00 No sign of *Duchesses* though it appears that *Hamilton* did make the Campbeltown sailing. Ate well, with tomato soup, mince with carrot, white turnip, potatoes and broad beans - most of the veg came from the back garden. Finished up with fruit and jelly. Took a cup of tea before venturing out into the storm. Took bikes but were blown about and carried off course! While I was cycling along the jetty on a brakeless, bell-less, rusty, lady's boneshaker, I had the misfortune to meet with a wire hawser across the path and several inches above ground. The front wheel got over but this caused the wire to spring, lifting both me and the bike into the air and down I came with the bike on top. I was unhurt but suffered injured pride! Helped to carry the dinghy into the garden for protection before turning in to bed at 10.30, leaving a party still in full swing in the front room.

Graham's crew spent much of the evening rescuing a yacht which was swept up on the rocks at Brodick.

Commentary Day 58

Back to Sundays without pay and spent actively in Corrie. As the diary records, this Sunday spent at Brodick was no day of rest for the crew.

Bad weather did nothing to dampen our spirits and we spent a busy day. Once again, the desire to swim got the upper hand and we enjoyed a short, stormy session at the local diving spot. There followed the inevitable walk, this time along the shore to Sannox. Here the white poles marking the end of the measured mile can be seen. This is the desolate area in the north of Arran where larger liners or fast naval ships show their paces on trial without disturbing populated areas with the wash from their propellers. When we returned later to the jetty, we had availed ourselves of bikes. Absence of any brakes made these rather hazardous forms of transport and my close encounter with the cunningly placed hawser proved the point when the bike went up and I went down. Still, bike and I were none the worse for the incident.

Meals at the cottage in Corrie seem to have been on the same lavish scale as I enjoyed in future visits with student pals to our Rothesay flat.

We had no vegetable garden at our wee flat there, but this did not prevent us making pigs of ourselves and putting a good lining on the stomach for the imbibing that invariably ensued. That night at Corrie differed only in the fairly modest drinking in which I indulged. I appear to have been more anxious to have an early night so that I would be ready for work on the Death run in the morning. Our seamen, struggling with the stranded yacht when they left the pub in Brodick, had no such inhibitions.

Day 59 *Monday 26 August*

Diary in red biro today - no other pen to hand.
Mainly dry but cloudy and fresh Nly wind persists. Sea slight.
Up at 6.15 and dressed hurriedly for the 6.30 bus to Brodick. All the passengers seemed alike untidy and dishevelled. Reached pier quite early and had time to take a look at the yacht which our crew had rescued and propped up securely on the shore. Hurried aboard and took over count without an enumerator. 390 in all, including Whiting Bay traffic. Took breakfast on crossing and sorted Saturday's tickets for putting ashore at Ardrossan. *Irish Coast* sailed and *Sannox* ran 30 minutes late on her early runs. Took on coal, then waited for a large tanker to be towed out by tugs. Then we made ready to leave at 12.30. This gave some bother as the bow rope burst. We swung round in the wind and went across to Winton Pier to get turned. It was 2.50 when we reached Rothesay, so that we were a few minutes late when we set off for Largs and our cruise Round Bute. 370 passengers sailed and we followed *Jeanie Deans* all the way, arriving back at Rothesay 5 minutes behind her. *Queen Mary* appeared fully 30 minutes late from Glasgow and was clearly being driven hard to catch up. Donald was in an unusually good mood. We proceeded blank to Gourock where I took the train up to Glasgow - my day off was to be Tuesday. On the SMT bus out from town, I caught my first sight of one of the new TB trolley buses on our route. My arrival caused a great surprise at home - the folks had come up from the coast in the morning. Still greater surprise when I arrived among my friends where both groups of girls were assembled. A happy reunion and a great night!

Commentary Day 59
Strong winds continued and a broken bow rope again caused us a bit of manoeuvring in Ardrossan harbour. But at least the coaling was finished and we were preparing to leave for up river. Before any of this happened, there had been the Death boat. I joined her at Brodick once she sailed along from Whiting Bay and did not bother to pick up a counter for the gangway - highly irregular and Donald would certainly not have approved. But at this time in the morning, I was not for bothering!
It seems remarkable that we should have been deliberately timetabled that summer to sail directly behind *Jeanie Deans* on the Round Bute cruise. The only explanation must be that it was supposed that Largs would make the difference, but we were not well supported on the few occasions we made the trip. As things turned out, we certainly were better employed when sailing out of Ayr.

My parents had returned to Glasgow that morning to be ready for the return to their respective schools where they taught and I followed them up for my day off. Nights at Rothesay were coming to an end. I was unexpected when I appeared, as my normal day off was Friday. My friends likewise - both sets of our girl friends being present, for some were school associates and near contemporaries while the others were younger and recently enlisted in our gang - were taken by surprise.

At this time, I was enamoured of the trolley buses which had replaced the tram cars on the Clarkston route. Hence my interest in the latest batch of trolleys numbered TB 35 to 134 which had appeared in the city. At this time, they were on our 107 route from Maitland Street. Sadly, these environmentally friendly vehicles were given a poor reception in Glasgow and they were destined to be short-lived.

Day 60 *Tuesday 27 August*

Sunny with some cloud.

Up at back of 9.00 and shaved. Went golfing in morning but limited myself to 9 holes of varying golf! Met two of my pals who were on holiday and joined them on my bike. After lunch, I cycled down to Muirend station with 3 of my pals who were working in town. Once their train arrived, I cycled along to the bank to catch up on business. Later I met a group of our local gang, both male and female, and we went first to the field and then to the park. There we had a merry time on the swings, watched all the time by the disapproving "parkie". In the evening, I started off with a visit to the Queens Park Café for a range of beers and rum. We walked from there to the dance in the Institute where the Vernon Jazz band was playing. Excellent. Took my leave of one friend who was returning home next day to England. Late home to bed.

Commentary Day 60

While the *Graham* spent her day idly at Gourock, I was given an unexpected day off. Friday was my usual day of release but I made the most of my freedom. First, I tried my hand at golf. I was now much less enthusiastic about golf than I had formerly been and 9 holes was my maximum for the day. I was too keen to join my friends and catch up on the gossip. Naturally, the quality of my play suffered with disuse and that gave another incentive to stop early. This done, I got on my bike and found various friends. We ended up in the Linn Park where Johnny, the long suffering park ranger, decided not to intervene though we were clearly over age for using the swings. He had decided, no doubt, that we might get up to something worse if redirected! Park rangers were still very much a part of the city's armoury in the supervision and maintenance of the parks at this time and they could be tiresome so far as we were concerned. Today, however, all was sweetness and light.

The final part of the day involved a visit to the splendidly named Queen's Park Café at Victoria Road. This splendid old howff had dispensed strong drink to all and sundry for generations. Many, like us, must have used reference to the Café as a cover for more serious drinking. It came in handy! Where better to charge up one's spirits for a session at the dancing to the music of the excellent Vernon Jazz Band in our local Stamperland Institute?

Day 61 *Wednesday 28 August*

A beautiful day with little cloud.

Up at 5.30 for an early trolley bus into town. Caught 6.25 train at Central and slept most of the way to Gourock where I joined the *Graham*. The old chief greeted me with the news that one of the lesser beings from the Kremlin had been down asking to see me. Nothing could be done but I took a second breakfast and we left at 8.50 for Largs, with the *Hamilton* coming out at our back, bound for Dunoon. From Largs I phoned Gourock, to be told that I would be of assistance on *Glen Sannox*, starting from Monday. The relief purser was aboard today so that I enjoyed a nice, easy day sunbathing up on the top after deck. Photographed *Montrose* and views of our funnel. We were quiet today, considering the weather, with only 470 to Glasgow and 495 back. But then, the schools are back in. Were presented with handbills advertising Billy Smart's Circus as we passed Gourock. Also got a letter from my local correspondent but the news was old, now that I had been home in person yesterday. Some River Steamer Club members were aboard today - probably because this is the last Upriver sailing of the season. *Queen Mary* was again running late and against the river flow when we met her, though we were keeping good time as the river tides favoured us. A pantry boy got me to buy him a half bottle of whisky as I looked more of the legal age. In return, I was rewarded with a bottle of Carlsberg Special out of the half dozen I also purchased for him. This got them going and they sang loudly to a skiffle group in the lower lounge. I joined them for some time before going off to my bed on deck.

Commentary Day 61

It was certainly an early start. In later years, I would have thought it better to catch her at Largs but at this stage I still watched my P's and Q's! The trolley bus service started early and so there was no difficulty in catching the train. The news from the Kremlin had been long awaited, as I had been wondering what would happen when the *Graham* came out of service on 2nd September. Would I be paid off like many of the other crew members? I had indicated that I was available till the end of September, if required. And so I was. My season was to end as it had begun, with a posting to *Glen Sannox* for the remainder of the season. The decision was logical: *Caledonia*'s Ayr programme terminated on 1st September and I had built up some expertise on the Arran crossing. Where better to send me? It was also the first definite indication that there was no reprieve at present for the *Graham*. Her Clyde service was to terminate on Monday.

This was the last Upriver sailing of the season. It had proved a worthwhile reintroduction and would continue in future years. Having the relief purser with us on a relatively quiet cruise was a godsend. I was still tired from my excesses of the previous night and the early start had not helped. It was just what the doctor ordered and I took every opportunity to relax on the upper sun deck.

But I was easily tempted! Having reached the giddy height of 18 years, hence achieving legal status, and with an impressive dark stubble on my chin requiring regular shaving, I was the obvious person for the pantry boys to approach. Anyway, my drinking was now well attested around the ship. So once again, I was the logical choice for the job. But this time the task was to place an order for a carry-out of drinks! My reward for successful fulfilment of the task was a beer and a place at the party until I left for the comparative comfort of my cancellation office cabin. You will note that the bunk below deck vacated by Dick held no attractions for me. I preferred the airiness provided by my office on deck and was not anxious to be any closer to big Donald or the chief in the fug below.

And don't forget Smart's circus! This will appear again later.

Day 62 *Thursday 29 August*

Cloudy but mainly dry. Slight W wind.

Wakened by relief purser at 7.00 in time for early departure to tender to *Carinthia* and again flying the Cunard house flag at our main mast. *Maid of Cumbrae* was already busy tendering to the *Stockholm*. She was busier and we carried a mere 200 or so from our liner. Managed to scrounge another log card of *Carinthia* from an official as evidence! *Saint Columba* had a steam pipe burst so that her departure from Gourock was one hour delayed. Donald rejoined us at Gourock from his day off and off now went our relief. Took up yesterday's tickets to the girls in the checking huts and had a blether. Next stop was Rothesay where we arrived at 1.25 in good time for our Arran Coast cruise. Only 46 from Rothesay and 100 plus out of Largs. Sailed as far as Brodick bay and were still 10 minutes early back at Largs. Left Rothesay again at 6.05 on a special run to Gourock for Smart's circus. Picked up 380 from Rothesay and a further 440 from Dunoon. Collected the tickets as they boarded and this enabled a free stampede on arrival at Gourock. The *Montrose* left Dunoon along with us but tied up at Gourock a good 4 minutes ahead. The company agent failed me over the free tickets for the circus that he had promised and he scuttled off with never a word. I contented myself by meeting up with other assistants and we had some drinks at the Ashton hotel. We gained an extra 10 at Gourock when the circus goers finally returned. The gangways were very steep.

Commentary Day 62

This was a near duplicate of our programme on the previous Thursday, with *Carinthia* substituted for *Sylvania*. We remained loyal to the Cunard house flag and left the *Stockholm* for the *Maid* to handle. Our numbers on the tender were not much better than our cruise figures as the season was drawing to a close! I was careful again to secure a souvenir of our involvement - the log card seemed most appropriate.

Numbers for the Arran Cruise were very disappointing but typical for the end of the season. It had to be something special to attract a crowd and the evening circus special did the trick. The promise of a midnight return sailing from Gourock made the circus visit attractive and 800 was a good crowd. The numerous handbills we carried, as well as advertising at the two resorts, clearly paid dividends. We were also promised free tickets to the circus for our support. But the baldy company agent played us false and slipped off among the crowd with never a word. No doubt he had passed the tickets to some one else. We were cheated and turned to the demon drink for solace! That, together with the darkness and the steep gangways, probably accounts for the extra 10 passengers counted aboard at Gourock. We were fortunate that it was not wet. Steep gangways and a few drams would have been quite lethal when it came to boarding at low tide. Chutes should probably have been provided! It would seem that the Kremlin was happy to have us running all the hours that God offered and knew that our skipper would be the last to object.

Day 63 *Friday 30 August*

Up at 9.00 and after breakfast I went ashore at Rothesay to photograph the *Graham* in her unusual berth at 1A round the front of the pier. We left blank for Ardrossan just after 10.00, arriving at 11.30. We were aiming for Jerry's quay for coal but a strong Westerly wind kept blowing us off, so that we were forced to lie facing seaward at the lighthouse and then reverse back alongside the quay with the ropes offering extra assistance. Fortunately, the *Sannox* had left just before our arrival or the manoeuvre would have been well nigh impossible. We then coaled and I went up to do a few messages and to complete Donald's car licence renewal and post it in town. He'll be lucky if he ever sees that licence! Wrote to my friend at home. Went over blank to do the 3.50 sailing from Whiting Bay. *Hamilton* passed on the Holy Isle cruise out of Ayr as we neared the Bay. Only 100 crossed back with us and a mere 78 joined us at 7.05 for the final run to Brodick and Whiting Bay. Had a chance to speak with the assistant on the *Sannox* about beds - I'll need to lodge a protest. My Corrie pal was aboard for Brodick so that I confirmed my intention to spend Sunday with him. Only 25 sailed on to Whiting Bay where we picked up our night watchman and sailed blank for Ardrossan. More delays berthing and it was 10.00 when we rushed off - a few of us reached our goal! Went with the luggage man and the pantry boys and tried two pubs before securing entry. Export, Carlsberg, stout and whisky were taken.

Commentary Day 63

The day started unusually with our unfamiliar base at Rothesay. Even more unusual was our berthing at the inside of the pier in berth 1A, where in years gone by the old paddler *Kylemore* once berthed and today was the customary berth for the little *Countess of Breadalbane*. She was elsewhere and so we were there to avoid disturbing the morning runs over to Wemyss Bay. Thereafter, our day was not profitably spent. Blank runs to Ardrossan, then to Arran and back again at night to Ardrossan. Our service runs themselves were little better than blank runs as we scarcely topped the hundred! The 25 passengers from Brodick to Whiting Bay hit a new low spot, closely followed by the sail back to the mainland with no traffic beyond our own night watchman. You see what I mean, then, about unprofitable sailing!

Having so much time in my hands made me available for other matters. Clearly, I was not confident that I had handled the motor licence renewal properly. Only Donald could answer that. But already concerns were arising about accommodation on *Glen Sannox*. Big she was but clearly she was not accommodating! I sensed problems ahead and knew from my numerous chats with other assistants that we must go on the offensive and confront the skipper.

Then there was the wind as well to contend with! It made things difficult on our first arrival at Ardrossan, so that only some extraordinary manoeuvring with help from the ropes enabled us to berth successfully. On our late return from Arran, the wind sprite was again in evidence and almost succeeded in denying us any time ashore and on pay day at that! It was closing time as we docked and the master would certainly not have revelled in the spectacle of various of his crew members leaping ashore before the gangway was positioned. Indeed, a few of the most desperate even leaped from the passenger rail! The old luggage man was with us - he and I at least waited till the gangway was in place - and off we sped up town through the coals and other encumbrances on Jerry's Quay, ready to run from one cry of "Finish your drinks" to another and to keep going until we found a pub willing to take pity and serve us. We must have made an entertaining sight as we rushed in a disorderly crowd from pub to pub. But we were no slouches when it came to placing a good range of orders!

Day 64 *Saturday 31 August*

Early mist and rain, becoming mild and dry later.

Was up to the ringing of the breakfast bell and after coaling we moved over to our customary berth by Montgomery pier. There I phoned Gourock and arranged for a free pass to Glasgow each day or, failing that, a bed on board *Glen Sannox*. Only then did I go for change at the bank. We carried only 150 or so to Whiting Bay but *Sannox* was quite busy and we had to make our way round her, as she was still loading cars. Took a walk on reaching the Bay before returning to the mainland with 450 passengers. There was the usual hand waving but more subdued than in the past. *Sannox* was still at Winton Pier when we arrived, so we went into Jerry's quay. She left soon after, so we moved over to put ashore 10 barrows of luggage. Had 1 car on 3.10 crossing and 3 more on the last 6.45 run to Arran. Once again, *Sannox* held us up for 10 minutes at Brodick. Did the ticket collection on crossing and there was little to collect. Bussed up to Corrie but found one of my pals was at the pictures. So I spent a costly night between the pub and the dance. Turned in very late.

Commentary Day 64

With my sojourn on the *Marchioness* rapidly coming to an end, my first priority was to reach a decision regarding overnight accommodation on the *Sannox* or daily travel. The skipper on the big ferry was not at all friendly to assistants - much more hostile indeed than I had experienced on the *Graham* and I thought ours was bad! He was absolutely determined to keep us out the designated cancellation office which was located right next his bridge cabin but doubled up as a VIP room for such celebrities as Lady Jean Fforde of Arran. His aim was to have this office restricted to use for guests and we certainly did not fit in with his plans. However, he was outmanoeuvred as one of us, the senior assistant from up river, managed to secure Gourock's agreement that a bed, one bed only, should be installed there, provided it was dismantled daily. This was much the position of my bed in the *Graham*, but there I had no option but to remove the mattress to allow us to use the mahogany desk surface for dealing with tickets. The situation on the *Sannox* was quite different in that a camp bed was set up in the corner of the room and there was no interference with the coffee table and lounge seats provided for visitors. Besides, we even had an old, disreputable table supplied for our ticket duties! Still, this was to be the arrangement and I was to be given free passes enabling me to travel daily from home in time for the *Sannox*'s 10.10 sailing. This seemed to me a most agreeable arrangement.

With all this settled, I was free to consider other matters, like going to the bank or planning a strategy for a quick get away for the Corrie bus at night. Collecting tickets while sailing was a brainwave - copied from the Smart's circus experience. I don't know whether Donald was even consulted! Taking in the tickets on the last crossing allowed me to change and go ashore with the passengers while the crew could deal with unloading the cars. They had all weekend to spend in Brodick! And how appropriate that the *Graham* should have carried cars in time honoured fashion on her very last crossing from Ardrossan to Arran! The comment about the 10 barrows at Ardrossan is interesting. The crew must have breathed a sigh of relief when the *Sannox* moved out leaving space for us at Winton Pier. The thought of manhandling the cargo along from Jerry's quay among the rails and obstructions would have been horrendous.

Day 65 *Sunday 1 September*

Glorious day with plenty sun. Strong Nly wind.

Caley on her last run of the season from Ayr round Holy Isle, while the *Graham* lay idly at Brodick. Was sick first thing but recovered and set off at 1.30 to climb. We went up Goatfell first via High Corrie. I was exhausted on the climb up! After taking in the marvellous view up and down the river, we walked along into the teeth of the wind and with the air noticeably thinner by way of the Pinnacles to North Goatfell and then along a tortuous "path" to Cioch na h'Oighe (the Maiden's Pap). Stumbled hastily back down from here and took a quick bathe in the altogether in a deep pool above Sannox. The water was refreshingly cool. Made ourselves a man sized dinner on our return to base at 7.00. Went out for a while at night before going back to do dishes and shave. On our way back, we raided a plum tree in the village and guzzled juicy plums by the fire till past 2.30am.

Commentary Day 65

Sunday was a time of retribution for the excesses of the previous night. But it was the end of an era so far as I was concerned and it had to be duly celebrated. Sickness was a small price to pay and it cleared my head. Yet it was afternoon before we felt fit for a climb and what a climb! Off we trekked through Corrie heading for Goatfell and the first long pause to take in the view. The weather was spectacular. First we gazed at the tiny *Marchioness* in Brodick before watching the *Caledonia* inching her way over to Holy Isle from Ayr. Then we directed our view up river, away from the mainland and taking in Bute, Cumbrae and the upper Firth. We could have spent all day there but adventure called. Ill clad as we undoubtedly were - for I certainly had no boots and was better kitted out for a walk in the park! - we picked our way by the pinnacles to North Goatfell and, incredibly, on to Cioch na h'Oighe. I doubt if I would tackle this today even with good climbing equipment! But then we were equipped with the bravado of youth and I was unaware that this was regarded by experts as "a dangerous venture" and to be attempted only by experienced mountaineers. We live to tell the tale, and the attractions of a deep flowing mountain stream for skinny dipping to remove the sweat could not be ignored on our downward tumble. Nor for that matter could we turn a blind eye to the ripe plums that night as we returned late through the village. It was all so natural!

Day 66 *Monday 2 September*

Another fine day with little cloud.

Up to the alarm at 5.45 and caught the bus for the Death boat with one of my friends who was heading for the city. We had to stand, as the bus was crowded with fellow sufferers. We sailed across to Ardrossan on what may (but I hope will not) be the *Marchioness*' last service run, during which time I took breakfast, got all my gear together and went round taking my leave of the crew including chief and skipper (who were both very pleasant). It was a sad day and everyone seemed affected by it - there were tears in the master's eyes, but it could have been the cold. We carried 407 sheep, penned in at the bow. These had been loaded at Whiting Bay well before departure so that we kept well to timetable. The skipper gave Brodick a final blast as he sailed out. Once the ship was cleared of passengers and sheep at Ardrossan, the decks were washed and the planks were laid on a barrow and taken back on board. The *Graham* then left with a final blast, moving astern out of the harbour. Even big Donald was there at the rail waving! I photographed the departure and then waited for the arrival of the *Sannox* at 9.20 where I was to start work at once.

Commentary Day 66

The Death run was never so aptly named as on this sad morning. The cars on the last Saturday crossing and now the sheep penned in at the bow seemed designed to highlight the wide range of the *Graham*'s services to Arran over the years. I had little time to get emotional. There was plenty for me to do if I was going to join my new charge at Ardrossan, but I was anxious to take my leave of all those with whom I had worked that summer and I also had to sign off formally with the skipper. Perhaps I now knew that there were happier ships to work on than the *Graham* but that was nothing to do with my *Marchioness*. Her only fault was that changing travel needs and a substantial trading loss for the company had rendered her redundant. Of course we all hoped she would be reprieved and return to service the following summer but the summer deficit would put paid to such hopes.

In what seemed like no time, the farewells were said and I was unloading myself and my belongings on to the pier at Ardrossan. I saw her off sadly as she left for the Albert harbour in Greenock awaiting news of her fate. My fate was already determined. My 66 days associated with the *Graham* were over and it remained for me to await the arrival of *Glen Sannox* at the pier head.

Preparing to leave Ardrossan for the last time on 2 September. The mate stands by the funnel and big Donald stands proud over to his left. The skipper commands the show from his eyrie.

Marchioness of Graham bows out of Ardrossan- stern first!

Change of Life - Aboard *Glen Sannox*

For the remainder of that month, I was to be found aboard the mighty *Sannox* and how different things were! The programme was easy if not profitable since I had no Sunday work. On the other hand, I had an additional day off each week and my free pass allowed me to leave home at 7.30 and to be back home again by 7.15 at night, giving ample time to meet up with my pals each evening. Before this, I might as well have been on Saint Helena, so rare were my home visits!

Glen Sannox was also a happier ship, except where dealings with the captain, John Cameron, were concerned. He was obviously very ill at ease with his new charge and obsessive about boat drills and ship inspections. The former had been extremely rare on the *Graham* and the latter unknown. But the wee man took these occasions very seriously, so that I readily fell foul of him when minded to photograph the lowering of the boats. I was sharply reminded that this was "not a circus!" The purser was delighted when I recounted my discomfiture and thought I had done well in the circumstances. Because of his diminutive stature, the skipper stood on specially raised platforms on the wings of the bridge to add to his height and improve his view of proceedings below. Yet, even there, he was not out of range of the toilet rolls hurled from the pier below at departures. He stood up there motionless, as one petrified by the Gorgon's glare, while the rolls coiled around him like the serpents round Laocoon. Again, I yielded to temptation and was about to take a photo when he rounded on me, declaring "this is a bridge, not a playground!" and I was compelled to beat a retreat. I would never have made so bold with our Colin! But the main and continuing confrontation with him was over the cancellation office beside his cabin on the bridge. He had failed in his effort to deny us the use of a camp bed in this sanctum but he retaliated by demanding that we must not use the lounge seats or carpets - these were for guests and only guests. Our radio too was forbidden as causing interference with ship to shore contact. But we could live with all these irritations. We were comfortable, far distanced from the public eye, ensconced in a modern room with a view and even equipped with curtains! If we had a complaint, it was the vibration. Otherwise, we could cope. We did in fact have one blow out when the Marine Superintendent from the Kremlin was called in. We were largely successful: there was to be one camp bed in the cancellation office but it was to be folded away daily; the transistor was quite acceptable if not played too loudly; our office was to be kept tidy in case of visitors. We were so pleased by this result that we were emboldened to complain to the skipper about the mess left by Lady Jean's party on one occasion.

My main task was with the cargo, while the other assistant, a tall lad of 4 years' experience as an assistant, took more to do with passengers. This brought me into contact with a wonderful new world. Pigs presented the biggest problem when handled and they were reluctant to stay put on the lift. Horses, cattle and, of course, sheep were more amenable to discipline. Then there were the increased numbers of cars. Things were made more difficult by the unpredictability of the hydraulic car lift. It was painfully slow and sometimes a ramp seized up so that all car landings were made on one side only. A new motor was fitted but it was still slow and unreliable. Sometimes the ship's crane was brought out of retirement and used to help operate the lift at times of crisis. At other times, when the tides made the gangways impossibly steep, the lift was employed for disembarking passengers. Provision of special gangways at the piers to address this problem came much later. Another reason for poor time keeping was the skipper himself. He seemed unable to get a take on the working of the screws and the ship's undoubted manoeuvrability was lost on him. She caught the wind badly with her high superstructure, and the skipper's tardiness in taking corrective action regularly resulted in fathoms of nylon rope stretching from the pier. The skipper was reluctant to let go when a rope was landed and relied on the rope to do what the screws might have achieved - hence the need for nylon ropes. Little wonder that he was a difficult man to handle with so much on his mind!

Meals were of a consistently high standard and I soon came to enjoy this new placement. The crossings were lengthy and could provide lively passages, the route and passengers were familiar and agreeable, the purser was extremely easy to work with and there was much to savour and enjoy, from watching the *Talisman*'s antics at Fairlie, when we moved out or else she came alongside, to delighting in the spray flying over our seemingly inaccessible tower up on the bridge deck. Indeed, when asked by Gourock if I would prefer an up river placement to avoid so much daily travel, I demurred and stayed put. I knew I was on a good thing! In fact, I returned to work on the *Sannox* on four future weekends at Easter, although by then the sparring captain had moved on to higher command. Pay may have remained poor but the open waters were attractive and the new skipper was delightful.

My spell on *Glen Sannox* ended abruptly. The Clyde fleet was struck by a flu epidemic and I succumbed. I failed to last out till September weekend and went home early on Friday 27. My uniform followed me home along with my pay, after appropriate deductions to defray postage. My cap and coat, together with those of the chief purser who was similarly smitten, were sent to Gourock, there to be burned in a conflagration which ravaged that nerve centre of the Clyde operation over that winter.

Festooned with toilet rolls, *Glen Sannox* at Brodick in September, 1957.

Wee John Cameron looks down from the bridge on the *Sannox* to the *Talisman* alongside her at Fairlie. Size matters! Compare above Illustration on page 69.

Metamorphosis - A Life Hereafter

But let us go back now to the *Marchioness*. On that fateful Monday morning of 2nd September, I disembarked and watched her reverse out of Ardrossan harbour, turn outside the breakwater and head off, blank as so often, for Gourock and thereafter the Albert harbour in Greenock to deposit seats. There was still a chance that she would reappear on the Clyde next season - after all, at 22 years, she was comparatively youthful and her condition was good. Indeed, there were rumours that she was to be improved with the fitting of a new top deck and life rafts as well as a new funnel, but these were offset by reports that her hull was too narrow to take the oil tanks required for her conversion to oil burning. For her to survive, expenditure was necessary, as the arrival of the car ferry on the Clyde had usurped her position. She could not compete now as a car carrier and her accommodation, as my account has illustrated, was not up to cruising standards. The speculation ended abruptly when a hefty operating loss of £200,000 was declared by the company for 1957. The *Graham*'s days on the Clyde were numbered and she was put on the market.

The Clyde fleet had reached its zenith that season with more services and cruises available than at any other time since the war. For this pattern to have continued, a fine season was essential. That summer of 1957 was not fine! Of my 66 days associated with the *Graham*, 30 were bright to fine and 36 were dull to wet. Of that total, 20 were windy and most rough in consequence. Thus cruising conditions were not often inviting. Then, there was our blank running which was excessive and costly. I counted 61 blank runs varying in length from 1 hour to as much as 2 hours. Bearing in mind that she was the only coal burner in the fleet, complex and costly provision was necessary to keep her in fuel, as coal had to be brought to various pier heads. It came as no surprise therefore that, when it was announced that tonnage must be shed, the *Graham* was identified for withdrawal. More surprising was the news that *Jupiter* too was to be withdrawn, despite her expensive conversion to oil burning for the 1957 season. *Jupiter* lay forlorn in harbour, till sold in 1960 to an Irish owner at a knockdown price of £8,000, considerably less than her conversion costs! She never sailed again, being scrapped early the following year.

The *Graham* fared better. At the very close of 1958, having languished in harbour alongside *Jupiter* all that summer, she was sold for some £15,000 to a Greek ship owner to take up service in the Aegean Sea. Stripped of her clock, which is said to have found a new home in the *Maid*

Marchioness of Graham and *Jupiter* awaiting disposal in Greenock's Albert Harbour.

Marchioness of Graham prepares to leave for Greece under new ownership, as signified by the Greek letter delta (D) for Diapoulis on the funnel.

of the Loch at Balloch, bereft too of the sign indicating CANCELLATION TICKET OFFICE which I purloined on a visit to her in September 1957, the *Marchioness* set sail in gloomy conditions on 10 February, 1959. Her funnel bore the addition of a broad blue stripe as indicator of change and blue Grecian skies ahead. She went under her own steam, with coal stock piled in all her alleyways and saloons and with windows boarded against expected storms en route. Pausing only at Gibraltar to refuel, the *Marchioness* proceeded on her marathon voyage, arriving safely at Peiraeus, port of Athens, on 2nd March.

In Greece she was transformed. Renamed *Ellas* (Greece), she was converted from steam to diesel and given a squat monstrosity of a funnel, appropriate for the space age. The funnel bore the Greek letter delta on a broad blue band to signify Diapoulis, her new owner. The hull was cut just above the belting and a whole new, expansive superstructure added, increasing her tonnage to over 1,000 tons. Derricks were fitted at the bow to service a new cargo hold. This was the wholly unrecognisable ship which confronted me at Peiraeus, when I succeeded in tracking her down on her new service run to Rhodes on 8 September, 1962. There was next to nothing left of the trim, little ship that I had come to know so well on the Clyde. I took an immediate dislike to the abomination of a funnel and she appeared to have a permanent list to starboard. I doubt the old chief's filled bath would have made no impression here! There was precious little time left before she was due to sail but I was anxious to find proof that this was really the *Marchioness* in a new guise. I managed to make my appeal in broken English and Greek and was permitted a brief sortie aboard. The wheelhouse came up trumps. There was the familiar steering wheel and telegraphs which once I had polished and, though I did not have time to see it, I was persuaded that the ship's bell out forward would confirm her former identity. Further information was poured upon me. Her journey out to Greece had been alarming but she was now fitted with stabilisers and was, allegedly, as steady as a rock! Her conversion had taken almost a year and cost £37,000 in Greece. Her new tonnage approached 1,000 and 2 German diesels could drive her at 19 knots - this I disbelieved! Her new sailing route took her from Peiraeus to Rhodes, a 19 hour journey with 4 hour turn around time at either end. Her passenger capacity was 820: 470 steerage and 350 in 1st and 2nd class. She had 80 cabins and a special cabin for the manager. Besides this, she carried 99 crew, of whom half were stewards. On board she appeared fresh and bright with a preponderance of mirrors. On the down side, it was admitted that vibration was bad, the funnel was given

Transformed to *Ellas*, now converted to diesel and serving Rhodes from Peiraeus in September, 1962 - yes, once our Clyde *Marchioness*.

That frightful funnel close up.

to emitting smuts and the new fittings were of poor quality. This then was the new creation.

The following year I was back in Greece and again I sought her out. This time she was temporarily laid up at Peiraeus, her owner being bankrupted by a "big damages case" or so we were informed. Her name was now *Nea Hellas* (New Greece), her whole hull was painted white as was her funnel but on this was embossed a dark blue letter delta with a trident superimposed. A small extra deck had been added beside the funnel and radar fitted on front of the bridge. A fine conceit was a small stairway forward which gave access to a tiny plunge pool located where once the cargo hold had been situated. The watchman viewed us with suspicion in our student holiday gear and refused access. But then there appeared a proud electrician from below and, on hearing our garbled account, he warmly welcomed us aboard and we saw around at leisure. He informed us that she was a good ship and currently on the market for new owners. Of Scots or Scotland he knew nothing - England was the *Graham*'s place of origin. Our visit ended with homage paid to the ship's bell which, though now silvered, bore proudly and unmistakeably the name *Marchioness of Graham*. So much for all that polishing on blank runs around the Clyde! Paint smothered all my efforts but at least the inscription remained clear.

This was to be my last sighting of the *Graham*, as subsequent summers took me to other areas of the Mediterranean. But her career continued. In 1964, she sailed under the name *Galaxias*. Then in 1966, again with different owners, she was renamed *El Greco* and sailed as a cruise ship, first out of Genoa and subsequently back again in Greek waters. 1968 saw her laid up yet again and as late as 1974 she was seen by a keen eyed steamer enthusiast as she lay, rusting and forlorn, in Eleusis Bay, almost certainly destined for the scrap yard. Her final fling was over - she was truly "Finished with Engines".

Renamed *Nea Ellas* in 1963, with new insignia on that awful funnel.

The plunge pool replaces a cargo hold belonging to pre-cruise days.

This concludes my account of the 66 days which I spent aboard the *Marchioness of Graham* that summer of 1957 on her last Clyde season, as well as including a brief glance at her final days spent in Aegean waters. As for me, her former partner, I remained on the Clyde, wondering where I would be placed for season 1958. Would *Glen Sannox* again seem the obvious choice or had the fates something better in store for me? Best make an early application and find out!

Still, I kept the wee ship's memory alive, in her Clyde role rather than in her transformed state among the Greek islands, when I addressed the River Steamer Club in January 1964 on the topic Memo on a *Marchioness*. I spoke for over an hour, reliving some of the glory days downriver and linking the *Graham* with *Queen Mary II* as another one funnel turbine with a definite Glasgow connection on her weekly upriver sailing. By that time, of course, my own link with the Glasgow run had been firmly forged but that is another story.

A backward look — a last look at the *Graham* that I knew.

Index

A

ABC ferries 45
ABC of Clyde Steamers 103, 122, 123, 124
Adamant 3, 38, 116
Adamson 6
Ailsa Craig 36, 95, 97, 130, 175
Ailsa Shipbuilding 45
Albert pier 127
Amended Sailings 110, 112, 150, 151, 162
Anderson 61
Ardarach 2, 9, 10
Ardentinny 89, 92, 94
Ardlamont Point 10
Ardrishaig 1, 36, 146
Ardrossan 13, 16, 19, 22, 31, 32, 42, 43, 51, 63, 64, 65, 70, 72, 73, 75, 76, 77, 78, 80, 91, 95, 97, 99, 100, 109, 112, 113, 118, 119, 130, 132, 134, 136, 138, 139, 140, 141, 142, 143, 146, 148, 151, 156, 160, 162, 164, 166, 174, 179, 181, 182, 183, 184, 191, 192, 193, 196, 203, 204, 206, 208, 209, 213
Ardrossan Dockyard 42
Arran mv 9, 11, 19, 32, 45, 46, 51, 64, 91, 99, 124, 130, 192
Arran ss 32
Arran 13, 16, 19, 22, 24, 30, 33, 40, 42, 48, 50, 52, 55, 62, 63, 65, 67, 68, 70, 71, 73, 76, 77, 79, 82, 86, 90, 95, 99, 112, 116, 134, 138, 140, 141, 143, 144, 148, 156, 164, 169, 170, 171, 172, 181, 184, 189, 193, 194, 199, 201, 203, 204, 205, 206, 208
Arrochar 42, 140
Ashton 45, 49
Ashton 201
assistant purser 13, 20, 24, 33, 47, 74, 100, 105, 107
Atalanta 48, 50
Ayr 13, 32, 40, 42, 51, 52, 55, 63, 77, 78, 79, 80, 82, 95, 97, 98, 99, 109, 112, 113, 115, 116, 118, 120, 122, 129, 130, 131, 132, 133, 134, 135, 136, 137, 138, 140, 143, 144, 146, 147, 148, 149, 151, 152, 153, 154, 156, 157, 160, 161, 162, 163, 164, 165, 166, 167, 169, 170, 171, 174, 175, 176, 177, 178, 179, 181, 183, 184, 185, 187, 190, 191, 193, 196, 199, 203, 207

B

baldy 91, 120, 127, 128, 183, 184, 186, 201
Ballast quay 166
Balmoral 6
Barclay Curle 39, 154
Bardic Ferry 168, 169, 186
BBC TV 67, 68, 72, 76, 84, 86, 89, 91, 94, 95, 124, 126, 127, 128, 142
Bennie 56, 62
Billy Smart's Circus 199
Bridge Wharf 10, 54, 84, 86, 135, 146, 153
Brigadier 169
British Rail 1
British Transport Commission (BTC) 13, 14, 15, 70, 80, 81, 151
Brodick 10, 13, 16, 19, 20, 21, 22, 24, 64, 65, 70, 75, 77, 78, 79, 80, 81, 82, 95, 97, 99, 109, 112, 116, 117, 130, 134, 141, 144, 145, 160, 164, 165, 174, 175, 181, 183, 189, 192, 193, 194, 195, 196, 201, 203, 205, 206, 207, 208, 212
Burns Laird 31, 65, 95, 151
Bute 45, 73, 89, 90, 91, 127, 138, 140, 141, 142, 175, 176
Bute 1, 40, 42, 62, 63, 79, 80, 84, 94, 103, 121, 122, 171, 172, 174, 178, 190, 191, 196, 207
Buteman, The 127

C

Caledonia ix, 5, 6, 12, 13, 20, 32, 40, 42, 43, 48, 51, 63, 77, 78, 79, 80, 81, 82, 89, 95, 98, 99, 100, 107, 108, 112, 113, 117, 118, 134, 138, 151, 152, 153, 160, 161, 162, 164, 165, 167, 169, 170, 171, 175, 176, 178, 181, 182, 183, 184, 185, 189, 190, 199, 207
Caledonian Steam Packet Company ix, 2, 13, 19, 23, 32, 36, 53, 63, 90, 162
Caley (see *Caledonia*)
Campbell, 55, 58
Cameron 6, 210, 212

Campbeltown 10, 33, 36, 40, 65, 67, 68, 69, 70, 105, 107, 108, 109, 112, 120, 137, 138, 140, 155, 156, 157, 162, 171, 172, 185, 191, 194
cancellation office 89, 99, 100, 103, 104, 105, 106, 119, 132, 139, 161, 164, 166, 200, 205, 210, 216
Carinthia 73, 105, 201
Carrick 117
Chapel Hill 2, 121
Chieftain 168, 169
Christian Institute 6
Cioch na h'Oighe 207
Citizen (see Evening Citizen)
City of Lichfield 169
Clan MacRae 169
Cloch 82, 103
Clydebank 12, 13
Clyde River Steamer Club ix, x, 6, 19, 121, 135, 199, 219
Clyde Steamers at a Glance 120, 121, 122, 123
Columba 178, 179
Corrie 75, 77, 78, 79, 80, 82, 95, 98, 148, 164, 189, 192, 193, 194, 195, 203, 205, 206, 207
counter 20, 57, 196
Countess of Breadalbane 45, 49, 107, 120, 127, 138, 188, 203
Cowal 21, 45, 64, 73, 86, 89, 90, 95, 99, 118, 141, 189
Cowal 175
Craigendoran 40, 42, 63, 101, 119, 187
Craigielea 2
Craigmore 4, 6, 13, 105
Cruiser 169
CSP (see Caledonian Steam Packet)
Cumbrae 5, 73, 178, 179, 207
Cunard 12, 189, 201
Cunarder 13, 73, 180

D

Davaar 67, 172
Death boat, Death run 64, 80, 90, 99, 116, 134, 148 164, 184, 195, 196, 208
Denny, Denny's 1, 9, 31, 36, 40, 45, 186
Diapoulis 214, 215
Dick 54, 59, 60, 67, 70, 71, 73, 74, 86, 87, 95, 97, 98, 103, 104, 105, 106, 107, 118, 126, 127, 128, 132, 134, 136, 138, 139, 141, 143, 144, 146, 147, 156, 157, 160, 162, 164, 166, 169, 170, 171, 178, 181, 182, 183, 184, 186, 189, 190, 200
Donald (see MacNaughton)
Doon the Watter 40
Duchess 1, 2, 4, 10, 33, 36, 37, 38, 40, 52, 53, 67, 69, 80, 83, 103, 105, 120, 138, 152, 155, 167, 172, 173, 191
Duchesses 48, 63, 64, 67, 80, 89, 100, 121, 161, 194
Duchess of Fife 1, 2, 4, 5, 9 52, 53, 152
Duchess of Hamilton 10, 38, 40, 64, 65, 67, 80, 86, 95, 99, 103, 105, 107, 112, 121, 134, 135, 138, 155, 156, 157, 158, 167, 171, 172, 173, 178, 191, 194, 199, 203
Duchess of Montrose 36, 37, 40, 82, 83, 97, 99, 107, 116, 117, 120, 130, 138, 139, 174, 191, 199, 201
Duckworth and Langmuir ix
Dunagoil Bay 10, 82, 101, 118, 151, 152
Dunoon 9, 24, 37, 40, 45, 63, 67, 83, 86, 87, 89, 91, 97, 99, 103, 104, 107, 108, 112, 116, 117, 118, 119, 132, 151, 153, 162, 169, 183, 192, 199, 201

E

Eddie 62
Eleusis Bay 217
El Greco 217
Elizabeth 2
Ellas 216
embarkation tickets 23, 95, 130, 143, 144
Empress (of Scotland) 64, 65, 66, 77, 116, 130, 175, 189
Ettrick (Bay) 140, 174
Evening Citizen 82, 99, 100, 101, 103, 137, 141, 142

F

Fairfield 40, 42, 47
Fairlie 22, 51, 63, 64, 67, 68, 69, 70, 71, 72, 73, 75, 76, 178, 192, 193, 211, 212
Ferguson ix, 75
Fforde, Lady Jean 24, 205, 210
Fife (see *Duchess of Fife*)
flag 12, 13, 23, 143, 159, 162, 189, 201

Flora (see Scott)
Flying Enterprise 9
Flying Merlin 168, 169
Flying Spitfire 169
Flying Tempest 169
Forger 169

G

Galaxias 217
Gantocks 103, 113
Gareloch 32, 97, 105, 132, 162
Garroch Head 10, 130, 138, 164
Gay Queen 120, 121
General Manager 19, 130, 143, 144, 151
Girvan 151
Glasgow and South Western 48, 97
Glasgow Fair 63, 95, 99, 100, 101, 124, 128, 130, 138
Glasgow University. xviii
Glecknabae 140
Glen Sannox mv 16, 18, 19, 20, 21, 22, 24, 32, 36, 40, 45, 48, 52, 63, 64, 67, 68, 70, 71, 73, 75, 76, 77, 79, 80, 86, 91, 95, 97, 99, 109, 112, 113, 116, 117, 118, 119, 130, 134, 136, 141, 142, 143, 144, 148, 151, 161, 164, 176, 178, 179, 190, 192, 193, 194, 196, 199, 203, 204, 205, 206, 207, 208, 210, 211, 212, 219
Glen Sannox ps 52
Glen Sannox ts 9, 50, 51
Goatfell 207
Gourock x, 1, 4, 6, 11, 13, 16, 19, 21, 24, 36, 40, 42, 45, 46, 49, 63, 64, 67, 68, 75, 80, 81, 82, 83, 86, 87, 89, 91, 92, 95, 98, 99, 101, 103, 105, 106, 107, 108, 109, 118, 119, 120, 124, 127, 128, 130, 139, 143, 144, 148, 153, 155, 165, 169, 173, 175, 176, 178, 181, 183, 186, 187, 189, 190, 196, 198, 199, 201, 202, 205, 211, 213
Graham, Marchioness of (see *Marchioness of Graham*)
Grannie Kempock 49
Greece ix, 214, 215, 217
Greenock 2, 49, 58, 82, 145, 153, 208, 213
Gunn 20, 90

H

Halliday 2, 7
Hamilton, Duchess of (see *Duchess of Hamilton*)
Harland and Wolff 40
Harris 9
Herriot ix
Hesperus 130
High School (of Glasgow) i, xviii, 12, 13, 162
Holliday 93, 94, 128
Hooch 56, 62
Hopper No.9 169
Horne 89, 91, 93, 94, 124, 127, 128
House 89, 91, 94, 128
Hughie 89
Hunter's Quay 183

I

Inglis 42
Innellan 11, 42, 101, 105, 107, 118
Inveraray 36, 83
Isle of Man 192
Iona 161
Irish Coast 151, 192, 196
Isle of Mull 161

J

Jeanie Deans 2, 40, 41, 42, 63, 80, 122, 175, 178, 196
Jerry's quay 43, 72, 77, 80, 118, 119, 136, 148, 151, 174, 183, 203, 204, 205, 206
Jimmy 61
John Brown 12, 13
Joseph Lykes 168, 169
Juno 97
Jupiter 6, 42, 43, 44, 57, 65, 67, 68, 70, 73, 80, 82, 86, 99, 101, 103, 105, 113, 118, 119, 120, 138, 140, 141, 151, 152, 153, 158, 160, 175, 176, 178, 183, 186, 187, 189, 192, 213

K

Kelly 153, 154, 192
Kelso 1

Keppel 67, 105, 107, 108, 151, 152, 178, 187
King George V 46
King GeorgeV (KGV) dock 169
Kilbrannan Sound 10, 67, 105, 172, 178
Kilchattan Bay 1, 9, 101
Kilcreggan 49
Kildonan 31, 32, 75, 91, 153
Kintyre 67, 172
Kremlin 13, 16, 23, 70, 82, 99, 127, 128, 139, 151, 187, 199, 202, 210
Kylemore 203
Kyles (of Bute) 40, 42, 63, 79, 94, 99, 124, 127, 134, 146, 154, 166, 178, 190

L

Lady of Man 141
Lady Jean (see Fforde)
Lairdscrest 31
Lairds Isle 31, 32, 64, 65, 70, 77, 109, 151, 153
Lamlash 192
Lamont 2, 49
Lamont's shipyard 2, 178
Langmuir ix, x, 6
Largs 1, 32, 42, 43, 63, 67, 70, 73, 80, 82, 86, 97, 101, 103, 112, 113, 116, 118, 120, 129, 132, 135, 136, 138, 139, 141, 146, 147, 151, 153, 154, 160, 162, 166, 169, 170, 171, 175, 178, 179, 183, 186, 187, 189, 192, 196, 199, 201
Leven 45, 49, 162
Linn Park 198
LNER 1, 40, 42
Loch Carron 8, 9, 13
Loch Fad 171, 172
Loch Frisa 188, 192
Loch Goil 99, 112, 118, 119, 151, 152, 183
Loch Long 89, 92, 99, 105
Lochranza 67, 68, 107, 120, 171
Loch Riddon 79, 112, 113, 124, 127, 146
luggage man 54, 61, 62, 156, 164, 203, 204

M

MacArthur ix
MacBrayne 1, 8, 9, 36, 46, 101, 179, 188, 192
MacCormick 32, 33, 87
MacDonald 60
MacKay 52, 53

MacLean, 54
Macleod 36
MacLoon 54
MacNaughton, Donald 58, 59, 60, 70, 71, 74, 77, 81, 97, 98, 99, 100, 103, 104, 105, 107, 108, 109, 118, 120, 127, 136, 137, 138, 139, 141, 146, 151, 156, 157, 164, 166, 169, 170, 171, 172, 176, 183, 186, 189, 190, 196, 200, 201, 203, 204, 206, 208, 209
McQueen ix
MacRae 178, 179
Maid of Argyll 11, 42, 46, 118, 173
Maid of Ashton 42, 146, 162
Maid of Bute 121
Maid of Cumbrae 42, 70, 82, 89, 99, 101, 118, 134, 146, 201
Maid of Skelmorlie 10, 42, 99, 107, 186
Maid(s) 10, 11, 36, 42, 45, 63, 71, 90, 121, 151, 171
Maid of the Loch 214, 215
Mallon 93, 128
Marchioness of Graham i, v, vii, ix, x, 6, 8, 9, 11, 13, 16, 17, 19, 24, 32, 36, 40, 41, 43, 47, 48, 50, 51, 52, 57, 59, 61, 63, 64, 67, 69, 70, 73, 74, 77, 79, 80, 83, 84, 86, 87, 89, 91, 92, 97, 99, 101, 102, 105, 115, 116, 121, 124, 127, 129, 131, 133, 137, 140, 141, 147, 148, 154, 155, 156, 158, 160, 161, 165, 167, 170, 171, 172, 174, 175, 176, 179, 181, 182, 183, 184, 188, 190, 191, 192, 194, 198, 199, 200, 203, 205, 206, 207, 208, 209, 210, 213, 214, 215, 216, 217, 219
Marchioness of Lorne 8, 9, 47
Marine Superintendent 19, 210
Martin 56, 94, 128
Maybole 151
Measured Mile 194
Meteor 169
MFV 1186 118
Millport 42, 43, 45, 51, 59, 67, 68, 82, 101, 112, 118, 119, 146, 151, 152, 162, 175, 178, 179, 183, 186, 187, 189, 191
Mona's Queen 32, 141
Montrose, Duchess of (see *Duchess of Montrose*)
Murdoch 40

N

Narrows 79, 127
Nea Hellas 217, 218
Netherlee 5
Norman 2, 7

O

O'Connor 128

P

Paddle Steamer Preservation Society, 42
Paisley 158
Passenger Luggage in Advance 1
Peiraeus 215, 216, 217
Pladda 156, 171
Pleasure boat 72, 76, 86, 90, 91, 92, 93, 94, 124, 126, 128, 134, 142, 165
Port Bannatyne 189
Portencross 130, 169
Port Glasgow 2
purser i, xvii, 13, 19, 20, 23, 24, 32, 33, 45, 47, 58, 60, 67, 70, 74, 75, 76, 89, 91, 100, 105, 107, 137, 153, 160, 162, 164, 166, 183, 185, 186, 190, 199, 200, 201, 210, 211

Q

Queen Alexandra 1, 36
Queen Mary 12, 36, 38, 39, 40, 45, 80, 99, 118, 119, 120, 122, 127, 134, 137, 144, 145, 153, 154, 161, 162, 166, 167, 174, 183, 186, 191, 196, 199, 219
Queen's Park Café 198

R

Raines (see also Dick) 54, 59
Ralston 13
Regal 174
relief purser 32, 33, 105, 153, 160, 162, 164, 166, 186, 199, 200, 201
Rhodes 215, 216
Rhodesian Star 169
River Steamer Club (see Clyde River Steamer Club)

Robbie 20
Robertson 6
Rodger 33, 87
Rosser 54, 57
Rothesay xvii, 1, 2, 3, 5, 6, 9, 10, 13, 24, 38, 40, 41, 42, 43, 44, 45, 46, 61, 63, 66, 67, 70, 73, 74, 75, 80, 81, 82, 83, 86, 99, 101, 103, 104, 105, 107, 112, 113, 115, 118, 120, 121, 124, 125, 126, 127, 128, 130, 134, 136, 137, 138, 139, 146, 147, 153, 154, 155, 157, 158, 164, 165, 166, 169, 170, 171, 172, 173, 175, 178, 186, 188, 189, 190, 191, 194, 196, 197, 201, 203
Rothesay Advertising Association 103, 153
Round Bute 40, 63, 80, 103, 122, 140, 178, 191, 196
Royal Ulsterman 95
Runabout 10

S

Saint Columba 1, 3, 10, 36, 81, 99, 101, 134, 136, 140, 164, 165, 166, 167, 174, 191, 201
Sannox (see *Glen Sannox*)
Scott, Flora 55, 61
Showboat 82, 99, 101, 103, 105, 107
Shrimpy 94, 128
Skelmorlie 1, 177
Smoky Joe 65
Somerville 6
South Beach 138, 141
Spencer 6
Stamperland Institute 198
Starlight 169
St Enoch 19, 22, 141
Stewart, 20, 90
Stirlingshire 169, 171
Stockholm 201
Stornoway 9
Strongbow 169
student pursers 47, 61
submarine(s) 116, 117, 118, 125
Sunday Post, The 32, 57, 147
Sunrose 169
Sunshine 70
Sylvania 180, 189, 201

225

T

Tail of the Bank 73, 189
Talisman 9, 34, 42, 43, 59, 69, 70, 73, 80, 99, 101, 120, 129, 134, 146, 147, 152, 160, 164, 166, 169, 175, 178, 179, 192, 211, 212
Thelma 166, 167
Thorburn 54
Tickets 22
Tighnabruaich 6, 10, 40, 107, 112, 136, 138, 166, 167, 172, 178
Tommy 54, 62
Toward 2, 105, 165, 175
Train 9
Troon 32, 45, 97, 102, 112, 113, 116, 118, 132, 134, 135, 136, 146, 151, 156, 162, 164, 166, 167, 171, 172, 183
TV (see BBC)

U

Upriver 63, 70, 86, 112, 134, 135, 138, 145, 153, 169, 170, 173, 185, 186, 189, 199, 200

V

Victoria hotel 120, 121

W

Warrior 169
Waverley xvii, 1, 3, 5, 42, 44, 52, 63, 66, 67, 70, 71, 80, 89, 90, 91, 99, 100, 101, 105, 113, 120, 121, 122, 124, 134, 140, 151, 164, 171, 178, 180, 191
Wemyss Bay 1, 2, 6, 42, 45, 63, 67, 73, 83, 99, 103, 105, 134, 138, 139, 141, 158, 160, 175, 178, 192, 203
Whiting Bay 19, 33, 64, 65, 75, 77, 95, 99, 109, 112, 115, 116, 117, 128, 130, 134, 138, 139, 140, 141, 143, 148, 152, 156, 157, 159, 160, 161, 162, 164, 171, 174, 175, 181, 192, 193, 196, 203, 205, 208
Williamson ix
Winton (pier) 19, 143, 196, 205, 206
Wrestler 169

Y

Yarrow 42

www.ingramcontent.com/pod-product-compliance
Lightning Source LLC
Chambersburg PA
CBHW080536170426
43195CB00016B/2584